LAST WINTER
IN
THE UNITED STATES

LAST WINTER

IN

THE UNITED STATES

BEING

TABLE TALK

COLLECTED DURING A TOUR THROUGH
THE LATE SOUTHERN CONFEDERATION, THE FAR WEST,
THE ROCKY MOUNTAINS, &c.

By F. BARHAM ZINCKE

BOOKS FOR LIBRARIES PRESS
FREEPORT, NEW YORK

College Library, Wayne. Nebr

First Published 1868
Reprinted 1970

INTERNATIONAL STANDARD BOOK NUMBER:
0-8369-5542-0

LIBRARY OF CONGRESS CATALOG CARD NUMBER:
76-130569

PRINTED IN THE UNITED STATES OF AMERICA

TO MY WIFE

I Dedicate these Pages

BECAUSE, WHILE OF ALL WOMEN I AM ACQUAINTED WITH SHE WOULD HAVE BEEN MOST CAPABLE OF ENTERING INTO THE INTEREST OF THE SCENES AND OF THE STATE OF SOCIETY THEY DESCRIBE, SHE DETERMINED, FOR THE SAKE OF HER ONLY CHILD, TO FOREGO THAT PLEASURE; AND URGED ME NOT TO LOSE, FROM CONSIDERATION FOR HER, AN OPPORTUNITY FOR CARRYING OUT A LONG-CHERISHED WISH TO VISIT THE UNITED STATES OF AMERICA.

WHERSTEAD VICARAGE:
    Nov. 24, 1868.

CONTENTS.

CHAPTER I.

PAGE

The Winter Voyage recommended—A Cabin to oneself may then be had at no additional cost—Advantages of Travelling in America in Winter—A Feeling in a Gale—The Americans on board the Steamer—Divine Service on Board 1

CHAPTER II.

New York—*Menu* at Fifth Avenue Hotel—How Travel in the States may be arranged for a Winter Tour—The Queen's Book in America—External Appearance of New York—Ignorance of English Immigrants—Industrial Schools—Children's Aid Society—Number of Churches—Broad Views general—A Service at the Rev. H. W. Beecher's Church—Episcopalian Broad Church Club—Chapels in poor Districts annexed to Episcopal Churches in rich ones—American Churches worked at High Pressure—An American Divine's Opinion of a Minister's Duty . . . 8

CHAPTER III.

Why an unreasonable Fancy was acted on—The History of the Cause of American Progressiveness—What passes in America important to us—The Northern States sown broadcast with Houses 24

CHAPTER IV.

The Locomotive in the Streets—In Baltimore Public Opinion first becomes Southern—Growth and Prospects of Baltimore—On Trading Politicians and Ill-will to England—Why an American Tutor thought necessary for an Englishman—Repudiation—The Masses and Middle Class in favour of it—Arguments in favour of it—An Argument used 2,000 Miles from Wall Street—Why Republicans bound to repudiate—Americans addicted to Abstract Reasoning—Instances 32

CHAPTER V.

Washington—Style of Speaking in Congress—Congress no Nursery for Statesmen—Society in Washington—Episcopal Church in Washington—Some Opinions of an American Bishop—Commissioner of Agriculture—Use of the Department—Its Museum gives an Idea of the Vastness of the Country—Its Natural Advantages—What Variety of Productions has done for England will be repeated in America—Special Excellence of Californian Productions—The Californian himself—California compared with Italy—Why Coloured Waiters preferable to White—Negro Funeral with Masonic Honours—American Birds' Nests—Bill for making Education compulsory—Coloured Schools—Comparative Intelligence of the Negro—Vulgar Errors about Americans—Night Attendants at Hotel read 'Oliver Twist'—Capitol—Treasury—Patent Office—What our Diplomacy in America should be—Use of Iced Water 44

CHAPTER VI.

Richmond—Way by the Battle-fields—Handiness of American Soldiers—Effect of Slavery on the Virginian Landscape—Appearance of American Forest—Republican Relations of Father and Son—State of Feeling in Virginia—Billiards in America—Why Richmond Millers undersold by Californian—Why American Cities are Large—American Living—Prospects of Richmond—Indications of Southern Climate in Richmond—Church-matters in Richmond—Interest that attaches to Richmond, and to the Heroism of the South 67

CHAPTER VII.

How Southerners describe their own Condition—Each State must be taken separately—Missouri—Tennessee—Kentucky—Texas—Virginia—Georgia—Florida—North Carolina—Arkansas—South Carolina—Louisiana—Mississippi—Will the Blacks get the Franchise?—No party considers them fit—They will have it for a time—This will weaken the repudiating party—Also the party hostile to this country—The Blacks will not all be republican—The South should have been left alone to settle the Labour Question—The Bureau suggested false ideas—There will be no war of races—What will kill out the Blacks—The rate of this—Fusion physically impossible—Means of Communication in the South indicate its condition 91

CHAPTER VIII.

First Sight of a Cotton-field—Spanish Moss—A Night on the Rails—Many kinds of sameness in America—Maize—Order of Succession in the Forest—Its extent—Evergreens in the Southern Forest—Poor land in the South may be more profitable than rich land in the West—Deadness of Charleston—Its Hotels—A Charleston Sam Weller—The Naples of the United States—Few English Travellers—Sufferings of Southern Families—Want of schools—How the deficiency is being supplied—Blacks should be put on same footing as Whites—Dialogue with Black Member of Convention—Another Convention—Able Black Member—South Carolina Orphan Asylum 109

CHAPTER IX.

Cold in South Carolina and Georgia—Curious appearance of Ice—Time not valued in the South—Why Americans will not cultivate the Olive—Tea might grow in Georgia—Atlanta bound to be great—Cattle badly off in winter—A Virginian's Recollection of the War—His Position and Prospects—Approach to Mobile by the Alabama River—Mobile—The Harbour—Why no American Ships there—A Day on the Gulf—Ponchatrain—New Orleans—French Sunday Market—French appearance of Town

—A New Orleans Gentleman on the Episcopal Church—Bishop Elect of Georgia—Mississippi—The Cemeteries—Expensiveness of everything—Transatlantic News—Fusion of North and South—French Half-breeds—Roads—The best in the World—Approach to New Orleans by land—Sugar Plantations—A Prayer for a Brother Minister 126

CHAPTER X.

My only Delay on an American Railway—No concealing one's Nationality—Railway Cow-plough—Pistols—Memphis—Emigration from the South deprecated—True Method of Resuscitation—The Minister's Study—Conversation with two Ministers—Invitation to 'go to Church' 150 Miles off—Luxury does not sap the Military Spirit—Mrs. Read—Entry into Eden—Share a Bedroom with a Californian—How California was civilised—How a Site upon the Swamp was created for Cairo—Decline the fourth part of a Bedroom at Odin—'Be good to yourself' . 146

CHAPTER XI.

Mississippi frozen over at St. Louis—Why the Bridge at St. Louis is built by Chicago Men—General Sherman—Ideas about Education at St. Louis—Liberal Bequests for Educational Purposes—How New Englandism leavens the whole Lump—The German Invasion will not Germanise America—St. Louis—Its rapid Growth—Its Church Architecture—An Idea on Mental Culture from the West Bank of the Mississippi—A Thought suggested by hearing the Skaters on the Mississippi talking English . 164

CHAPTER XII.

Instance of American Kindliness—Red-skins and Half-breeds on the Rails—Cincinnati and its Inhabitants—What may be made of Pigs—The influence of its Pork-crop—Machinery for Killing and Curing—Improving effect American Equality has on the highest and lowest Class—Churches only unprosaic Buildings in American Towns—Schools—Merits of Philadelphian style of City-building not obvious—In what it consists—America has but one City—No. 24, G Street, corner of 25th Street 172

CHAPTER XIII.

The Valley of the Ohio—Much of the United States will produce Wine—Illinois at Night—First View of Lake Michigan—Chicago—A Sign of outward Religion—'Small-pox here'—Fire Alarm—Liberality of Chicago Merchants—The Dollar not all-in-all—A Church lighted from the Roof—A handsome American—America has developed a new type of Features—Chicago Schools—An exception to the American way of denouncing the official Class—Chicago Sunday Schools—Programme of one I attended—Excellence of Water at Chicago—How supplied—Lifting up the City—Post Office Arrangements—A disadvantage of frequent change of Clerks—Americans on Aristocracy—How the Germans, the masses of the people, and the upper class feel towards it . 182

CHAPTER XIV.

Prairie from Chicago to Omaha—Plains from North Platte to the Mountains—Omaha, the intersection of the Pacific Railway and the Missouri—Temporary Bridge over the Missouri—Indifference to Risks affecting Life—A Prairie Fire—The Forest on the Mountains on Fire—Fire the cause of the Treelessness of the Prairies—First found Animal Life abounding in the Valley of the Platte—'The hardest place, Sir, on this Continent'—Its Predecessor—How it is possible to establish Lynch Law at Shyenne—My first Night in Shyenne—A second Night in Shyenne—Necessity and advantages of Lynch Law—'The use of the Pistol'—A Man shot because 'he might have done some mischief'—Newness of Aspects both of Society and of Nature . . . 202

CHAPTER XV.

The Armament and Experience of a German Herdmaster—A Stage Coach on the Plains—The Party in the Coach—The only Colonel I met in the United States—The Colonel's Wife—A Colorado Herdmaster—A Philadelphian Graduate—Two jocose Denver Storekeepers—Advantage of having one's Rifle in the Coach—A Californian's account of a Skirmish with Indians—Manners and Life at a house on the Plains—A Lady of the Plains—American Society judges Men fairly—Between Shyenne and Denver 221

CHAPTER XVI.

The City of Denver—The Ladies give a Ball—Manners of Denver—' Quite our finest Gentleman '—The Plains will be to America an improved Australia—The advantages they offer for Flocks and Herds—Will soon be clear of Indians—Markets now opened to them—Size of the Runs—Wealth of the Region . . . 233

CHAPTER XVII.

The Rocky Mountains—Golden City—Golden Gates—Mining Towns—Neighbouring Mountains stripped of every Tree—What grows on the Mountains—American Horses—Roads and Bridges they have to pass—How, six-in-hand, we went down a Hillside in the Mountains—A nice Distinction as to Accidents on this Hill—Climate—Wind-storms—Birds—Dogs 241

CHAPTER XVIII.

Rocky Mountains a Field for Sporting—Great variety and abundance of Game—Wild Fruit—Excellence of Climate in the shooting season—How the Mountains may be reached, and how much seen by the way, in 15 days from Liverpool—Cost of the Expedition—The best Camping Ground is the South Park at foot of Pike's Peak—The Route by Chicago and Denver recommended—Other Route by St. Louis and Leavenworth—Route into the Park—The North Park easier work—The more enterprising may go to Laramie Plains—Will deteriorate every year. 249

CHAPTER XIX.

Hotel Cars, real First-class Carriages—An Editor on his Countrymen's Knowledge—American Grandiloquence—Of whom this is said—Necessary to repeat some of what one hears—' Have you seen our Forest?'—' The Pacific Rails will carry the commerce of the world '—Large Acquaintance Americans have—An American on Letters of Introduction—Niagara—The American and Canadian Falls—What is in the mind magnifies what one sees—The Stone Trough it has chipped out—Ice Bridge—How Niagara is pronounced—A Week of Canadian Weather—A Snow-bound Party at Niagara 258

Contents. xiii

CHAPTER XX.

PAGE

Educational Department at Toronto—Canadian Arguments against Common Schools—A Canadian's Opinion on Secular Schools in England—How the Canadians' Objections are met in the United States—Upper Canadians not yet a People—Advantages possessed by Upper Canada—Service at the Romanist and Anglican Cathedrals—Unmannerly Behaviour permitted on Canadian Railways—Badness of their Carriages—Why Canada is not 'the Land of Freedom'—Yankee Smartness in Train-driving—Picturesqueness of Vermont—Travelling on American Railways not fatiguing 269

CHAPTER XXI.

Boston is the Hub of America—Mr. Ticknor—Professor Rogers and the Technological—Mr. Norton—Professor Agassiz—Mr. Appleton and Mr. Longfellow—Mr. Philbrick—A Grammar School Commemoration—Humility of the better Literary Men of Boston—Regret at leaving Boston 279

CHAPTER XXII.

American Hotels—Why some People in America travel without any Luggage—Conversation at Tables-d'hôte should be encouraged—The Irish, the African, and the Chinese—Can a Republic do without a Servile Class?—What will be the ultimate Fate of these three races in America—No Children—Motives—Means—Consequences—Why many young Men and young Women make Shipwreck of Happiness in America—The course many Families run—America the Hub of the World 286

CHAPTER XXIII.

On American Common Schools—Conclusion 299

INTRODUCTION.

No one would now think of writing a continuous narrative of travel in the United States of America. The only alternative hitherto adopted has been that of Essays on American subjects. But towards these the opinion of the reading public has not been so favourable as to make one desirous of adding to their number. There appears, however, to be another form, as yet, I believe, untried, in which he who has travelled in a country, about which people know much, but from which they are still desirous of hearing something more, may present to the reader what he has to say. He may write, I mean, somewhat in the fashion of a book of table-talk. This he may do by confining himself just to what he knows would be listened to with interest in a company of intelligent persons who had some acquaintance with the subject; and by putting what he has to say of this kind with the conciseness, and, if possible, with the point, required in conversation. This would render it necessary that the book should consist rather of paragraphs than of chapters; and that these should frequently have little or no connection; many of them being very brief, because they will contain merely some observation, or the notice of some fact, for which half a dozen lines will suffice. It is in this way that I now propose to write about America, trusting that by so doing I shall spare my readers' time and patience.

A WINTER IN THE UNITED STATES.

CHAPTER I.

THE WINTER VOYAGE RECOMMENDED—A CABIN TO ONE'S SELF MAY THEN BE HAD AT NO ADDITIONAL COST—ADVANTAGES OF TRAVELLING IN AMERICA IN WINTER—A FEELING IN A GALE—THE AMERICANS ON BOARD THE STEAMER—DIVINE SERVICE ON BOARD.

I WOULD RECOMMEND the man who begins to feel the effects of long-continued professional labour, or of an idle and luxurious life, if his constitution is still capable of amendment, to try what may be gained by a voyage across the Atlantic, and back again, in winter; with such an interval between the two as he might be able to allow for a tour in the United States. In the summer the weather is likely to be so fine that the only benefit he would derive from his two voyages would be that of breathing the air of the ocean for as many days as he would spend in making them; but in winter there would be almost a certainty of some rough weather; and if after a few days he should prove capable of resisting the usual disturbing effects of such weather at sea, and come to take a pleasure in facing and battling against boisterous winds and tossing waves, I do not know what could more rapidly brace up within him what had begun to fail. Even the mere finding of one's sea-legs, and the subsequent use of them under difficulties, would not be unattended with advantage, for I suppose it would bring into action and develope muscles not much used at other times. In winter, too, the air would be cool (it is not at all necessarily cold at that season on the track between England and America, except when one nears the American coast), and this coolness of the air would of itself have with many constitutions an invigorating effect. But be the process what it may by which your two ocean voyages bring about their renovating result, that result is that you return to your home a stronger and a hungrier man than you were before you left it.

There is always much inconvenience and discomfort in sharing at sea the few square feet a cabin contains with another man, however gentlemanly he may be; and it is not improbable that one taken promiscuously from a hundred and fifty Transatlantic travellers would possess some habit or infirmity which would render such close companionship almost insufferable. In summer you cannot avoid this misery except at a great cost. To be alone at that season you must pay the fare of the one or two additional berths in your cabin which you wish should remain unoccupied. But in winter the number of passengers being always less than the number of berths, you can stipulate for a cabin to yourself without being put to any additional expense. There are now so many competing lines of steamers to America, that neither on the outward nor homeward voyage will you find any difficulty on this head. And you need not scruple about asking for this accommodation, for it may be granted to you without at all lessening either the profits of the owners of the ship, or the comforts of any one of the passengers.

Travelling also on the *terra firma* of America in winter has its advantages. At this season of the year you find everybody at home; and if your object is rather to see the people than the country in which they live, this will alone outweigh all other considerations. The Americans being the most locomotive people in the world, are seldom to be found at home in summer. I travelled through the States in the winter and the early spring, and had letters of introduction to persons in every city I stayed at, and in no instance did I find anyone absent from home, with the single exception of a gentleman who happened to be just at that time discharging his duties as Member of Congress at Washington, whereas the letter which had been given me was directed to him at his house at Chicago, where I presented it. In winter, also, one escapes the persecutions of the mosquitoes, and of the creeping things that bite in beds, of the withering heat, and tormenting dust—those inevitable concomitants of travel under an American summer sun.

What is lost by confining one's travels in America to the (botanically) dead season of the year is, that nothing is seen of the summer and autumn aspects of the vegetation of the country. Its winter aspect, however, is not without interest to the Englishman, whose eye is accustomed to the perennial green of his own parks and meadows, which are generally, indeed, even greener at Christmas than at Midsummer. While in America I did not see in the winter and early spring a blade of grass that was even faintly tinted with green, from Canada to the Gulf of Mexico, or from New York to the Rocky Mountains. I was told that the blue grass of parts of Kentucky and Virginia is an exception, but of this I saw nothing myself. I found the roadsides, pastures, and prairies everywhere clothed in unrelieved drab.

To look out from one of the Cunard Company's magnificent steam-ships, where everything is going on with the precision of clockwork, while a gale is raging on the ocean around you, and to see that in the Mid-Atlantic you are master of the winds and waves, makes you feel that it is something to be a man.

As I was going to America to see the Americans, I took the first opportunity which presented itself—that of the voyage to America—for weighing and measuring the specimens of that very compound race who happened to be on board the ship in which I was sailing. About half the passengers, forty-five in all, were of German extraction; and about half of this half were of the Hebrew persuasion. One young fellow among these latter, who I suppose might be regarded as a representative of the broad synagogue, delivered it as his opinion, that the time had come when the Jews should give up all their peculiar practices which modern knowledge had proved to be founded in misconceptions and mistakes. He in-

stanced their abstinence from pork, and from the
blood of the animals they used for food, and their
method of killing animals. One of these Teutonic
Americans, a youth with such a width of shoulder,
and massiveness of neck and head, that no one could
look upon him without being reminded of a buffalo,
was an Indian trader from the borders of Kansas.
His practice was to give the Indians four dollars'
worth of goods for such a buffalo robe as sells in
London for fifty or sixty shillings. It was his
opinion that Indians were vermin which should on
every opportunity have a dose of lead administered
to them. When asked if this was justifiable, 'Well,'
he replied, ' they are a set of bloodthirsty, treacherous
skunks; and they must all die out, or be shot down,
and it can't matter much to them which it is. It
comes to much the same in the end. They shot my
brother, and my plan is to take a shot at them
whenever I have a chance.' All these German
Americans spoke English as fluently as they did
German. Their most prominent idea appeared to be
hatred of all aristocracies. That of the United
Kingdom of Great Britain and Ireland they regarded
with their purest hatred, because it seemed to them
the most developed and the most powerful. The
best mannered people of the party were the Yankee
and New York traders; some of these were buyers
for large wholesale and retail houses, others on
their own account. There were about a dozen of
them on board. They were very careful about their
dress, and their conversation was pleasing and
intelligent. The majority of them were entirely free
from the Yankee tone of voice. They were the very

reverse of pushing, and they never guessed. In appearance and manners they would have passed amongst ourselves for gentlemen. We had, however, among the passengers one genuine Yankee of the received type. He had been a successful inventor of improvements in machinery, though medicine, not mechanics or engineering, was his business. He thought that anything by which he could make money was as much his business as his profession was. He was always talking, and ready to argue on any subject: if unacquainted with it, that made no difference—he still had a right to express his opinion. His favourite idea was that discussion led to knowledge, and that books came after knowledge, and that therefore they were not of much value. This dictum he fearlessly applied to everything—to history, to science, and to religion. Theoretically he was a strong Negrophilist. He believed that the patriarchs and prophets, that the Saviour of the world and His apostles were all Negroes. He thought that the amount of wealth a man had been able to accumulate was the true measure of a man, because all pursued wealth, and employed in the pursuit the whole of their power. If a man was idle or stupid, he employed what power was left him, after so much had been cancelled by his idleness or stupidity. And therefore—for this was his conclusion—if he could produce several blacks, which he was sure he could do, who had accumulated more wealth than anyone present, then they were better men than any of the present company. I say he was theoretically a Negrophilist, because, although he liked the Negro, he liked him best at a distance. In politics, he held that clever men, and men with ideas, were the bane of the country. They had already got their constitution and their laws. The people did not want a letter of either altered, or anything added to either. All officers, therefore, elected by the people, whether for the general or the local government, were in the position of servants with written instructions. No one would tolerate a domestic servant who, in the face of his instructions, thought for himself; nor ought the people ever to re-elect a public servant who acted in this way. Indeed he held that no man should ever be re-elected, but that all public offices should be made 'to go as far as possible' in bringing into notice deserving young men, and in helping them on a little, and in rewarding in a temporary way those who had exerted themselves on behalf of their party. He was always joking; his jokes consisting of grotesque impossibilities and laughable exaggerations. But his unconscious and unfailing conceit, and his assumptions of omniscience, were as ridiculous as his jokes.

On Sunday Divine Service was celebrated in the saloon. The service was that of the Established Church. The Germans absented themselves. The Americans were all present, and behaved very well, many of them making the responses audibly. The Bishop of Ontario read the prayers, and an English clergyman preached. Some of the Americans proposed to him that he should, as they expressed it, 'hold another meeting' in the evening; but it would not have been right to drive the Germans a second time on to the deck.

CHAPTER II.

NEW YORK—MENU AT FIFTH AVENUE HOTEL—HOW TRAVEL IN THE STATES MAY BE ARRANGED FOR A WINTER TOUR—THE QUEEN'S BOOK IN AMERICA—EXTERNAL APPEARANCE OF NEW YORK—IGNORANCE OF ENGLISH IMMIGRANTS—INDUSTRIAL SCHOOLS—CHILDREN'S AID SOCIETY—NUMBER OF CHURCHES—BROAD VIEWS GENERAL—A SERVICE AT THE REV. H. W. BEECHER'S CHURCH—EPISCOPALIAN BROAD CHURCH CLUB—CHAPELS IN POOR DISTRICTS ANNEXED TO EPISCOPAL CHURCHES IN RICH ONES—AMERICAN CHURCHES WORKED AT HIGH PRESSURE—AN AMERICAN DIVINE'S OPINION OF A MINISTER'S DUTY.

DURING my first visit to New York I stayed at the Fifth Avenue Hotel, which I had been told was the largest and best managed of the monster hotels of the city. I arrived just in time for dinner. On being shown into the dining-saloon, I found between two and three hundred people at table. I had lately been staying at Paris at the *Grand Hôtel du Louvre*, where it was thought we were treated rather liberally in having seven *plats* at dinner, including two sweets, and one cream or water ice. The ice was served in infinitesimal morsels; and if you asked for a second morsel, it was represented by an additional franc in your bill. With this experience of a great European hotel fresh in my mind, a waiter in the dining saloon of the Fifth Avenue Hotel placed in my hand the bill of fare for the dinner then going on. Seeing almost an interminable printed list of *comestibles,* and not knowing how these things were managed in America, I supposed that this was the list of dishes the hotel undertook to prepare; and that, had I arrived some hours earlier, and then made my selection, what I might have ordered would have now been ready. The *menu* contained turtle soup, venison, turtle steaks, soft-shelled crabs, canvas-back ducks; in short, whatever fish, flesh, fowl, vegetable, and fruit were then in season. But the attendant informed me that the paper he had given me was the bill of fare for that day, and that everything mentioned in it was then actually ready; and that I might order whatever I pleased, and it would be immediately brought to me. I made my selection; and while he was bringing what I had ordered, I counted the number of dishes provided that day for our dinner, and found that the total amounted to seventy-five. Nothing was supplied in the scanty way in which everything was doled out at the *Grand Hôtel du Louvre;* but as a general rule more of everything was set before you than you could require: for instance, instead of setting before you a morsel of ice-cream, a whole mould was left with you till you ordered it to be taken away. The next morning I found fifty-two things mentioned on the bill of fare for breakfast. Luncheon, tea, and supper are also supplied to its guests by this establishment. On the ground-floor are placed the bar, the billiard-room (containing twelve tables), and a kind of after-hour Stock Exchange, in which operations are commenced at eight o'clock P.M. The charge for living in this palatial hotel was five dollars a day in greenbacks;

that is, about sixteen shillings, at the then price of gold.

One frequently hears the severity of their winters urged as a reason for not travelling in the United States at that season of the year. My own experience of the unusually severe winter of '67–68 would go some way towards proving that those who press this consideration do so under a misapprehension. It is possible that by a singular run of good luck I may have always been at a warm place when the weather was cold elsewhere, but it is literally true that during that winter I never once had occasion to put on an overcoat, excepting when I was in Canada at its breaking up. I left New York early in January; went through the South, where I gathered ripe oranges from the trees on which they were hanging; ascended the Mississippi; crossed the prairies and plains to the Rocky Mountains, at the foot of which I found the thermometer, at Denver, standing at 70°; recrossed the prairies to Chicago; and during the whole of this time, whether on foot, or in a railway car, or on or in a coach, did not on any occasion find the weather disagreeable on account of the cold, though I frequently found it in railway cars and in hotels very much warmer than was agreeable. By what I have just said I do not mean that I never fell in with weather that was thermometrically cold, for I walked over the Mississippi on the ice at St. Louis, but that it never felt disagreeably cold. It so happened that whenever the thermometer was low, the air was still, and the sun bright. During this winter it only rained twice, and never snowed but once, at the places at which I happened to be staying. It rained once at Washington, and once at New Orleans, and it was snowing on my return across the prairies to Chicago. On my outward journey over them they were entirely free from snow. Of course if I had remained during the whole of this time at any one place in the northern part of the Union, I should have seen some bad weather. My conclusion, however, is that the traveller may so arrange his tour even for the winter as to be put to very little annoyance by the cold or wet.

Everybody in New York had read the Queen's book; in every society I found people talking about it; and I never heard it mentioned without expressions of interest and approval, always uttered without any qualifications, and with unmistakable heartiness. They said it made royalty appear to them in a new and more human light, in which they had never regarded it before. They spoke of her as the head of the Anglo-Saxon race, almost as if they had as much part in her as ourselves. I believe that her Majesty's work has had a greater number of readers, and that a greater number of copies of it have been sold, in the United States than in the United Kingdom.

The exterior appearance of New York is at first disappointing. We are accustomed to find in every capital we visit large and stately buildings, which, as in the case of royal or imperial palaces, public offices, and the hotels of a territorial nobility, are the results of our own existing institutions; or, as in the case of cathedrals, churches, town-halls, and castles, are the result of a state of things belonging to the past history of Europe; and so when we walk through the streets of a city larger than most European capitals, and find none of the buildings we are in the habit of seeing everywhere else, we condemn it as architecturally poor. This feeling is increased in New York by the fact that there is nothing very striking in Broadway, its main street, except its length. The shops, or stores as they are called, are rendered externally quite ineffective by the narrowness of their frontage, and by the way in which they are converted into an advertising frame for names and announcements of various kinds. When you get inside the door you find as extensive and rich an assortment of goods as can be seen in the best shops of London or Paris: there is, however, little indication of this from the outside. But a better acquaintance with the city qualifies to a great extent this first feeling of disappointment. It is irrational to condemn a place for not having what it is impossible could ever have been there. New York cannot have imperial palaces, or mediæval cathedrals, not even great public offices; but in the part of the Fifth Avenue, and of the contiguous streets, which is occupied with the residences of private citizens, it is not surpassed by anything of the same kind in any city of the world. Certainly Belgravia can show nothing like it. There is no stucco, nor are the houses built, as is the case in our streets, in rows of monotonous uniformity, but in some places each separate house differs in design from its neighbours. Sometimes you may find three or four that are alike, but seldom more than half a dozen; and probably those that are alike in general design will vary in the ornamentation of the doors and windows; thus indicating that they are not run up to order, as in Paris, or on speculation, as in London, but that they were built by the people who inhabit them. This variety of façade, where nothing is mean, of course contributes very much to the effect of street architecture. The materials, too, used for building in New York are better and more varied than those used by ourselves. In the best quarters a chocolate-coloured stone is the most common. Brick, which is always painted, and dressed with stone, comes next in frequency; then a stone which in colour is compounded of a yellowish-white with a very perceptible trace of green. Some of the largest stores and hotels, and occasionally a private residence and church, are of white marble. Of this latter material is constructed the imposing office of the New York Herald—I suppose the most magnificent newspaper office in the world.

The great glory, however, of the city is its Park. It is on the central ridge of the island—on very uneven ground, with the native rock everywhere cropping up through the surface, and with many depressions, in which are pieces of water peopled with various kinds of waterfowl; it is between two and three miles in length, and is throughout kept in faultless order; it has already cost the city twenty millions of dollars, and is one of the more than imperial works of the American democracy.

An English merchant, carrying on business at New York, and who had for several years been the president of the St. George's Society of that city, and in that capacity brought very much into contact with the English immigrants, assured me that he had often had to blush for the ignorance of his countrymen. 'Of all the immigrants,' he said, 'who came to the United States the Englishman was the least educated, and so the most shiftless. Even the wild Irishman had generally been better taught, and knew more.'

Among my letters of introduction for New York was one to a gentleman who is personally and actively engaged in the working of some of the most useful institutions of the city. Under his guidance I visited and examined several of their industrial schools, in which the children of the lowest and most vicious part of the Irish and German population of the city are educated. Sixteen of these schools have already been established, and are now at work. They do not at all enter into competition with the common schools, but are a supplement to them, occupying very much the place of our ragged schools. They are partly supported by the city, and partly by voluntary contributions. This is far better than that the city should take upon itself the whole of the cost; because in that case everything would be done by paid agents, who, as experience proves, are seldom able to establish an influence over the classes for whose benefit these institutions are designed; while good and Christian people are generally to be found, who will, for love's sake and for the work's sake, go among the disorderly and depraved, and endeavour to awaken whatever dormant sparks of parental affection, of religious sentiment, and of the sense of responsibility may remain within them, and will thus induce them to send their children to school. And not only will these ministers of good words, illustrated and expounded by kindly acts, aid the regular teachers in bringing children into the school, but also in attaching them to the place where they were first made comfortable and happy. In all these schools I either found ladies actually present at the time of my visit, or heard that they were in the habit of being present almost daily. Their chief effort is to instil into the minds of the children a good moral and religious tone, and to bring them to feel that there are such things in human hearts as kindliness and regard for others, and that this kindliness and regard is being directed towards themselves. They also generally superintend the musical instruction, for which purpose each school is supplied with an harmonium. It is thought that music will both attract and humanise children accustomed at home to so much roughness and coarseness. They also teach the girls to make their own clothes; the materials for which, in the case of the poorest and most neglected, are given either at the cost of the school funds, or by some of the well-wishers of the school through these voluntary assistants. This, and meals provided two or three times a week for the most destitute, are used as allurements by which the most neglected children, which are precisely the cases the managers are most desirous of getting hold of, may be brought in.

None of the children found in these schools would ever attend the common schools—their rags and habits would alone render them inadmissible; and it is only by such means and exertions as I have just mentioned that they can be attracted to and fitted for the industrial schools. I was told that notwithstanding the success I witnessed, there was still a lower depth that could not be reached, in which the children remained untaught in the lessons of any school excepting that of vice.

In these matters, then, they have in the great commercial capital of the New World, where land is a drug, and where there are employment and food for everybody, just the same difficulties we have to struggle against in the capital of the old country, and they endeavour to meet them much in the same way as ourselves; though perhaps they may set about doing what they see ought to be done, with more system and energy than we have yet shown.

The same gentleman also took me over the establishments of the Children's Aid Society. The object of this association is to collect from the streets the news-boys, and any others who may be growing up uncared for, and who have no prospect of being trained up to any employment or trade by which they may gain an honest livelihood, and by the inducement of comfortable lodgings, and some other advantages, to get them to submit to regular habits, and to a certain amount of instruction; and then, when they have become qualified for such situations, to give them an outfit, and find them homes in the farm-houses of the West. This institution was under my friend's superintendence. It appeared to be a very valuable one, and to be effecting a great deal of good among a large class that could have no other chance of being rescued from degradation, and launched favourably into life. On each of my two visits to New York I saw a band of healthy and hopeful-looking youths it had trained and taught, and had just fitted out, on their way to the railroad which was to take them to their new Western homes.

I have mentioned these industrial schools and the Children's Aid Society in connection with my first visit to New York, because I did not meet with institutions of this kind elsewhere. I shall say nothing about the common schools I saw here, because as I had letters to the superintendents of schools in all the chief cities I visited, and so had opportunities for inspecting these schools wherever I went; and as I intend to bring into one summary the conclusions I arrived at after an inspection of schools from New York to Denver on the plains at the foot of the Rocky Mountains, and from Denver back again to Boston, it will be better that I should only make separate mention of my visits to schools which appeared to possess some peculiarity of method or object.

'We wish everybody to have a chance, and to enjoy life. We wish for nothing for ourselves which we should not be glad to see others have.' I first heard this sentiment enounced in the above words by a gentleman whom I met in one of my visits to the Children's Aid Society. I afterwards heard it expressed by other persons in widely distant parts of the Union. There is nothing new in the sentiment itself to those who are familiar with a book for which deep reverence is professed on both sides of the Atlantic; but I felt —perhaps I was wrong in feeling so—that there was something new in hearing it proclaimed as a principle of conduct, and in finding myself among people who in their system of public education, in many of their charities, and in other matters, distinctly acted upon it.

Few people can have visited the great and wealthy capital of the French empire without being struck with the paucity of churches it contains. Few can have visited New York, which is not even the capital of the State whose name it bears, without being struck with the opposite fact. The latter city abounds in churches, still I saw many additional ones in course of construction. Many of these churches have cost large sums of money, and are of good architectural designs. As a general rule, those who minister in them are very liberally maintained: I was astonished at hearing the amount of the annual collections in some of them.

The clergy are allowed much freedom of expression in America. A gentleman residing in New York, while conversing with me on this subject, made the following statement of what he supposed was the general practice:—'The way in which we deal with the clergy here is to pay them well, and to encourage them to say exactly what they think. What we pay them for is not other people's ideas and opinions—that we can find in books—but their own. We expect them to devote a reasonable portion of their time and all the mental powers they possess to theological study, and then to give us the result.' This broad construction of the duty of a clergyman, as a religious teacher, coincides very much with what I was frequently told, that the broad way of thinking was becoming the common way of thinking in almost all the American churches. Mr. Henry Ward Beecher, though a Presbyterian, is very broad, and never has a seat empty in his church. Sunday after Sunday, three thousand people assemble to hear him preach. In American society religious questions are frequently discussed. No one feels any disposition to avoid them, because expression of opinion is perfectly free. An American lady once said to me across the table, and was heard by everyone present, that 'every thinking American was of opinion that religion, if not in conformity with the knowledge and sentiments of the times, was a dead thing.' In New York this expression of opinion appeared perfectly natural; but I suppose that if an English lady entertained ideas of this kind, she would not think it allowable for her to enunciate them in company.

The most celebrated preacher in America is Mr. Henry Ward Beecher. On the subjugation of the South he was the man selected by President Lincoln from all the great speakers of the United States to pronounce at Fort Sumter, where the war had commenced, an oration which would signalise its conclusion with an eloquence worthy of the occasion. The three thousand sittings his church contains, I was told, are let by auction for sums which on this side of the water would appear fabulous. He returns his income at 8,000*l*. a year. Of course I went to hear him, and through the assistance of one of his congregation obtained a seat.

The church is very much in the form of a theatre. The stage is occupied by Mr. Beecher himself. Over the stage, however, is a gallery for the organ and choir. There was not, on the occasion upon which I was present, a vacant place in the building. As one looked down from what corresponded with the gallery of a theatre, there appeared to be no aisles in the body of the church, because as soon as the occupants of the pews had taken their places, seats that had been fastened up against the outside of the pews were opened out and instantly filled. The service commenced with the Te Deum, chanted by a choir of ladies and gentlemen. A short prayer was then offered. This was followed by a short lesson from the book of Ecclesiastes, which was all that the service contained from the Holy Scriptures. Six or seven children were now baptised. The baptismal service consisted of several texts bearing more or less on the subject, which were chanted by the choir, Mr. Beecher afterwards sprinkling water upon each in the name of the Trinity. This was succeeded by a long prayer, which was rather a thanksgiving for domestic happiness than a prayer. A hymn was then sung, during the singing of which very few of the vast congregation rose from their seats. There was, of course, no kneeling during the prayers, or in any part of the service, which was concluded with a sermon of more than an hour's length, taken from the few verses in Ecclesiastes that had been previously read. The sermon was an essay on ' the art of making old age happy and beautiful.' This was in connection with the administration of the sacrament of baptism. He spoke very eulogistically of a certain admiral, whose name I could not catch, now residing at Brooklyn, in the neighbourhood of Mr. Beecher's church, and whom the preacher announced as the specimen old man. He inveighed strongly against all forms of dissipation, on the ground that 'they take too much out of a man. They are,' he said, ' cheques drawn by youth on old age.' He said ' he had no objection to balls, provided they were held in the middle of the day and in the open air.' He should like to see young people dancing on the green turf in summer. But crowded rooms and late hours were prejudicial to health.' He thanked God that he had never used tobacco in any form. He said, 'the use of it was a filthy, beastly habit, wasteful of health and of animal power.' In speaking of excessive drinking, he said 'that the American had not the excuse which the Englishman had, for the latter had so much water outside, that there was a reason for his never taking any inside.' This was received by the congregation with great laughter, as were some other sallies contained in the sermon.

According to our ideas, there was a great want of reverence in the service. People talked—some who were in my hearing, of dollars and investments—till the service commenced. One of the officers of the Church wore his hat till the congregation were more than half assembled. Mr. Beecher appeared to me to have but two tones, a very loud one and a quiet impressive one. The latter was very much the better of the two. His manuscript was placed on a desk on the stage. He could leave the desk with his manuscript on it whenever he pleased; and this he frequently did. One has no right to express an opinion of a preacher's power after having heard only one sermon; all, therefore, that I will say of Mr. Beecher is what I heard said of him. I was told that his popularity never flagged, and that his originality had hitherto proved inexhaustible; for that during the many years he had been before the public, during which time everything he had said had been reported, he had never been known to repeat himself. I was also told that he had been a useful man in

calming, as far as the great influence he possessed
allowed, the storms both of religious controversy and
of political animosity. It must be remembered that
a clergyman of Mr. Beecher's energy and talents has
much more prominence and influence in America,
where there is no governing class, than it would be
possible for him to attain in England.

There is a club—perhaps we should call it a society
or association—of Episcopalian Broad Churchmen,
the members of which reside in the cities of New
York and Philadelphia. I believe clergymen only
are members.

Almost every Episcopal church in New York has
a chapel attached to it, exclusively for the use of the
poor. This has been done because it has been
found there, just as is the case with us, that in the
cities the poor will not use the same churches as the
rich. We have in London, in a few cases, attempted
to cure the same evil with the same remedy. The
remedy, however, has not been fairly applied, for a
better class of persons (the very thing that indisposes
the ill-clad poor to be present) has been allowed to
appropriate to themselves a large proportion of the
sittings in these chapels.

I will mention here a conclusion to which I was
brought by my observation of what was going on in
the Episcopal Church in different parts of the Union.
Among ministers and congregations there are, just
as with us, some High Church, some Low Church,
some Ritualistic, and some Broad Church. I think
the proportion of those that are High Church is
greater with them than with ourselves. The real and
important difference between us on this head is,

that in the American Church every minister and congregation belongs distinctly to one or other of these parties, and that every Church is worked at high pressure.

One of the leading divines of America whom I met at New York (he was not a minister of the Episcopal Church) remarked to me that the view taken in America of a minister's duty was, that he was a teacher. He occupied towards the adults of the congregation precisely the same position that the schoolmaster held with respect to the children. What he had to teach was the history and theory of religion; and to show how, as a rule of life, it bore on the ever-varying circumstances of the day. If he could not teach the people these things he was of no use to them.

This ignores altogether that view of the service which makes it an expression of the devotion and of the religious feelings of the congregation itself.

CHAPTER III.

WHY AN UNREASONABLE FANCY WAS ACTED ON—THE HISTORY OF THE CAUSE OF AMERICAN PROGRESSIVENESS—WHAT PASSES IN AMERICA IMPORTANT TO US—THE NORTHERN STATES SOWN BROADCAST WITH HOUSES.

I HAD had good times at New York, and I was rather eagerly looking forward to good times at Washington, and so was somewhat disinclined to tarry on the way thither. Still I thought it would be unwise to lose an opportunity which offered itself for seeing something of the second city of the Union, which lay upon my route. I therefore stopped at the place, and having secured comfortable quarters at the best hotel (in America there is a wider difference between the best and second-rate hotels than there is elsewhere), I sallied forth to get some idea of the external appearance of the town. There are occasions, it is said, when imagination overpowers our judgment, and makes fools of us all. I now became, I suppose, an illustration of this process. As I walked along the streets they appeared to me distressingly straight. Their nomenclature, too, was painfully dull and formal. This is a place, I began to think, where men and women profess a form of virtue too exalted for ordinary mortals. Such a city as this appears to be, must be inhabited by people who are not so human as to err, nor so divine as to forgive. If I had not been alone, it would probably have been impossible for so groundless a fancy to have taken possession of my mind. Still I was rational enough, when I had finished my breakfast the next morning, to think of delivering some of my letters of introduction. It seemed best to begin with one addressed to a gentleman whose official position need not now be mentioned. On finding the house I was in search of, I sent in my letter. The gentleman was not himself at home, but his wife opened the letter, and sent out to say that she would see me. I have not the slightest idea that she had any thought of being rude or discourteous. If so, I should not say anything about what passed; for then it would have been the only instance of discourtesy I met with in my travels through the United States, and a single instance of discourtesy would be obliterated by the recollection of helpfulness and kindness everywhere else. It was, however, an instance of precisely what my fancy had been suggesting of the kind of virtue which would be the natural growth of the place. 'Sir,' said the lady, without asking me to be seated, or taking a seat herself, and in a tone and with a manner which proclaimed that she belonged to the order of beings who cannot err, and who regard the disposition to forgive as one of the weaknesses of ordinary mortals: 'Sir, I will not attempt to conceal from you that our feelings are completely changed towards Englishmen. Formerly we used to think that England was always on the side of right. But since we found that, during the late war, she sided with the South, our opinion of England has been reversed; and the reversal of our feelings has accompanied the reversal of our opinion.'

'Madam,' I replied, 'it is true that there were many in England who felt towards the South, just as the schoolboy feels, while he reads Homer's "Iliad," about Hector, when he finds him battling manfully against destiny and a host of heroes. His sympathies, if he has any generosity in his character, are naturally enlisted on behalf of the brave man who is acquitting himself so well, and who must in the end be overwhelmed.'

With these two little speeches the brief interview ended. For the moment my fancies seemed hard and established facts. What could I gain by remaining longer in such a place?—and so I left it by the first train.

People look upon the progressiveness and enterprise of the Americans as if it were something *sui generis*. This, however, is a mistake; the difference is only one of degree, and not of kind. The character of the American, just like every other product, whether in external nature or in man, is the result of a chain of precedent events. In his case the links of this chain can be traced back to dates and events long anterior to the dawn of history, or even to the twilight of tradition, but which, thanks to modern science, are not altogether irrecoverable. Philology reveals to us that race of mankind to which the American belongs, seated at a very remote date somewhere in Central Asia. As there is no ground for supposing that it came from the South, which was occupied by another and very different branch of the human family, or from the West or the North, for reasons with which the philologist and ethnologist will be familiar, we must conclude that if it had not sprung from the soil, it must have come from a more distant east. If then the Aryans of Central Asia had been the product of a migration, of course only those had come who had had the enterprise and the hardihood to go in quest of a new home. This then was the spirit which presided over the race at its birth, and launched it upon its long career. Again and again—we know not how often, for the records of history had not yet begun—the same process must have been repeated. Of this hardy and enterprising race, the most hardy and enterprising again renewed their westward movement. All the while the characteristics of the advancing race were being confirmed and strengthened; the infirm and feeble in body or purpose were ever being left behind, and the primeval and now hereditary impulse to move on at all risks was becoming in those who from time to time sought new homes an ever-strengthening instinct. At last—and this is when ordinary history first takes cognisance of them—we find them settled on the southern and northern shores of the Baltic.

After a time the day arrives for another movement, for another winnowing and sifting, far more searching than any of the previous ones. Greater hardihood and enterprise are needed than were ever called for in any of their past movements. The sea has now to be crossed—a new form of danger to be confronted. Those who venture in their open and half-open boats on this great enterprise, to establish a new home for themselves on the other side of the storm-swept waste of waters, must be men who know no fear, and in whom the instinct of moving onward is irrepressible. The result of this supreme effort is the great English nation—the product of all that is best in Angles, Jutes, Saxons, Danes, and Northmen. Such was the long process by which the men were formed who fought at Crecy, Poitiers, and Agincourt; at Blenheim, and Ramilies, and Malplaquet; at Trafalgar, and at Waterloo; on the Ganges, the Nile, and the St. Lawrence; who produced a Bacon, a Shakespeare, and a Newton; who first tried men by their peers, and first governed themselves by their representatives; who broke the papal yoke, and established freedom of religion, of speech, of the press, and of commerce. In their little island they proved themselves the grandest race the world had seen.

But the great drama was not yet complete. The original impulse had ever been gaining strength, and now appeared to culminate. But it was not so. One more effort had to be made. In grandeur and hardihood it transcended all that had yet been achieved. Not a narrow sea, but the broad Atlantic had to be crossed; not a small island, but a new world had to be occupied. The English race must itself be sifted, and none but those who have nerve as firm as that of the Pilgrim Fathers, and the most active instinct of progression, can take part in this mighty enterprise. And so it comes to pass that America is peopled with that which is most enterprising and progressive in that race in which these qualities had been most highly developed. In these respects she receives the cream of the cream, the purest selection of that which was most select.

The long series is now completed. The circuit of the world has been made. The hardy, the inventive, the go-ahead American looks out on the Pacific and towards that side of the old continent from which his first ancestors started on the long career which in his person is now consummated.

The like of this has not been done by any other race of men, or in any other part of the world. In human history it is something quite unique. It is the main stream in the history of man. All other series of events—as, for instance, that which resulted in the culture of mind in Greece, and that which resulted in the empire of Rome—only appear to have purpose and value when viewed in connection with it, or rather as subsidiary to it. Their true place in history is that of affluents to this main stream. And even Christianity itself, which so loudly proclaims its indifference to all national or ethnological distinctions, and its equal regard for every branch of the human family, while it has been rejected by the race to which it was first revealed, has become to the more advanced parts of the Teutonic race, in a greater degree than to any other people, their educator and their strength.

A moment's comparison of the tone in which we write and speak about America with the tone in which we write and speak about other countries, and of the feelings with which we regard what is passing there with the feelings with which we regard what is passing elsewhere, will show that we look upon American events as fraught with a greater amount of good and of evil to ourselves, than what is happening in all the world besides. Much, for instance, has of late been said and written about what is called the resurrection of Italy, but who expects from that resurrection anything that will affect either the hopes or the fears of mankind? Everybody, however, feels that the future of humanity will be greatly influenced by, and in no small degree depend upon, what is going on in America. Or if we turn to that country which has hitherto been more influential than any other in disturbing, or, which it claims as its right, of directing the course of events on the Continent of Europe, we do not find any causes now in operation which we can suppose likely to result in improving the material circumstances of the French petty proprietors, that is, of the bulk of the French nation, or in giving them more freedom and intellectual energy than they at present possess. The form and character of their government, their church, the division of property that obtains among them, the accepted arrangements and spirit of society, all tend to immobility. In America everyone understands that the stream is all the other way. Mental activity is universal. Public opinion is the opinion of those who in the open arena of public discussion are able to influence the greatest number; and public opinion sweeps away every obstruction.

The aspect of the country between Philadelphia and Baltimore took me very much by surprise, as I suppose it would anyone whose previous travels had been confined to Europe. I had imagined that old and densely peopled countries, like England and France, must necessarily present to the eye of the traveller an appearance of their being more closely inhabited than a new country like America. But the very reverse of this is the case, and most strikingly so. All the way from Philadelphia to Baltimore I found the country sown with houses. This arises from the fact that every 100 or 150 acres belong to a separate proprietor (large estates being unknown) who has his house upon his small farm, which he cultivates with his own hands and the assistance of his family. As far as the eye can range over the country you see these white farmhouses. And you may now see them all the way from New York to Omaha on the Missouri, 500 miles beyond Chicago, and 1,500 from New York. The traveller in the United States generally derives his idea of the wealth of the people from what he sees in the towns. The rapidity of their growth, the amount of business done in them, the dimensions of their shops, the goodly appearance of the houses of their merchants, justify him in supposing that the Americans are a very wealthy people. But all this wealth of the towns is in fact only a measure of the wealth of the country. The towns become wealthy and flourishing in proportion to the wealth of the country. These tens of myriads, then, of farmhouses, each of which is evidently the home of a well-to-do family, and of which one is never out of sight in the settled districts of the North, are the truest and most interesting indications of the nature and of the amount of the riches of the United States.

CHAPTER IV.

THE LOCOMOTIVE IN THE STREETS—IN BALTIMORE PUBLIC OPINION FIRST BECOMES SOUTHERN—GROWTH AND PROSPECTS OF BALTIMORE—ON TRADING POLITICIANS AND ILL WILL TO ENGLAND—WHY AN AMERICAN TUTOR THOUGHT NECESSARY FOR AN ENGLISHMAN—REPUDIATION—THE MASSES AND MIDDLE CLASSES IN FAVOUR OF IT—ARGUMENTS IN FAVOUR OF IT—AN ARGUMENT USED 2,000 MILES FROM WALL STREET—WHY REPUBLICANS BOUND TO REPUDIATE—AMERICANS ADDICTED TO ABSTRACT REASONING—INSTANCES.

WE very often find a difficulty in getting our horses to take quietly the sound of a railway train in motion. It was at Baltimore that I first saw the locomotive dragging a train along the main street of a city. All the precaution that was taken was merely to ring a bell on the top of the engine to warn foot-passengers and drivers of carriages. Many horses were passed, and many crossed the moving train, but I did not observe that in any instance they took the least notice of it. I afterwards saw the same arrangement at Chicago, at New York, and at many other places, and did not anywhere hear that accidents resulted from it.

Baltimore was the first place in which I found the general sentiment strongly Southern. Balls and bazaars were being got up, while I was there, for the openly avowed purpose of collecting funds to support those families in the South which had been reduced

A Marylander's Opinion of Government.

to poverty by the late war. This made me feel as if I were among another people; for in the North I had heard the South spoken of very vindictively, as 'that they needed more suffering to take their pride out of them;' and 'that nothing could be done with the South till the present proprietors had all been swept away, and Northern men substituted for them.' I am not aware, however, that I ever heard any remarks of this kind made by persons whom we should describe as of the upper class.

There has been a large emigration to Baltimore, from the States of the late Southern Confederacy, of people who would not live under negro domination as long as they had the means of living elsewhere. Many Northern men also had lately settled there, in expectation that the business of the place would rapidly increase. As it has a fine harbour, and the development of the railway system is now connecting it with the whole of the interior, there appears to be no reason why it should not, at no very distant day, become a dangerous rival of Philadelphia and even of New York. I understood that as many as 4,000 houses were built here in the last twelve months.

'Sir,' said a Maryland planter to me, 'many Americans, of whom I am one, think that the English government is the best in the world. No system of government which, like ours, can breed nothing better than trading politicians, can be either generous or just; and must sooner or later fall, overwhelmed by the hatred of some and the contempt of other sections of the community.' The same gentleman was of opinion that the animosity felt towards

England after the revolutionary war had now almost died out among native-born Americans; for instance, there is, he said, not one Fenian lodge in the whole of New England. Whatever ill-will there may be existing at present originates in the Irish, and radiates from them, if in any instances it has spread beyond them. An Englishman who had been long settled in America, and who took part in the conversation, thought differently. He was of opinion, that at all events a strong prejudice existed in the minds of native-born Americans against the English.

While at dinner at my hotel, a gentleman who was seated opposite to me—he was one of the few stout men, I believe the only one, I saw in America —accosted me with the remark 'that he could not believe what he understood me to say, that I had not yet been a month in the country, because'—for this was his reason—'I spoke the language so well. Or if I am to believe it,' he went on, 'I suppose you had an American tutor to teach you our language.' I assured him that he had understood me rightly, and that I had never had the advantage of the instruction he considered necessary, nor was there such a great difference between the language of America and that of England as to make Englishmen feel the need of American tutors. 'That, sir,' he replied, 'is by no means in accordance with my experience. I have myself conversed with Englishmen, and found their language very unlike our own. They seldom know where to use and where not to use the initial H. And their language is full of ungrammatical and vulgar expressions, from which ours is entirely free.'

This gentleman's mistake can be easily explained; and the explanation will show that it is one into which an American may very possibly fall. It is a remarkable fact that the English spoken in America is not only very pure, but also is spoken with equal purity by all classes. This in some measure, of course, results from the success of their educational efforts, and from the fact which arises out of it that they are, almost to a man, a nation of readers. But not only is it the same language without vulgarisms, in the mouths of all classes, but it is the same language without any dialectical differences over the whole continent. The language in every man's mouth is that of literature and of society; spoken at San Francisco just as it is spoken at New York, and on the Gulf of Mexico just as on the great lakes. It is even the language of the negroes in the towns. There is nothing resembling this in Europe, where every county, as in England, or every province and canton, has a different dialect. Of this the philological observer I was dining with was ignorant. He only knew that all Americans spoke uniformly one dialect. He naturally therefore supposed that all Englishmen must do the same; and as his acquaintance with Englishmen was confined to poor immigrants, he imagined that their dialect was the language of all Englishmen.

Often, in parts of the country most remote from each other, in wooden shanties and the poorest huts, I had this interesting fact of the purity and identity of the language of the Americans forced on my attention. And at such times I thought, not without some feelings of shame and sorrow, of the wretched vocabulary, consisting of not more than three or four hundred words, and those often ungrammatically used, and always more or less mispronounced, of our honest and hard-working peasantry. As language is the vehicle of ideas, these poor fellows have not been fairly used, and are being deprived of a large portion of the rich intellectual patrimony of Englishmen.

Before I went to America, I felt as certain as one can feel about any future event, that the Americans would pay every cent of their debt. I think still they possibly may. For their own sakes and for the honour of the race I hope they will. But I am not now so positive on this point as I was. Wherever it was allowable in conversation, I introduced the subject of the debt. At first, to my surprise (but after a time I got so accustomed to the expression of the sentiment that I should have been surprised had I heard anything to the contrary), I never met a single person in railway cars, or in hotels, who was in favour of complete payment. Many were in favour of complete repudiation; but far the greater number advocated the plan of immediate payment, by an issue to the public creditors of, as I heard it sometimes put, cartloads of greenbacks. This, of course, would not be very far from repudiation pure and simple: though nominally a payment in full, it would really be only the payment of a few shillings in the pound, as so large an issue would enormously depreciate the value of the greenbacks. This is the plan of Mr. Pendleton of Ohio, who is now the democratic candidate for the next presidency. It must therefore be approved generally by his supporters. The people, at a knowledge of whose sentiments I arrived in the way I have just mentioned, belonged chiefly, I suppose, to the class of storekeepers and travelling traders; though I have sometimes heard persons whose position I knew was better announce the same opinions. On the other hand, however, I never met with any flourishing and respectable merchant, and I may almost say with anyone whom we should describe as belonging to the upper class of society, who admitted for a moment the possibility of repudiation in any form. It seems, then, that in forecasting the probabilities of this question, the class that has numbers on its side must be regarded as pitted against the class that has on its side cultivation, intelligence, and wealth. But even from these few, some, as was once observed to me, ought probably to be discounted; because it is possible that some may be making a cheap profession of honesty, which they know will not, and have no wish ever should, be acted on. And the more certain they may feel of ultimate repudiation, the louder they may declare themselves in favour of payment. The South, whenever it shall have resumed its place in the councils of the Union, will, as most people seem to think, be in favour of the use of the sponge; for how can people be expected to tax themselves to pay for what was the instrument of their humiliation, conquest, and ruin? The question, then, between payment and repudiation, complete or partial, cannot now be decided so clearly and peremptorily against the latter as one could wish.

Of course the argument most commonly used

against payment is, that it necessitates such a burden of taxation as is no longer tolerable, that it is impoverishing the whole community, destroying both the home and the foreign trade, and pressing with peculiar and insupportable weight on the humbler classes.

Again, it is urged by many that the amount of their taxation is the one undoubted cause, both of the cost and of the corruption of their government. If they go back to their old amount of taxation, there will be no work for, and, what will be more to the purpose, no funds to maintain, these armies of official bloodsuckers.

I found, too, that there was floating before the minds of some an entrancing vision of what would be the wealth of the country if production were cheapened and trade revived, and if everybody had twice as much money to spend as at present.

Another argument I frequently heard, was made to rest on an attempt to separate in idea the bondholders and public creditors of all kinds from the people; and while it spoke of them as an extremely wealthy class, living in luxury, and doing nothing (a very unrepublican position for anyone to occupy), it suggested the idea that their wealth was derived from the burdens, that is to say, the sufferings, of the masses of the people, who, all the while, were struggling very hard for a bare subsistence. The object of this comparison is to make the bondholder an object of odium, and the tax-payers of the humbler classes objects of commiseration, in the hope that by so doing a rankling sense of injustice might be implanted in the breast of the latter.

Arguments for Repudiation.

At an hotel in a town on the very frontiers of civilisation, two thousand miles away from Wall Street, I heard the question of 'to pay or not to pay' debated, and the conclusion in favour of the latter alternative was clinched by the proof of the impossibility of paying. The speaker was an ex-judge, and was a man who spoke and reasoned well,—I mean in such a way as to carry his hearers along with him. His argument on this point was very concise. 'Just before the war,' his words were, 'the Government of the United States published a return, collected by its own officers, of the value of all the property of the people of the United States. The correctness of this return is unquestioned. We know from it both the saleable value of the property of the people and the annual income of that property. The property of the whole people is for purposes of taxation a single estate, but the debt we have incurred, plus the capital represented by our ordinary taxation, is greater in amount than the value of the whole of the property of the people of the United States; and the interest to be paid on the debt, plus the taxation required for other purposes, general and local, is greater than the income of the property of the whole people. And as no private estate can carry a debt greater in amount than the value of the estate, so no country can bear burdens that represent a property, if they were capitalised, greater than the property of the country, and an annual amount of taxation greater than the income of that property. I will not say, then, that the debt must be repudiated, for that would imply that we had some option in the matter;

I will only say that it is impossible that it should be paid, either capital or interest. The estate can't do it. It is an impossibility.' Both the statements of this argument and the inference drawn from them appeared to the audience unquestionable. There was a murmur of assent, and conviction was expressed on every face.

I will report the firing off of one more shot against the payment of the debt which I was so fortunate as to witness. It is worth mentioning, both for the sake of the *entourage* and because it involves a style of argument I found very frequently used, and with convincing effect, among the people of the United States.

The Governor of ———, one of the largest States in the Union, had been so good as to invite me to call upon him, that I might be introduced to some friend of his who would be with him on the following day. On being shown into the reception-room, I found the Governor seated in a kind of state, with his back to the fire and his feet on the table. On the opposite side were seated in a row eight or ten persons. They appeared to be a deputation from some town or association, who were then having an interview with the Governor. When the interruption caused by my entrance was over, a tall grey-headed man who had been speaking as I entered resumed his argument. He had rather the look of a well-to-do farmer, not of our stolid type, but of the keen American type. He was quick and incisive in his style of speaking, and dealt much with interrogatories, as is common with persons who have been mastered by an idea, and cannot but think that it must appear to others just in the light in which it appears to themselves. He proceeded:—'What I want to know is, whether this is not a republic?' He looked round, and was satisfied with the amount of apparent assent. 'The next thing I would ask is, what is the meaning of a republic?' No one was prepared with an answer, and so he proposed one himself. 'A monarchy is a government where everything is contrived for the advantage of an individual. An aristocracy is a government where everything is contrived for the advantage of a few. But a republic is a government in which whatever is for the advantage of the greater number either is or ought to be law. And now I ask another question: would it not be for the advantage of the greater part of the citizens of this State, and for the greater part of the citizens of the United States, that we should have no debt?' This was an unassailable position; and so he at once proceeded to the conclusion. 'Well then, I say, that if this is a republic there ought to be a law passed to free us from this debt. If we are not repudiators we are not republicans.' I am unable to report any other arguments that were urged by the deputation, for at this point the Governor conducted me into another room.

The method of reasoning contained in the gaunt old gentleman's argument against the payment of debts by republicans is, as I observed, very frequently used and very well received in the United States. It is worth noticing, because it is a method that is seldom used and never accepted on this side the water. It proceeds by assuming the truth of some abstract propositions, of which neither truth nor falsehood can properly be predicated, but which a half-instructed audience is always ready to accept, and then goes on to apply them to some question on which they appear to have a bearing, and which happens to be interesting at the moment. For instance, I was speaking on the subject of negro suffrage with one of the leading supporters of that concession in the South. An Englishman would probably have confined himself to the consideration of the fitness of the African for so important a part in the government of the country. My American friend contented himself with a kind of numerical formula. 'Suppose,' he said, 'the grown-up male population of the country is represented by the number 100. By excluding the negroes from the franchise, you reduce the voters to about one-half, that is 50. But, in a constituency of 50, a majority of 26 will rule. That is to say, 26 will rule 100. That is bad, but it is not all the evil of the restriction. In small bodies it is generally found that one resolute mind takes the lead. The result therefore would be that one would rule the 100. All this would be the consequence of departing from the simple republican rule of giving the vote equally to all.' The gentleman had this formularised argument in favour of the admission of the African to equal political power with the white race drawn out on a paper, which he took from his pocket-book and showed me—I quite believe, with the idea that I should find it unanswerable. It was all in vain that I pointed out to him that his argument was so abstract that it omitted all consideration of every one of the actual conditions of the question. He himself was thoroughly persuaded of its conclusiveness.

Another argument of just the same kind, but which aimed at the opposite conclusion, was frequently urged upon me. 'Have you read,' I was asked, 'Bishop ——'s book?' I forget the name of the ingenious prelate. 'He has demonstrated that the negro is not a man. No human being was saved from the Flood except Noah's family, and it is quite impossible that he could have had a negro son. The negro must therefore at that time have been regarded as a brute beast. And as Noah was acting under Divine guidance, he could not have been wrong in his estimate of the negro. And the negro cannot be any better now than he was then, for a brute beast can never become a man. We therefore are justified in looking upon him just as Noah looked upon him, and in supposing that he is of the gorilla race, only a little improved.'

I do not mean that a well-educated American would be at all more disposed to accept this kind of argument than a well-educated Englishman, but that it goes down with multitudes of Americans who have from their youth up had very little time for acquiring any knowledge but that of their business, yet feel themselves called on by the circumstances of American life to form and express opinions on almost every subject; and this is a call to which few are slow in responding.

CHAPTER V.

WASHINGTON—STYLE OF SPEAKING IN CONGRESS—CONGRESS NO NURSERY FOR STATESMEN—SOCIETY IN WASHINGTON—EPISCOPAL CHURCH IN WASHINGTON—SOME OPINIONS OF AN AMERICAN BISHOP—COMMISSIONER OF AGRICULTURE—USE OF THE DEPARTMENT—ITS MUSEUM GIVES AN IDEA OF THE VASTNESS OF THE COUNTRY—ITS NATURAL ADVANTAGES—WHAT VARIETY OF PRODUCTIONS HAS DONE FOR ENGLAND WILL BE REPEATED IN AMERICA—SPECIAL EXCELLENCE OF CALIFORNIAN PRODUCTIONS—THE CALIFORNIAN HIMSELF—CALIFORNIA COMPARED WITH ITALY—WHY COLOURED WAITERS PREFERABLE TO WHITE—NEGRO FUNERAL WITH MASONIC HONOURS—AMERICAN BIRDS' NESTS—BILL FOR MAKING EDUCATION COMPULSORY—COLOURED SCHOOLS—COMPARATIVE INTELLIGENCE OF THE NEGRO—VULGAR ERRORS ABOUT AMERICANS—NIGHT ATTENDANTS AT HOTEL READ 'OLIVER TWIST'—CAPITOL—TREASURY—PATENT OFFICE—WHAT OUR DIPLOMACY IN AMERICA SHOULD BE—USE OF ICED WATER.

WHILE at Washington I was frequently present at the debates in both Houses. I was not much impressed by the style of speaking either in the Senate or in the Chamber of Representatives. I heard much good common sense, and many of the attacks and defences which are necessary in party warfare, but I heard no eloquence, and nothing even that on this side we should call good speaking. Where eloquence was attempted, it seemed to me to result in declamation. I went away with the idea that both senators and representatives spoke, not like persons who were in the habit of addressing cultivated audiences, but whose style had been formed by the practice of canvassing-speeches and mob-oratory.

The most striking difference between our parliamentary system and the American Congress is, that ours is as perfect a school as is conceivable for statesmanship, while theirs can never be anything of the kind, except accidentally and in a very slight degree. With us a man who is destined for public life enters Parliament while still young. If there is anything in him, he is generally able to retain his seat. Thus he is all his life through learning the routine of administrative practice and the science of statesmanship. All along every word he utters is set down in black and white, to stand in evidence for or against him, and to be weighed by the House and by the public. And it is the opinion of the House and public, thus formed, that assigns him his place in the hierarchy of party. If he is capable of becoming a statesman, with time and training he becomes one. If the House and the country know that he has shown himself one of the ablest men of his party, high office is his right. He has to thank no one for it but himself. If he has proved himself the ablest man of his party, the first place is his. He has established his claim to it in the face of the world. Nothing of this kind goes on in the American Congress. It may be said to have no personal continuity. A large proportion of Congress—and this happens every fourth year—are new men, thrown up to the surface by the action of local political causes in their respective States; and most of these new men will themselves be superseded by other new men in the ensuing Congress. The idea of forming statesmen does not at all enter into the aim of the American Congress; it hardly seems to regard itself as standing in need of statesmanship, wherever and however acquired. It is rather a machine for ascertaining and carrying out the opinions of the people. A successful local politician, be he a grocer or a shoemaker, a rail-splitter or a tailor, will find his way into the Senate.

The society of Washington, while Congress is sitting, is remarkable for its great variety. There are the heads of the civil and military departments with their subordinates; and the senators and representatives from all parts of the Union, from California, the great West, the highly educated States of New England, and from the commercial and manufacturing States of New York and Pennsylvania. At present we have only to regret the absence of the gentlemen of the South. Many of these persons bring with them their families. The society thus formed is not so vast as that anyone should be lost in it; nor is there much tendency to break up into sets. The influence of the White House, which acts as a centre, and the practice of general receptions, which is universal among official people and persons of distinction, prevent isolation. The variety just mentioned in the component parts of the society of Washington is very perceptible, and contributes largely to its interest and picturesqueness. The only difference I observed between the manners of these republicans and our own, was that they were easier and less constrained than we are; for no one is haunted with the idea of maintaining or of establishing a position, because no one supposes himself better than anybody else; they appeared, too, to possess, in a greater degree than is common among us, that great requisite of good breeding, the double facility of being pleased and of pleasing. I would only add that there seem to be few dull people in American society. There is with them more general animation and *enjouement* of life than with us.

On attending morning service at the Church of the Epiphany at Washington, I found on the seat a printed paper containing a letter from the congregation to the minister, announcing that they begged that for the future he would consent to receive an increase to his salary, raising it to £800 a year; and one from the minister to the congregation, thanking them for their liberality. In addition to this salary they had presented him with a furnished house.

Washington, with a population of 120,000, has in the city eight Episcopal churches, and four in the suburb of George Town. There were when I was there two additional congregations in process of formation. At that time they were meeting in an upper room, but it was expected that they would soon be strong enough to build churches for themselves, and to become fully organised. An effort is being made to obtain a bishop for the district of Columbia, and, if possible, to get the consent of the bishops to his being made an archbishop and metropolitan of the American Church.

At the service I attended, there was not a seat vacant in the Church of the Epiphany; but they were all filled with well-dressed persons. In the afternoon of the same Sunday I went to the church of St. John's, to be present at a Bible class held by the Adjutant-General of the United States army, a man whom any church might be thankful to have among its members, and to hear the catechising conducted by the rector. The children catechised were those of the upper class, for here also I found no ill-dressed people among the congregation. In the evening I went to Trinity Church, where I was told I should see a congregation of the humbler classes. I heard a clergyman conduct the service and preach, who I thought possessed just the qualities which would adapt him for obtaining an influence over those classes, but I saw very few of them in the church.

As I am not aware that any bishop of the American Episcopal Church was at Washington while I was there, I will take this opportunity for offering to the consideration of English Churchmen some remarks that were made to me elsewhere by an American bishop. I run the risk of doing this without permission, because I believe that here at home we are far too ignorant of, not to say indifferent about, what is passing in the minds and hearts too of our American brother-churchmen. He thought that the Episcopal Church in America was the natural, or at all events now the chief, bond of union between the old country and the United States. With very few exceptions, and they are exceptions that are not worth considering, the Episcopalians cherish the recollections of the old country most fondly; whereas it is notorious that the American churches which are connected with English dissent are more or less actuated by feelings, if not of animosity, yet certainly of coldness towards the old country.

The Episcopal Church is a great power in the United States, and is more respected, and more influential in forming and guiding public opinion than even the government and legislature. Its members comprise the great bulk of the most refined and educated class in the country. Those who join us from that class come to us because they regard Romanism as a religion not for men, but only for women and children, while they look upon the other churches as having little devotion and less stability.

The Episcopal Church was opposed to the late war, and though pressure was put upon it, it would not give in to the fierce mania of the moment. This was the case in both sections.

The clergy of the different churches, but more particularly of the Episcopal Church, are, in the existing state of things on this continent, the natural and only aristocracy. The lawyers come next. The politicians are nowhere. The American people have had plenty of time and opportunities enough for weighing the latter, and have found them wanting in everything for which man respects his fellow-man: all the while their respect for the clergy of the Episcopal Church has constantly been becoming deeper.

The five Yankee States, with the exception of Connecticut, which is the most Episcopal State in the Union, are rapidly becoming Unitarian and Universalist. This in some degree accounts for the equivocal character of their acuteness, and for their singular want of magnanimity.

When he was in England, he was struck with the fact that the members of the Government took no notice of the American bishops. In this they showed their ignorance of the public mind in America. They also showed their disregard of the advance of the church to which they profess to belong. He did not suppose they neglected them because they were afraid of giving offence to the other religious communities of America, but simply because they were ignorant about America, and careless about their own church.

The Americans, being a practical people, have established, in connection with the general government at Washington, a department of agriculture, presided over by a commissioner. One of the objects of this department is to form a perfect museum of the agriculture of the United States. This is the act of a practical people, because as America is a new country, in the process of settlement, there must always be immigrants starting, some for one locality and some for another, who are in need of information as to what kinds or varieties of grain, vegetables, and fruit would be most suitable for the soil and climate of their proposed new home; and as to the best methods of cultivation for each crop; and what will be the difficulties they will have to contend with, and what have been ascertained to be the best remedies for these evils. It is possible that each year the value of the information distributed throughout the Union by this department may be many times greater than the cost of the department. If so, the cost is a small price to pay for a very great advantage.

My reason, however, for mentioning this museum of agriculture, is that it contributes very much towards making distinct in one's mind the idea of the vast extent of the territory of the United States, and its great range of climate. This it does by ocular demonstration. Here are collected into one view specimens of the agricultural and horticultural produce of every State in the Union, from Maine to Florida, and from Massachusetts to California. These specimens range through all the products of the temperate regions of the earth, and descend far down into the list of the products of tropical climes. All the cereals we grow in this country, Indian corn in many varieties, the grape, every description of European fruit—in some cases, as in that of the apple, greatly improved by its transference to America—tobacco, rice, the sweet potato, the sugar-cane, the orange, the banana, ending with the cocoa-nut of the South of Florida.

Here is a region larger than the whole of Europe, which if it were transferred to the part of the globe which Europe occupies, only retaining its latitude, would reach down to the Sahara of Africa, covering the whole of the Mediterranean. This vast territory contains an inland navigation which is the grandest in the world, and has in no way taxed the labour of man. From its extremest point at the north, at the head of the navigable stream of the Missouri, to its southern point at New Orleans, there is an open course of three thousand miles without a single break, a distance as great as the space which separates London from Timbuctoo, or from Bokhara. And this main artery of communication, the value of which is enhanced a thousand fold by the fact that it runs from north to south, enabling the produce of so many climes to be exchanged, instead of running along the same line of latitude, where there would be little or nothing to exchange, is supplemented on the right and left by 23,000 miles more of the natural navigation of its great affluents. And the vast valley which this system of rivers opens to traffic and travel is so extensive and fertile that it could support the whole population of Europe, and probably will support some day as large a population in far greater material well-being, and with far more highly cultivated intelligence.

If everything throughout this vast territory had been arranged by the most intelligent of mankind, with a view solely to the convenience of its inhabitants, we cannot imagine how it could have been made to contribute to those ends in a higher degree than it does at present. Not only is it capable of producing to a practically unlimited extent every plant that man cultivates, but it is also inexhaustibly rich in the precious and the useful metals, and in mineral fuel. The configuration too of the continent is such as to aid man in many ways in subduing and utilising the soil, for on each side of the grand central valley rises a long range of mountains, the one descending to the Pacific, the other to the Atlantic, which give birth to multitudes of rivers, which connect these vast districts with the two oceans, and supply harbours for carrying on intercourse with all the world.

One of the causes that has most contributed to the wealth and commercial aptitude of the inhabitants of the old country is, that the productions of no two districts in it are precisely similar. The districts, for instance, that breed cattle and sheep are not always those that fatten them, and never those that consume them. So with cereals, one district is good for wheat, another for barley, another for oats, another for beans and peas. Fish that is taken on the coast is consumed in the interior. A similar remark may be made of the various kinds of minerals with which different parts of the island have been enriched. Even the granite of Scotland is wanted in London for its streets. Every town must get its

CH. V. *A Consequence of Variety of Productions.* 53

flag-stones from a distance. Each kind of manufacture has certain requirements which render one district more suitable for it than another; so that for the article produced in each manufacturing locality there must be trade between that locality and all others. Hence it comes about that there is a larger interchange of home productions in this country than in any other in the world. In this respect compare Italy with ourselves. All its districts have much the same productions; the result of which is the minimum of home trade. How enormous must be the differences which must result to Italy and ourselves from this dissimilarity in our respective circumstances! I apply this to the United States of America. The cause which has contributed so much to make us wealthy, intelligent, and commercial, is to be found in the United States—with the difference, however, that what has been done here on a very small scale, is there done, and has yet to be done, on an enormous scale. Their variety of products is far greater than ours, and will have to be exchanged to far greater amounts, and so will employ a proportionately greater number of agents. What a vast traffic will it be when the wheat consumed throughout the Union shall be supplied by what are now the North-western States and California, and the mutton and beef shall be supplied by the Western prairies, and the pork by the maize-growing States, and the various metals, precious and useful, and the different forms of manufacture, each by different localities to all the rest!

This Museum of Agriculture and Horticulture gives one the means of comparing the size and quality of the fruits, vegetables, and cereals grown in different parts of the Union. The effects of climate and soil are, as might have been expected, very perceptible. A variety of the apple, for instance, that produces very large and good fruit in Illinois and Michigan, will deteriorate as one goes farther south, till at last it becomes not worth cultivating; while one sees specimens of other varieties, which their nature adapts to the sunnier States. The variety and excellence of the produce of the whole country is very striking, for everywhere in the United States there is light and heat enough and to spare; but what strikes one most of all is, the peculiar and extraordinary excellence of everything that comes from California; for instance, the pear La Belle Angevine, without any of the minute attention that is bestowed on its culture in France, very commonly attains the almost incredible weight of between three and four pounds. And all other kinds of fruit, and every kind of vegetable, grow in the same luxuriant manner. This is something that must be seen to be believed; but when seen, it enables one to understand how in the short space of twenty years this State has passed from an uninhabited wilderness to one of the richest and most powerful States in the Union. With such a climate and soil, to say nothing of its enormous mineral wealth, 'it is bound,' to use the local word, to leave New York, and Pennsylvania, and all the old leading States of the Union far behind, and, indeed, every other part of the world, whether new or old.

One cannot become acquainted with half-a-dozen Californians without seeing that man himself has been improved in this wonder-working region—the finest, not only that the Anglo-Saxon race, but that any race of man has ever inhabited. There is a quickness and determination of mind, and a calmness of manner, a quickness of eye and a cleanness of limb about a Californian that you cannot but notice. They have in a thousand ways shown enterprise which astonishes even Americans themselves. But in nothing have they shown it to such an incredible degree as in their agriculture. Their wines are of many kinds, as may be seen in this museum, and some of them are very good. Their garden produce is quite unrivalled. But I will only mention what they have done in the culture of wheat. Twenty years ago there was no agriculture in this State. Twenty years are not time enough here to enable us to make up our minds as to whether we will use the steam-plough. But in these twenty years the clear-sighted and undaunted Californian has learnt how to grow enough wheat to feed the inhabitants of his own State, and in a great degree of the neighbouring States of Oregon and Washington, and the whole population of our British Columbia. And not content with this, he has undertaken the supply of Chili and Peru, and the other republics on the sea-board of the Eastern Pacific. This comes to a great deal—to what is almost beyond belief. To the Californian, however, it is nothing at all. He has for several years been sending wheat the length of the Pacific and Atlantic Oceans to England. Eight years ago, I saw cargoes of Californian wheat selling at a profit in Liverpool. And last year he capped even this, for he sent both flour and wheat to New York, selling the former at eleven dollars a barrel—that is, two dollars a barrel cheaper than the great millers of Richmond can afford to lay it down at, whose mills are, as it were, just outside the gates of New York. And the latter they sold at a price which, had there been enough of it, would have completely excluded Chicago and the great wheat-producing States of the North-west from the market, and so would have swept away, at a single stroke, the chief part of the business of the great Erie Canal.

Any little change at our own door appears great to us, while the mightiest changes at a distance affect us little: if, however, we are disposed to weigh events in accordance with their intrinsic and real importance, we might compare the rising of the star of this extraordinary community with the lately recovered unity and independence of Italy, which has of late engrossed so much of our attention and interest. California at the present moment contains a population of between six and seven hundred thousand souls —Italy one of twenty-four millions. But if the old Nation and the new State were to try their strength against one another, I believe that this handful of keen-witted and intrepid men would go just where they pleased, and do just what they pleased in any part of Italy; while the Italians, however much of their strength they might put forth, would find themselves quite unable to do anything of the kind with California. How much would a Californian population of twenty-four millions make of Italy! They would have no armies of officials, no brigandage, no debt; their ships would sail on every sea; their influence would be felt all over Europe and throughout the world.

At Washington, as at Philadelphia and Baltimore, I found the waiters at the hotels were coloured men. I very much preferred this to having the white waiters I had fallen in with at the Fifth Avenue Hotel in New York: the latter, I thought, felt the degradation of their position. In America, waiting in hotels and railway cars, being domestic servants, and keeping barbers' shops, are the only employments, with the exception of field-labour in the South, which are really left open to the coloured race. For a white man, therefore, to become a waiter at an hôtel, is to sink himself to the level of the black. It is impossible to conceive a native American placing himself in such a situation. It is too poor an employment for him; it is of a servile character; and it is one which, in public opinion and by general practice, has been assigned to the African. Even here, in England, one pities the man whom circumstances have made a footman—when one sees the hosts of men occupied in this way in London and elsewhere, and compares what they are, and their sad prospects, with the fine manly fellows they might have been, and the independence they might have secured for themselves and their children in Canada, the Western States, Brazil, on the Rio Plata, in Natal, Australia or New Zealand, or in other places where the climate is fine, land a drug, and the only thing wanted is men who can work as Englishmen and their descendants alone can and do. The feelings, however, of commiseration with which in England we regard the man whom circumstances have placed in such a position, become in America dashed with somewhat of contempt for the whites who voluntarily place themselves in it. One does not feel in the least degree in this way towards the coloured waiters. It is not in the nature of the black that he should ever work hard enough to cultivate the soil, where the climate is such that the European is capable of labouring in it. He has it not in him to become, and never has become, a settler. One cannot imagine half-a-dozen negroes voluntarily submitting for half-a-dozen years to the incessant toil—the ploughing, the sowing, the weeding, the harvesting, the threshing, the cattle-tending of a Northern farm. It is not only that they are constitutionally lazy, but that they are also of too volatile a disposition for such a life. Nature, however, has fitted them for such employments as domestic service and waiting in hotels. In their case there is an obvious congruity between the employment and the person. When you thank the willing and cheerful black for changing your plate, or ministering in some way to your personal wants, and get in return the almost universal 'Vara welcome,' you do not feel in the slightest degree that a good and likely man is being wasted and degraded just for the promotion of your own comfort and convenience.

On a Sunday while I was at Washington, I saw a grand negro funeral. The deceased had been a minister in one of their churches, and also a Freemason. He was therefore buried with Masonic honours. They chose for the procession the streets in which, and the day and the hour of the day when, there would be most people to witness it. The order was as follows :—First came a negro on horseback to open the way; then a powerful band. These were succeeded by two hundred Masons, all well dressed, with aprons, scarves, and badges. After these the corpse in a handsome coffin. In order that this might be completely seen, the sides of the hearse were of plate-glass. The corpse was followed by twenty carriages, each drawn by two horses. These carriages contained the ladies of the *cortége*. I saw no attempt among them, by drawing down blinds or the use of the handkerchief, to conceal their grief. Their bearing, I rather thought, indicated the presence in their sable breasts of the very ancient desire to see and be seen. No whites took any part in the funeral. A great many, however, had assembled to see it pass, all of whom appeared to behave very decorously. There was evidently a great effort on the part of the blacks to appear to advantage. It was a curious and interesting sight. Some of the mulattoes were tall and good-looking, but far the greater part of them were intensely ugly. In the procession was every shade of colour, from ebony to what might have easily passed for the complexion of an European; for in the United States not even light hair and blue eyes with a fair skin can rescue from social exclusion the man who is known to have in his veins a drop of negro blood.

Wherever in the South I mentioned this negro funeral, the same remark was made on the Freemasonry of the negroes. Everyone professed himself ignorant of how the negroes had come by it. No one knew who had admitted them; and no one would acknowledge them as brother-Masons.

On going over the Smithsonian Museum, I was much struck by the superiority of the birds of

America to those of Europe in the architectural skill and beauty of their nests.

While I was at Washington, a bill was before Congress for depriving of the franchise every father whose children (up to a certain age) did not attend school at least twelve weeks each year.

It was here that I first saw something of the Freedman's Bureau. Probably in the first days of emancipation some agency was needed for regulating the movements of the negroes, and for supplying them with information as to their newly acquired rights. I am, however, disposed to think that so extensive a department as this bureau was altogether a mistake. It has cost much, and, as far as I could judge, done some harm and very little good. But of that anon: I will only speak now of my visit to one of the coloured schools I found at Washington under its superintendence. Like all the American schools I visited in towns, it was graded; that is, as we should express it, the school was divided into classes, each class having its own teacher and its own school-room, and being in every particular entirely distinct and separate from all the rest. There were about four hundred children on the books, and the usual number, about fifty, in each grade. It is impossible to exaggerate the advantages of this method of teaching. Each teacher has but one class; therefore the whole of the school-time is actually and actively employed in teaching. One class is not idle while the teacher is attending to another. No child is neglected. All parts of the school are equally cared for. There is much emulation among the teachers, each desiring that his part in the general system shall be done well. Each teacher having only one step or grade to teach, perfects himself in it, and teaches it thoroughly. When it has been completely mastered, the child is passed on to the teacher of the next step or grade, who in his turn goes through the same process; till at last the child, at the end of three years —for each grade requires six months—leaves the school, having passed through all it professes to teach, and generally having acquired it all thoroughly.

As I am not one of those who believe that the intellect of the longest civilised and most highly cultivated race in the world is no better than that of a race of which no branch has ever been civilised or cultivated in any way or degree—or, to put it in other words, that those who have given greater proofs of intelligence than any other race of men are (which is a contradiction in terms) on a level with those who have never given any proofs whatever of intelligence —I carefully notice everything that appears in any way to militate against my side of the question. For this reason I must mention that I was taken by surprise at the quickness and attainments of these four hundred coloured children. I never saw a school in England in which so much readiness was shown in answering questions as to the meaning of words that occurred in the reading lesson, and questions as to the meaning of what had been read. I must, however, remark that this may perhaps have been owing to the excellence of the teachers, who at present are chiefly enthusiasts in the cause of the negro from New England, and to this method of grading the schools. Of course the children were not readier or better taught than white children are in America.

And here, besides, comes in the doubt whether the intellectual development of this race, as all travellers in Africa assert, does not stop at the age of fourteen. There was in connection with these schools one for adult negro scholars, which may be regarded as to some extent a contradiction of this opinion, for I will not call it fact.

A great many of our ideas about American manners are mere traditions of an utterly gone-by state of things, as far away from their present manners (for changes are rapidly effected in America) as our own present manners are from those of Squire Western's and Parson Trulliber's day. In travelling 8,000 miles, through all parts of the Union, I never once saw, even in the woods of the South, or on the prairies of the West, any more than in New York or Boston, a *table d'hôte* dinner, served, at the sound of a bell, at one time for all the guests of the house, upon which a scramble ensued for every dish. I should be surprised to hear that this practice now existed in a single hotel in the Union. The method of proceeding, which is now universal, is for every single person, or party of persons, to be served separately. Nor are the middle-class Americans, who are the chief frequenters of hotels, more rapid in despatching their meals than we are. They are the reverse of talkative. They are not inquisitive. They are far more civil and helpful to one another and to strangers than Englishmen are. Those whom we should consider in good society are in a very high degree quiet and unassuming. I never heard an American use the word 'Siree' for Sir; nor did I ever hear one 'guess'; nor was I ever asked to 'liquor.' And so one might go on with many other things which were once American practices, but have been utterly abandoned. The fact is that the Americans are the most reasonable and teachable people in the world. Prove to an Englishman that he is wrong, and he will cling to his mistake more closely than before. Prove to the Americans that they are wrong, and the whole people will, as if they were one man, readily abandon their mistake.

I left Washington by an early train. Trains, as is the case with the hours for breakfast and for business, are earlier in the United States than in England. On coming down to the bar of the hotel at 5 A.M., I found that the night service of the hotel had spent their long watch in listening to Mr. Dickens's 'Oliver Twist,' each reading aloud in his turn.

In our diplomatic intercourse with the Government of the United States our method of proceeding ought to be founded on a right appreciation of the character of the people, because it is mainly with the people themselves that we have to do. Everybody reads the newspapers; everybody has his opinion, and what is the opinion of the majority is what is done. Now, speaking generally, the character of the people of the United States is such that the simplest style of diplomacy, or rather no diplomacy at all, is requisite in dealing with them. The Americans are an eminently reasonable people, and can be made to understand what is right. It is not as if we had to deal with Austrian, or Russian, or French diplomatists, with whom, unless we have long been much mistaken, reason and right are not the first considerations. What is requisite, then, in dealing with our cousins on the other side of the water, is, that we should ask for nothing but what we are clearly entitled to—what is our due, and our own; and that having asked for no more than what is rightfully ours, we should not concede one jot or one tittle. In two words—right and firmness—are comprised all that we have to attend to. It is absurd to suppose that we are incapable of making them understand what is our right; and they will respect us if we maintain our right with firmness, and they will despise us if we do not. They would never go to war with us knowing themselves to be in the wrong.

But, just as in trade they are always ready to take advantage of every slip or oversight on the part of those with whom they deal, deeming that men, whether themselves or others, must pay the penalty of carelessness, or ignorance, or even of want of sagacity—carrying this to a point beyond what we should consider quite justifiable—so also in diplomacy they will see what can be made out of all kinds of claims and demands such as their politicians are ever ingenious and forward in suggesting. But they are too just and reasonable a people to persist in being misled, after things have been fully and fairly put before them. Having, then, right clearly on our side, all the art that is required for the double purpose of maintaining our right, and of securing their respect, is firmness.

In its public buildings Washington has begun to resemble an European capital. Everyone has seen engravings of the Capitol. It is a large marble building with a central dome, very well placed on an eminence at one end of the city. From some reason arising out of the proprietorship of the land, no private residences or shops have sprung up in its immediate vicinity. The main street, of about a mile in length, connects it with the Executive Mansion, as the President's house is called in newspaper language. This also is of white marble. It is about as large as the country house of an English gentleman who is in receipt of an income of 10,000*l.* a year. The ground sinks between the Capitol and the President's house. Most of the public offices are in the immediate neighbourhood of the latter. The chief part of the city lies around and beyond the President's house. The Treasury, which has been built since the war, is in its dimensions worthy of the enormous business carried on in it—that is, the printing and issue of the greenback currency. It also is of white stone, I believe a kind of granite. The only other building worthy of notice, either from its dimensions or uses, is the Patent Office. In this is contained a model, or specimen, of everything for which a patent has been issued in the United States. One ought at least to walk through the numerous and spacious and well-filled apartments of this building, to get an idea of the activity of the inventive faculty in America, and of the great honour in which it is held.

I understood from Americans that every facility and security possible are given to persons desirous of taking out patents. Not only is there this museum to enable them to see whether or how the thing has been done before, but there are also persons whose business it is to be thoroughly acquainted with the specifications and objects of all former patents, and who are ready to supply any information on the

F

subject to all applicants. I could not but contrast this instance of American intelligence and wisdom with our English methods for discouraging invention, notwithstanding the fact that mechanical inventions are among the chief foundations and glories of our manufactures.

The Americans are a population of very thirsty souls. I do not know whether the cause of this is the dryness of the climate, or the habits of the people, or both combined. All day long, throughout the winter as well as the other seasons of the year, people are drinking water with ice floating in it. Many persons finish their breakfast with a large tumbler of this. Wherever men congregate, whether in the drawing-rooms of hotels or of private houses, or even in railway-cars, there is to be found the ever-present and ever-needed iced water. I found myself thirstier, and drank a great deal more in America than I had ever done before; and, like the natives, I felt a repugnance to drink water, however cold the weather might be, without ice in it. Now again in England, I am satisfied with perhaps one fourth of the water I needed in the United States, and I have no desire for the ice I regarded almost as a necessary there.

CHAPTER VI.

RICHMOND—WAY BY THE BATTLE-FIELDS—HANDINESS OF AMERICAN SOLDIERS—EFFECT OF SLAVERY ON THE VIRGINIAN LANDSCAPE—APPEARANCE OF AMERICAN FOREST—REPUBLICAN RELATIONS OF FATHER AND SON—STATE OF FEELING IN VIRGINIA—BILLIARDS IN AMERICA—WHY RICHMOND MILLERS UNDERSOLD BY CALIFORNIAN—WHY AMERICAN CITIES ARE LARGE—AMERICAN LIVING—PROSPECTS OF RICHMOND—INDICATIONS OF SOUTHERN CLIMATE IN RICHMOND—CHURCH MATTERS IN RICHMOND—INTEREST THAT ATTACHES TO RICHMOND AND TO THE HEROISM OF THE SOUTH.

In going to Richmond I made the circuit by Gordonsville, that I might visit the battle-fields of the late war which lie so thickly on that route from Washington. I went by Bull's Run, Culpepper Court House, Manassas Junction, the Rapahannock, the Rapidan, &c. This ground was several times contested. Nothing strikes one now in these sites except the extent of the breastworks and rifle-pits, and of the earthworks for batteries. I was told by a general of engineers who went through the whole war, that American soldiers, especially those in the Northern armies, were always eager of themselves to throw up these defences. It was their custom to set to work upon them even when tired with a long day's march or severe fighting; and there were occasions when they did this without tools. They acted in this way because they had sufficient intelligence to be fully aware of the advantage to themselves of earthworks of this kind, and therefore were desirous of being provided with them as speedily as possible. Most of the men, too, being young farmers or sons of farmers, had been accustomed to felling timber, and working on the land, so that every regiment was full of ready-made pioneers.

Another advantage possessed in a preeminent degree by the Northern armies, was that—their soldiers having been drawn from all classes and trades—if a corps for wheelwrights', millwrights', harness-makers', or almost for any other kind of work required on the field, was suddenly wanted, it was always to be had ready-made at a moment's notice.

On passing over these battle-fields one quickly understands why in the late war cavalry was so little used for improving a victory, and why also the attacking army generally appeared to have so great an advantage. In this part of Virginia—and I found it to be so everywhere throughout the South—the clearings are small and few, and far between, all the rest of the country being covered with forest, or with abandoned clearings returning to forest. In such a country cavalry could not have acted, even if, which was seldom the case, the victorious army had had more than was required for outpost duty and other work of the kind. And there being cover everywhere, an advancing force, in coming up for an attack on the enemy, could everywhere find concealment and shelter.

As soon as you enter Virginia you see unmistakable evidences of the recent existence of slavery. The country is not cleared, cultivated, and inhabited in the marvellous manner which so much surprises and pleases one in the North, where each man holds a

CH. VI. *How Slavery Modified the Landscape.* 69

plot of about a hundred acres, more or less, with his neat homestead planted in the middle of it. Here only a very small proportion of the land is under cultivation : far the greater part has, on the wasteful Southern system (where men owned large estates of several thousand acres, many times as much as they could keep in hand), been worked out, and then abandoned and allowed to return to wood. A respectable house is hardly ever seen along this line of railway. One gets tired of the monotony of the forest, and of the ever-recurring reflection how differently things would have looked, if this glorious State, blessed so highly in its soil and climate, had not been cursed with the blight of slavery.

I was surprised to find how closely the American forests resemble those of Europe. I suppose this settles the point that at some remote epoch of geological time the two continents were united. The two commonest species, and which often constitute the whole forest, are the never-failing pine and the oak. They both reach from Canada to the Gulf of Mexico. The former, to unscientific eyes, is only a small edition of the Scotch fir; and the oak, in its several varieties, as you pass along the railway, has much the same physiognomy as our English oak. The same may be said of the elm, the ash, the birch, the maples and the poplars. In the woods there is generally no undergrowth ; on the embankments and outskirts of the woods a rubus, very like some forms of our English blackberry, is abundant. What is most striking in the forests is the want of fine trees. Except in the Rocky Mountains, I never saw one in the United States. Their oaks and pines die at the top before they have got much beyond what we should call poles. They never seem to branch freely. I suppose their progenitors having grown in the forest for so many thousand years, the race has acquired the habit of growing straight. In the heart, however, of the city of New York, in Broadway between the Fifth Avenue Hotel and the Coleman House, I noticed the trunk (for not much more is now left) of an occidental plane that must once have been a noble specimen of its kind. I was told that in Kentucky and Ohio there were fine trees, but I saw none. I have heard from travelled Americans similar remarks to those I have just been making on the dearth of large trees in the United States. This of course is said of those States that lie to the east of the Alleghany Mountains.

We are in the habit of regarding Americans as less domestic than ourselves. I would suggest that their ideas on this subject are somewhat different from ours. It struck me that with them a little republicanism had passed from the State into the home—that children assumed and were allowed a greater degree of independence and equality than with us. This doubtless arises in a great degree from the early knowledge all children have that they will be able and must soon begin to provide for themselves. But it is greatly promoted, I believe, by the fact that the sons do not, as a general rule, leave the paternal roof when they go to school. With us the father never sees his children except in the holidays, and therefore continues to regard them as children, and never learns to regard them as companions. In America the father never loses sight of his child, who thus grows up as his companion, and is soon treated as a companion, and as in some sort an equal. I was often struck with this while listening to conversations between fathers and sons. The father, evidently quite in good faith, would ask the child's opinion, and inquire of him what he was going to do; as if he had some right to opinions of his own, and to independent action in matters in which he was himself concerned. A little incident in the train as I was on the way to Richmond, illustrated, I thought, this state of things. A father and son of about fourteen years of age were among the passengers, and in the next seat to myself. They had long been talking on a footing of equality in the way I have just mentioned; at last, to while away the time, they began to sing together. First they accompanied each other. Then they took alternate lines; at last alternate words. In this of course they tripped frequently, each laughing at the other for his mistakes. There was no attempt at keeping up the dignity of a parent, as might have been considered necessary and proper with us. There was no reserve. They were in a certain sense already on the equal footing of persons of the same age.

I should have been glad to have fallen in again with this gentleman, as, from the casual conversation I had with him this day in the railway car, I found that he was one of the most cultivated persons I met in my tour through the United States.

I arrived at the Spotswood Hotel at Richmond after dark, and was immediately shown into the supper-room, and placed at a table already occupied by three other persons. We soon entered into conversation. They knew at the first glance, as I found everywhere was the case, that I was an Englishman. 'Sir,' said the youngest of the party, who did not appear to be yet twenty years old, 'you have come to a God-forsaken country. Those who lately had riches are now in want; and the whites are now ruled by the blacks.'

Another gentleman I had met during the day had said to me, that 'he and many others wished they were living under a king of the English royal family. That Virginians deeply regretted that they had ever been separated from England; but that it was their own doing; for, if they had not helped, the Yankees never could have brought about the separation alone.'

Before I left Richmond, I had heard some of this gallant and most unfortunate people give utterance to the sentiment, 'that they were so stung by the sense of defeat, that they were ever wishing themselves dead. That everything had been so completely set on the cast of the die, that now, when it had decided against them, they could not find anything to live for. That their sense of honour had been crushed by defeat. That their property had been taken from them. That their black slaves had been made their masters.'

I afterwards met with other Virginians, who, having been impoverished by the war, had voluntarily expatriated themselves that they might, if possible, find elsewhere some support for those who were dependent on them. They were men who had been in the first and the last fight, and had lost everything they possessed. But I never heard from their lips one word of disloyalty to the Union to which they had returned in perfect good faith. They had appealed to the arbitrament of the sword. The decision had been against them; and they had submitted without any reservation to that decision. Their bitterness was only for those trading politicians who, being, as they thought, incapable of understanding honourable men, had sent a Freedman's Bureau and an army of occupation to oppress and torment those who were now quite as loyal to the Union as themselves, and if they were not, yet were utterly incapable of moving a finger against it.

The rage for athletic exercises, which has spread like wildfire over England, has made some feeble and unsuccessful efforts to lay hold of the mind of Young America. It is quite in harmony with the English love of field sports and outdoor games, but not at all with the habits and predilections of Americans. Their climate, which covers the ground with snow in winter, and is so hot in summer, may be unadapted to, and therefore indispose them for these things. But I believe the chief cause is in their indoor pursuits, which engross so much of their time and thoughts, and in the almost total absence among them of a class possessed of leisure, which from the times of the barons to the present day has always been a large and constantly increasing class amongst us. Billiards appear to have taken very much the place in America which field sports and athletic exercises occupy here. The large billiard rooms of their large hotels are of an evening always full of players and spectators. The American tables have no pockets, except in the four corners. At the hotel at which I stayed while at New York, I saw a man who played his game without cue or mace, merely spinning his ball between his thumb and middle finger. He had attained to such skill in doing this, that he appeared to be able to send the ball just to any point he pleased, with the greatest ease and certainty. I suppose, like Blondin, he had made a single muscular feat the work of his life. I saw billiard tables set up in wooden shanties on the plains of the North Platte, and beyond the plains at the foot of the Rocky Mountains.

I inquired here about the truth of what I had heard at Washington, that the great millers of Richmond had last year been undersold in the market of New York by the millers of California; and I was assured by one of the oldest and largest firms in the city that it was so. This firm, who had so short a water carriage from their own mill to the quays of New York, whose appliances of business were all perfected before the fathers of those now their rivals in California were born, who carry on business on such a scale as to make between seven and eight thousand barrels of flour a-week, cannot sell a barrel of that flour in New York at less than two dollars more than the price at which the Californian sells it. They account for this in the following way. At the time the Californian's harvest is ripe, he knows for a certainty that for two or three months no rain will fall. He therefore merely cuts his wheat without putting it into stacks or barns, without even gathering it up into sheaves. All this expense in harvesting he is saved. When he has cut the whole of his crop, he takes his machine into the field, and threshes it from the swarth. But this is not all. He gains still more largely in another way. He ploughs his land for wheat, and puts in his seed. The land is naturally so clean, and the climate so favourable, that the dropped grains of the first harvest will give him another crop next year, without a cent of cost, for there will be no ploughing or seeding required. Thus every second crop is a pure gift of nature. It is this that makes Californian wheat, and therefore Californian flour, so cheap. I tell the tale as it was told to me. I remember, however, that Sir Alexander Burns mentions that he saw wheat in the neighbourhood of Bokhara which was a biennial, and that the Bokhara farmer got two crops from one sowing. It is possible he may have got two crops from one sowing, not because on the banks of the Oxus the wheat plant was capable of bearing seed twice, but in this Californian fashion.

American cities are not in the position of our country towns, but of the capitals of European kingdoms. Richmond, for instance, till the disruption of Virginia which took place during the late war, was the capital of a State as large as the whole of England and Wales, with the addition of almost the half of Scotland. And as the sites of these cities were always chosen on account of the facilities they offered for trade and commerce, they have in almost every instance become the emporia for the chief part of the foreign and domestic business of their respective States. This also has generally led to their becoming manufacturing towns. In this way each has come to engross almost everything in the State that contributes to the building up of a great city. Bearing this in mind, we shall cease to wonder at the rapid growth in population, wealth, and trade of such a place as Chicago. It is a measure of the population, the wealth, the production and consumption of the great State of Illinois. Just so also with Cincinnati, St. Louis, and all their other great cities. They are made by the States to which they belong. This of course is not the case with New York, which is the commercial capital of a great part of the Union, or with New Orleans, which is the warehouse through which a large proportion of the produce of the valley of the Mississippi must pass. We must also remember that these large cities are at enormous distances from each other. In some instances, as notably in those of New York and New Orleans, the chief town in the State has not been able to retain the presence of the State legislature; this loss, however, has proved of no great consequence to them.

We are often told that the character of a nation in some degree depends on its kitchen. A traveller therefore who understands all that will be expected of him when he returns home, will not pass by unnoticed the style of cookery, and the materials with which it deals, of the people among whom he makes what I heard in this country called, not unaptly, 'a tour of observation'; and cookery, whether he chooses to observe it or not, is a matter which at all events is submitted to his observation two or three times a day.

The fact that first struck me in American 'living' was its abundance. Butchers' shops and poulterers' were, particularly the latter, of more frequent occurrence and better stored than I had ever seen elsewhere. Everybody appears to have plenty to eat, and few appear to neglect their opportunities.

But as this is a prosaic subject, I must begin at the

beginning. On my voyage out, before I had had time to generalise a conclusion on such a subject, a gentleman among the passengers confided to me, as the result of his own experience, that New England young ladies (of course he did not mean this of the young ladies who belonged to the upper ten thousand) never appeared less amiable than when at breakfast. A long and large experience enabled him to speak with some authority on this subject; though, as I afterwards discovered, he was not a quite unprejudiced commentator. I declined to accept his conclusion, notwithstanding his pointing out to me two young ladies who seemed to confirm it by disposing, each of them every morning, of a beefsteak, while they were considering what they would order for breakfast, and then going through a performance of varieties which was in very good keeping with the prologue.

One ought to be sparing of comment on a neighbour's way of managing himself. You are not acquainted with his constitution, or with the atmosphere he has to live in, or with the kind of work he has to do; and these things may render advisable in his case what would not suit yourself. But if you know that some of his habits are such as do not generally conduce to a sound sanitary condition, and then see that the doctor is the most frequent visitor in his house, you can hardly help coupling the two facts together in the relation of cause and effect. Now it happens that wherever one is in the United States, the most prominent and abundant *affiches* are those that recommend different kinds of 'bitters.' There are 'Red jacket bitters,' and 'Planters' bitters,' 'French

'German,' 'Mexican' and 'American bitters,' but no English, which I am disposed to take as a compliment implying that Englishmen need no such restoratives, for it can hardly mean that the name would be no recommendation. And there are bitters from the four quarters of the compass, limiting the range, I suppose, to American soil. All this of course implies that in our neighbour's case 'perfect order does not reign in the interior;' and it struck me that his constant habit of beginning the day with a breakfast that for its variety and solidity would be sufficient for a dinner on this side, had something to do with it. I hazard this, though the reply is obvious that one does not know what is requisite in this way in America. It is possible too that these bitters may not always mean what the traveller is likely to suppose. I say this because, on an occasion when a fractured rail delayed the train on the banks of the Mississippi for several hours, and every one produced what he had in the way of resources for passing away the time, an American I was then with produced from his hand-bag a bottle of what he called 'Angostura bitters.' I was rather surprised at his offering me a glass of it, thinking from its name that it must be something medicinal. I found it, however, to be merely a better kind of whiskey a little fortified with spice.

But though one may not be quite up to the mark in judging of the significance of these numerous species of bitters, one at all events is able to understand the constant complaints of Americans themselves on the subject of their health. One never elsewhere met with people who so frequently impart to you the information that they are suffering from dyspepsia. They do things in America on a big scale, and here they have a bigger amount of dyspepsia than any other country in the world. There may be other causes for this, but I still, perhaps very ignorantly, think the breakfast sufficient to account for it. It is a good rule in dietetics, as in many other things, to begin the day quietly. A certain amount of breakfast means a certain amount of work for the digestive machinery; and just the same rule that would apply to your horse will apply to this animal part of your own system. If you were going to give him some work in the afternoon, and again in the evening, or at night, you would spare him in the morning. One's stomach cannot always be working hard any more than one's horse can. I heard of a Southern planter who (before the war) never sat down to breakfast with less than six-and-twenty farinaceous preparations before him. I forbear to call them six-and-twenty kinds of bread, as my informant did, because they included dough cakes, buckwheat cakes, slap-jacks, fried hominy, &c. It was by no means meant that the gentleman who was so profuse in furnishing 'the bread-kind' department of his breakfast table confined himself to what he found there. These were merely the garniture, and not the substantial part of the replenishment of his matutinal board.

I heard of another gentleman, who bore a name well known in the Union, and who made it his daily practice to conclude this meal with a large bowl of cream; and of a third who, when, in Homeric fashion and phrase, he had appeased the rage of his appetite, would conclude with as many buckwheat cakes as he could lift at one time on his fork, which it was his custom to strike for this purpose through a lofty pile of them. Americans, sooner or later, find breakfasts of this kind harder to digest than they have hitherto found their national debt.

As buckwheat cakes are the usual finale of an American breakfast, I will explain what they are, and how they are to be eaten. The cakes are made from a batter (as the name implies) of buckwheat meal. They are done on a griddle. Each is in diameter about the size of the palm of one's hand, and in thickness about the sixth of an inch. The usual way of serving them at hotels is three cakes, one on the top of another, to each person; not from any wish to limit the number consumed, but because they cannot be eaten in perfection if more or less than three are brought at one time. You then prepare them yourself, by lifting the uppermost one with your fork, and buttering the upper surface of the middle one (if they are not hot enough to melt the butter they are worthless) you then reverse your pile of three, and lifting what had been the bottom one, repeat the process of buttering. That completed, you pour upon them from a jug, which is always brought with them, enough maple-syrup, or that failing, enough clarified syrup of sugar to cover them. They are now ready, and are by no means to be despised. As the buckwheat, however, is a little oleaginous, the cakes are a little leathery—so much the better, many will say; but this, and the combination of butter and syrup, must, one would think, render them somewhat dyspeptic. Still they are universally approved of, and it is the waiter's business at an hotel, when he sees you are finishing your breakfast, to ask you 'if you will have some cakes.' There would be something to say in favour of concluding a moderate breakfast occasionally in this way, but to make the cakes a daily addition to a varied and solid meal is to presume too much on one's strength. Who but would be appalled at contemplating the amount of work which half a century of such breakfasts would impose upon himself?

Where buckwheat meal, as in the Western prairies, cannot always be had, a good and orthodox substitute is the slap-jack, which is made and served in precisely the same way, the only difference being that of the material, which is wheaten flour. As this latter preparation is capable, and I think worthy, of acclimatisation, I will mention that the batter from which it is made has no other ingredients than flour, water, and soda. The griddle must be rubbed with a piece of suet before it is heated, and again before it is used. Serve in threes—very hot—with butter and syrup, as with the buckwheat cakes. I picked up this bit of culinary lore at a solitary ranche on the plains, where, having exhausted all the more obvious resources of the place, there was nothing else to do.

At the great hotels five meals a day are allowed. This is too much, not for the hotels, for such liberality is attractive (of course they all have a fixed price per day, ranging from three and a half to five dollars, for bed and board), but it is too much for the guests who avail themselves of it.

I need not go into particulars as to how the great American nation dines. If a man has breakfasted as he ought, and spent the day as he ought, he may dine as he pleases. No people in the world have a greater variety of materials for dining well than they have; perhaps no people so great a variety. Their beef and mutton are (thanks to our climate) not quite up to the English mark, but they are better than any on the continent of Europe. In variety, however, of materials they far exceed us. In Ohio and Kentucky they have naturalised the pheasant. The domestic turkey, as might be expected in the native region of its race, is so abundant as to be almost within everybody's reach. The same may be said of all kinds of poultry. This results from the great number and smallness of the farms in America, and from the abundance of Indian corn. There is also no scarcity of prairie game and quail. Wild venison is to be had everywhere, which, when properly kept and cooked, as I have seen it at Southern tables, is as tender as chicken, though entirely devoid of fat. I once saw terrapin soup and stewed terrapin on the *menu*; and thinking that I should frequently see them there again, I let that opportunity for qualifying myself to form some opinion of their merits pass by, and no other opportunity occurred—I suppose because it was not the season for it. I let pass in the same way all opportunities at New York for making myself acquainted with the merits of the buffalo, thinking that I should frequently meet with it in the West. When at Denver I received an invitation to sup on buffalo, which was the only chance I had in the West; and this invitation I was unable to accept. Stewed clams and clam soup are not bad. Soft-shelled crabs are not good. There is a very great variety of wild fowl: at Mobile, and in a still greater degree at

New Orleans, I was astonished at the number of species I saw in the market. At the head of all these stands the world-renowned canvas-back. No one, I believe, ever found him inferior to his reputation: of all the feathered tribe he is the tenderest and the most juicy. If he has come from the Potomac, he has a fine flavour of the wild celery, which is there his chief food. The red-head duck has the second place in point of excellence.

But what I put first on the list of all the good things of America is its oyster. It is two or three times the size of the European bivalve; I think more tender, and certainly of a more delicate flavour. It has also the great merit of being entirely free from any trace of a coppery taste, which habit and necessity only have brought us to tolerate in our own mollusk. To all its other merits it adds this great one—that it exists in incredible and inexhaustible quantities: and we know that it was abundant in the remote epochs of the past; because on the coasts of the Southern States we find long ridges of its shells, which must have been the slow accumulations of the thousands of years during which some savage race, that has left behind it in these mounds no record of any capacity for improvement or progress, was in the habit of fishing it from the contiguous beds, and leaving its shells on the nearest beach. This race has passed away without having left any record of its existence except these heaps of oyster shells. But the descendants of the oysters they lived upon still exist, and their shells are dispersed, by the aid of the locomotive, over the whole continent. How interesting and suggestive a contrast is here! But to keep to our subject: these oysters exist in such abundance that in the Gulf of Mexico I saw them bailed into the boats as fast as the men who were taking them could work their rakes. There are enough of them taken for a large trade with the towns in the interior, to which they are sent either fresh or in tins. Wherever you go you have them in some form or other—scalloped, stewed, uncooked, or in soup—every day; at some places you see them on the bills of fare for breakfast, dinner, and supper. As on my return to England we were supplied with them throughout the voyage, and as our own oysters have of late been selling at a famine price, I do not see why we should not import a part of our supply from America.

As far as I was able to judge from what I saw (my experience was confined to the winter), I thought that in fish we had the advantage of the Americans, both in variety and quality. Their white fish and bass are good. The latter is best when broiled. I mention this as I am not aware that we cook our bass in this way.

Maize enters largely into the dietary of Americans, and is used in a hundred forms. Well-prepared hominy is a good substitute for rice as a vegetable adjunct to roast meat or stews. It ought to be as white as paper, but to prepare it in this way requires a tedious process, for it must be soaked for a long time in a strong lye, to get rid of its yellow skin. Maize bread is good only for a few minutes after it is taken out of the oven. As soon as it ceases to be warm, moist, and soft, it ceases to be eatable. The sweet potatoes of America are as superior to those of Algeria and the south of Europe as Stilton cheese is to that of Suffolk. The best are grown in the sandy soils of the South. In South Carolina from two to five hundred bushels per acre are harvested. Pigs will fatten on them, and men can live on pork and sweet potatoes. But no dependence can be placed on this root, as in some years, for reasons that have not been discovered, they will not keep.

To those who are desirous of introducing a little variety into their Christmas dinner I would recommend an American practice of serving the turkey with hot apple jam. I need hardly say this is a very different thing from apple sauce. There may, however, be some difficulty in getting the jam made, as I do not recollect having often seen it in England. I would also recommend for that festive season an American method of improving mince pies. On this side it is sometimes objected to this time-honoured institution, that there is a ha'p'orth of mincemeat to an intolerable quantity of crust: with their unfailing readiness of invention they have hit on the method of uniting what with us would be two or three dozen small pies, almost all crust, into one large raised pie, which they help in pieces or slices. This completely meets the objection.

The fire which the Confederates kindled in Richmond to destroy the tobacco that was in the city at the time the Northern army were about to enter spread rapidly, as there was a strong wind at the time, and destroyed the whole of the lower part of the town. This was the quarter that was chiefly occupied by the large flour-mills and other manufactories of the place; it contained also many of the largest stores. A great part of what was burnt has been rebuilt, chiefly, I understood, by Northern capital. At the time, however, of my visit the work of reconstruction was at a standstill; and I saw considerable spaces occupied only with the *débris* of former buildings. One might have expected that factories would not be rebuilt just yet, as trade has been dull everywhere since the war, and as the Virginians themselves, like all the Southern people, are utterly ruined. But that any part of Richmond will ever remain in ruins it is difficult to believe, for one cannot imagine a city more advantageously situated. Nature has made it the commercial centre of a State which in climate, soil, and abundance of water communication is unrivalled in the Union. It may be regarded as the inland point upon which a great extent of natural navigation converges. In the rapids of the James River it possesses within the city great manufacturing power. In tobacco also it has an agricultural product for export which is already enormous, and which, as all the world wants it, may be increased to a practically unlimited extent. Nothing, I think, is needed for enabling it to go ahead as fast as any Western city but just a little time for arranging matters in the town and in the neighbouring country on the new basis, and so launching it on a career of prosperity which nothing henceforth will be likely to check. As far as I am able to judge, the two best speculations in the United States are buying land in Virginia (where it may now be had in abundance at two or three shillings an acre—land that must soon be settled in the Northern fashion) and in California, which will be flooded with immigrants as soon as the Pacific

Railroad is opened through, and this is advertised for next year.

The upper part of Richmond is occupied with private residences. I was at first surprised at their number, and at the indications they gave of what had been till lately the wealth of their inhabitants. But this surprise ceases when one remembers that it is the capital of, and the only great city in, a rich and large State. Like most American cities it has rows of trees in the streets, and here it is that you first begin to see in the live oaks and magnolias unmistakeable indications of the commencement of a Southern climate. Some of the magnolias in the little plots of ground in the fronts of the houses were true specimen plants. I was never tired of looking at them. They had grown with such uninterrupted regularity that there was not a twig, I might say not a leaf, missing in them, to mar the symmetry of their form, which was that of a large cone of the deepest green. Each leaf in size and depth of colour was a noble object in itself. I thought, what would not one give to see these noble trees in flower, and if a man could only have such a tree on his own lawn in England?

Here, as I did wherever I went, I inquired into the position the different churches, and especially the Episcopal Church, occupied in the place; and here, as everywhere else, the Methodists and Baptists appeared to be in the majority. I was taken to hear a very celebrated Presbyterian preacher. As far as I could judge from a single sermon, I thought that he preacher's excellence consisted entirely in his style, which was more polished and highly wrought than usual. As to his matter, there was not an idea or a sentiment but what one might have heard in the humblest chapel at home.

Of course sermons of this kind indicate the theological calibre of the congregation as well as that of the minister; for ministers and sermons are in the long run made by the congregation. In the evening of the same day I attended service at an Episcopal church. The interior of the building was profusely decorated with Christmas evergreens, and the sermon showed that the preacher was a man of learning and thought.

There are five Episcopal churches in this city. Those who minister in them appear to be well paid. I was told that the two highest salaries were 4,000 and 3,500 dollars. I heard, however, but I do not know to what denominations my informants belonged, and so possibly they may not have been well acquainted with the subject, that the Episcopal Church here is not so active as it is in the North. Of course in the North there is greater intellectual and religious activity, just as there is more doing in agriculture, manufactures, and trade; but if there was to be any exception to this rule, I should have expected to have found it in the Episcopal Church in Richmond, because here the people in bearing and conversation far more closely resemble Englishmen than is the case in the North. They speak, too, more frequently, and with more regard, of the old country, its people, and its institutions. Everybody I saw in the churches in Richmond, just as in the churches of the Northern cities, was well-dressed. The humbler classes appeared neither to have churches for themselves nor places in the churches of the rich. This, as everybody knows, is the weak point in the American voluntary system in their great cities.

Richmond possesses just now an especial interest for the traveller, which attaches to no other city in the United States. It is the city against which the North launched so many mighty hosts, and which was defended with such bravery, skill, and success by Lee, Jackson, Stuart, and other good soldiers whose names will live in history. It was in the streets and houses of this city that the civil and military leaders of the unfortunate Confederacy might have been seen. Here it was that those resolutions were debated and formed which enabled them with such slender resources in materials and men to stand at bay so long against the overwhelming myriads of the North.

In talking, too, with Southern men about the war —the soldiers of the North will understand, and even sympathise with the feeling—you are more deeply stirred than in talking with Northern men. Those who throughout wished the North well, and rejoiced in the issue of the struggle, must still feel in this way. These Southern men fought for a greater stake, for a country and for their property, against fearful odds, and at great disadvantages. The issue was to them that they lost everything except their honour. When you talk to these brave men, and hear of the cruel privations and hardships they went through, of their personal sufferings, of the brothers and sons they lost; when you see them writhing under defeat, and paying heavier penalties than vanquished men have ever paid in modern times, you regard them with mingled feelings of admiration and pity, which cannot be awakened by anything you can hear from those whose warfare has been crowned at every point with complete success.

CHAPTER VII.

HOW SOUTHERNERS DESCRIBE THEIR OWN CONDITION—EACH STATE MUST BE TAKEN SEPARATELY—MISSOURI—TENNESSEE—KENTUCKY —TEXAS—VIRGINIA—GEORGIA—FLORIDA—NORTH CAROLINA—ARKANSAS—SOUTH CAROLINA—LOUISIANA—MISSISSIPPI—WILL THE BLACKS GET THE FRANCHISE?—NO PARTY CONSIDERS THEM FIT— THEY WILL HAVE IT FOR A TIME—THIS WILL WEAKEN THE REPUDIATING PARTY—ALSO THE PARTY HOSTILE TO THIS COUNTRY—THE BLACKS WILL NOT ALL BE REPUBLICAN—THE SOUTH SHOULD HAVE BEEN LEFT ALONE TO SETTLE THE LABOUR QUESTION—THE BUREAU SUGGESTED FALSE IDEAS—THERE WILL BE NO WAR OF RACES—WHAT WILL KILL OUT THE BLACKS—THE RATE OF THIS—FUSION PHYSICALLY IMPOSSIBLE—MEANS OF COMMUNICATION IN THE SOUTH INDICATE ITS CONDITION.

I HAVE been frequently asked what I found was the condition of the South? And the question has been put in such a manner as to imply that the speaker regarded the South as a homogeneous entity, and that he supposed that the causes of its suffering—the war and the abolition of slavery—affected every part of it equally. But the reverse of this would be nearer to the truth. The Southern Confederacy was composed of States very differently circumstanced from each other, except in the one point of their system of labour; and the late war, and the overthrow of their system of labour, have affected those different States very differently. It is difficult to understand to how great a degree this is the case without having oneself gone through the South and seen these differences with one's own eyes. This is what I did, and I shall now attempt to give a short account of what I saw and heard. My route was through Richmond, Petersburg, Weldon, Wilmington, Charleston, Atlanta, Augusta, and Mobile to New Orleans; then up the valley of the Mississippi by way of Jackson, Memphis, and St. Louis. I had a superabundance of introductions for all the places I visited. I had obtained at Washington letters to all the Generals holding commands in the South, and which were in many cases fortified by duplicates from other quarters. I had also brought with me letters from New York and elsewhere to merchants whose firms ranked among the leading houses of the South, and to others who had been through the war; to men who were endeavouring to resuscitate the industry of their fallen States, and to a gentleman who held one of the highest offices in the late Confederate Government. I had therefore sufficient means for obtaining the information I required.

But the question is, what did one see and hear, and what were the conclusions to which one was brought by personal observation? The fact that first forces itself on the eye in the towns, and often in the rural districts you pass through, is that there are multitudes of negroes loafing about, doing nothing. You see them at every station. When you come to make inquiries as to what they are doing, and how they subsist, and generally as to the state of the country, you are told that they are to be found in shoals in every town where there is a Freedman's Bureau. They expect something from the Bureau; and, like so many coloured Micawbers, are drawn to the towns in the hope that something or other will turn up. So in the towns; but that in the country districts, where there is no power to restrain the idle and ill-disposed, things are in an actively bad condition—that this class has taken to stealing, and has not left on many properties a sweet potato or head of maize, or the pig that would have fed upon them—that they have made a clean sweep of everything edible. As to the state of the whites, that their condition is far more dreadful both to bear and to contemplate; for the blacks, as soon as they please to do the work they are accustomed to, may escape from their present distress, but that tens of thousands of white families, who lately were living in affluence and refinement, not knowing what it was either to want anything or to do anything for themselves, are now in a state of abject penury, positively of starvation; that many are without the means of procuring hominy and salt pork, the humblest fare in the country. And about this point there can be no doubt; for you have as evidence of the statement not only what Southerners say, but, as I afterwards found on returning to New York, the corroborative evidence of those good Northern people who are themselves subscribing largely to keep these destitute Southern families alive. In addition to all this, everyone tells you that he expects the unspeakable horrors of a war of races, which in their opinion cannot be adjourned for more than two years, as the coloured population are becoming day by day more and more dissatisfied with what the great change has hitherto done for them.

The first observation to be made on these statements is, that they cannot be equally applicable to all the very differently circumstanced States of the late Southern Confederacy. For instance, the State of Missouri, which is one of the most fertile in the Union, and by its climate thoroughly adapted to the Northern farm-system, was instantly benefited by the abolition of slavery. Tennessee and Kentucky will soon be in the same position, for both may very well be cultivated by white labour. The slow rate of progress made by the latter, when compared with the State of Ohio, which is only separated from it by the Ohio river, and has a colder climate, and not a more productive soil, is a proof that slavery, in which alone they differed, was the sole cause of its retardation. Texas was even at the moment very slightly affected by the change, and will now become a more attractive field than ever for white immigration. Here cattle-breeding is the chief occupation, which is one that does not at all require slave labour; and here also cotton has for many years been cultivated by the whites without the compulsory aid of the blacks. Virginia having passed through all the distress which is implied by the passage from the estate to the farm system, will emerge from its present distress a far richer and more populous state than it was before. General Lee's son, and many others of the noble Virginian race, have already set the example, and are themselves holding the plough and doing all the work of the farm with their own hands. How much more pleasing a picture will the valleys and plains of the Old Dominion then present when every hundred acres shall have its homestead, and support a family of the noblest race of mankind! And in truth how sad a picture have they hitherto presented, while held in large estates, rudely cultivated by the enforced toil of that race which was the lowest and most incapable of all! The northern part of this State is very fertile, and is everywhere intersected with navigable streams, such as would enable the farmer to ship his produce generally from his own door. This is what is called the tide-way district of Virginia. And as all vegetables and fruit grown here, in the natural home of the magnolia, are at least a fortnight earlier than they are to the north of the Potomac, they would command the markets of New York and of the Northern cities. This advantage cannot be snatched from them by any more southern State, as it is the combined result of the character of their soil, of their climate, and of their abundant means of water communication.

In Georgia, particularly in the upper part of the State, where the ground rises considerably, I heard and saw that successful efforts were being made to effect the change from the estate to the farm system; and, instead of trusting entirely to cotton, to try what could be done by growing wheat and maize, the latter to be turned into pork—in short, to do whatever could be done to adapt their industry to existing circumstances. Florida at present is rather occupied by wild deer than by man; but as it is capable of becoming the chief winter *sanitarium* for the consumption-scourged North, and also of producing tropical fruits and sugar for the whole Union, it has a fair prospect before it. Mrs. Harriet Beecher Stowe, the writer of 'Uncle Tom's Cabin,' and sister of the celebrated Brooklyn preacher, has gone to Florida, with her brother, Mr. Charles Beecher, for the purpose of attempting the cultivation of the sugar cane with free labour. North Carolina is endeavouring to follow the example of its neighbours Virginia and Georgia. Arkansas, which was settled chiefly by the sons of Georgian planters, is showing much of the Georgian spirit. In Alabama great efforts had been made to re-establish the cultivation of cotton on the basis of freedom; and things were promising well, when at the end of 1867 the price of cotton, by a concurrence of adverse accidents, fell to 15 cents or $7\frac{1}{2}d.$ at Liverpool. This depression to a point below the cost of production in any part of the world was felt, I believe, by most of those who attend to these matters, to be only a temporary mishap. The same cotton was selling at the end of the following March at 25 cents—a fully remunerative price; but in most cases the planters had not been able to hold, so that the low price they were obliged to accept has ruined many, and discouraged more. I was told by a Tennessee cotton planter that a price of 20 cents would have contained an ample margin for profit on the cotton he had himself grown, on a large scale, with hired black labour. His contract with those he employed was that he should give them high wages, with more than a proportionate deduction for every hour of absence from work.

There now remain unmentioned only the three States of South Carolina, Louisiana, and Mississippi. As far as I could judge, South Carolina was utterly and hopelessly crushed. Its best estates were in the Sea

Islands, which, as they were very fertile, and their produce fetched exceptionally high prices, were densely inhabited with blacks; in many of them, however, no white man could live, or even pass a night with impunity. Under these circumstances it might have been expected that as soon as the negroes were emancipated they would take possession of the land in these islands. And so it happened in most of the unhealthy ones; while in those that were healthy the original proprietors equally lost their property by confiscation or forfeiture, or by being ousted in some way or other. The result of this, and of the other losses that arose out of the war, and the utter overthrow of the Confederacy, is that throughout South Carolina the most abject and irrecoverable poverty reigns precisely where formerly there was most abundant wealth. I heard of one gentleman, who before the war had been unable to spend the whole of his large income, being now a porter in a dry goods store; and of another, who formerly had possessed everything which riches could supply, dying in such penury that his family had to beg of their friends contributions for his funeral. For this State there appears to be no resurrection, except in some new order of things, under which a new set of proprietors will occupy the land, and cultivate it with Northern capital, and somewhat in the Northern fashion.

In Louisiana also things were so bad that it was hardly possible to see how they could be worse. In New Orleans I found families who formerly had lived in noble mansions, and exercised a grand hospitality, now occupying quiet lodgings. In some instances I knew of several families clubbing together, and living

H

as it were in common. But here there was a great difference—hope was not dead. They talked confidently of the re-establishment, at all events, of their sugar industry, and of the trade of the city. I saw several sugar estates not far from New Orleans, the very costly machinery upon which had been destroyed during the war. I was told—though, of course, I cannot vouch for the accuracy of the figures—that the machinery had been broken up and burnt on twelve hundred out of the seventeen hundred sugar estates of this State.

As far as I could see and hear, the State of Mississippi also was in a very bad way. This seemed to arise from two causes. A larger proportion of the white inhabitants than is the case elsewhere belong to the class called in the South 'mean whites,'—that is, persons without property, education, or enterprise. And then the planters are unable to borrow what is requisite for enabling them to work their plantations. No one will lend them a cent. This is but a natural consequence of the act of repudiation they adopted at the instigation of Mr. J. Davis, late President of the Southern Confederacy, and whom this State has either the honour or the dishonour of reckoning among her best known men.

This, however, is not the only light in which the South has to be regarded. There is the question of political as well as of industrial reconstruction, and the former is now throughout all the North shaking the very foundations of the Union, and setting the son against the father, and the brother against the brother. The question is being dealt with entirely and exclusively on party considerations, and this Mr. Thaddeus

The Negro Franchise.

Stevens and other leaders of the Republican party have acknowledged in speech and print. They say universal suffrage, whatever the consequences to the Southern planter, must be conceded to the blacks, in order that the South may return to the Union, not as of old, on the Democratic side, but on the Republican, as the present exigencies of that party and of the Union require. Nothing can secure this except the black vote. All considerations of the fitness of the late slave for the exercise of the franchise is thus dismissed, and nothing insisted on but what is needed by the necessities of the dominant party.

Of course no man who knows anything of the capacity and of the history of the black race, even if he be of the Republican party, abstractedly thinks that they are qualified for taking part in the government of the country, and of legislating for and governing many of the Southern States.

Will it then be conferred upon them? It may be taken for granted that it will. Many talk of a secret compact—an underground railway, as it is called on the other side—between the President and the Southern leaders, to defeat by their joint efforts the Congressional plan, he being rewarded by the support of the South, when, as Democratic States, it returns to Congress. If such a compact has any existence, it is very unlikely to have any results. As the blacks have been admitted to the conventions throughout the South, for forming the new constitutions under which they are to exercise the franchise, and as the present Congress is determined that they shall have it, one does not see what is to prevent its extension to them. Whether the possession of the boon will be continued to them is another point. But be that as it may, we must, I think, regard the immediate possession of the franchise by the blacks as a certain event, and consider what are likely to be its consequences.

Its first and most obvious effect will be that which it was intended to produce—the weakening, and perhaps the exclusion from power for some time, of the Democratic party. Will this be an evil or an advantage to the Union? As far as I am able to judge, an unqualified advantage. The Democratic candidate of to-day for the Presidency, Mr. Pendleton of Ohio, and so of course the Democratic party itself are in favour of a partial, but very considerable, repudiation of the debt. This would be so disastrous a policy, that no one who wishes well to the Union can wish well to the Democrats. But this plank in their platform may be reshaped or entirely removed. Their permanent distinguishing principle is resistance to the policy of strengthening the central Government at the expense of the liberties and privileges of the separate States, whereas the reverse of this is the distinguishing principle of the great Republican party. It is evident that the Republican policy is that which is best adapted for commanding and calling out for immediate use the resources of the nation, and so during their great war it was decidedly in the ascendent. And since the war, the tendency of legislation and of administration has been in that direction: and this tendency will probably become stronger, at all events it will be more needed, as the United States increase in area and population.

Englishmen also may be reminded that almost all the abuse and insults Americans have heaped upon us have been the manufacture of Democratic brains, and, till Fenianism arose, came chiefly from Southern men. We cannot wish success to that party from which we have never received fair and courteous—I would even say, rational—treatment, and which now encloses in its bosom all our deadliest enemies in the United States. If formerly we regarded the accusations they brought against us, and the motives they imputed to us, as the hallucinations of disordered minds, we must now expect still livelier sallies, in order that they may not fall below the mark of Fenian animosity. In any difficulty which may arise between this country and the United States, the Democratic leaders are precluded, for the sake of the Irish vote, from recognising right or reason; and they must go on in this groove. The Republicans are under no such demoralising necessity. Of course it would be unwise in a traveller or a diplomatist to show decided preferences for any particular party; but it is well to know where you are likely to find friends. The manufacturing and commercial element of the Republican party is alone disposed by circumstances to feel ill-will towards us. But all this will die out as soon as the good sense of the American people has made the discovery of the degree to which they are crippled and impoverished by the pestilent heresy of protection.

But to go back to the subject of the black vote. It does not appear to me that this will always be given on the Republican side. The African will be too ignorant to judge for himself; and though he will never want for Northern advisers, he will have others nearer home, and in some cases will, I think, be influenced by those who employ him; and not unfrequently he may even wish, as the negro is the most imitative of all the races of mankind, to vote, not as his sable brethren, but as his old master votes. The whites will act as one man; the negroes will never be able to do so; and in States where the colours are pretty evenly balanced, a few deserters would incline the scale in favour of the old Southern party.

I mentioned that while in the office of the Freedmen's Bureau at Washington, before I entered the South, it struck me that its establishment could not be justified on grounds of wisdom. What I saw in the South confirmed this supposition. Mischief, I thought, had been done by it. The whites might safely, and ought in good policy to, have been left to settle the labour question with their old slaves. They quite understood that it would be ruin to themselves if they failed to satisfy them, and that they could only do this by making them feel that they were fairly and kindly treated. The future of the whites entirely depended on this; and they saw the necessity of it so clearly that they might, without any interference on the part of the North, which could do no good, have been left to arrange with the blacks how the new system was to be worked. These were the two parties to the new labour-and-wages contract; and the Freedmen's Bureau could have no voice in the matter.

The industrial question evidently came first, because it is on labour primarily that the existence of a nation depends. But the Bureau establishes itself in some town; and what does this mean? That the blacks need protection—of course from their old masters, for there are no other people on whom to cast this imputation. And what does the Bureau itself give out that it will do? It proposes to educate the negro. This implies that the first thing to be attended to is not labour, but something else, and that a matter which in the order of nature occupies only a secondary place. It implies too that during the time education is being carried on, labour must be suspended, for one cannot be in the school and in the field at the same time. And what is the use and value of education in the eyes of the negro? Just this—that it will fit him for the situation of a clerk, or for keeping a shop. At all events it is no preparation for field labour. In these ways it appears that the Bureau implanted, at a most critical time, false and mischievous ideas which will inflict much suffering both on blacks and whites, and which it will be very difficult to counteract. There would have been no reason why the Government should not have sent, without any flourish of trumpets, a commissioner into each State of the South, to see that the blacks were fairly treated, if the whites had anywhere shown a disposition to treat them otherwise.

As I have already intimated, I frequently heard Southern people expressing an apprehension that a war of races was imminent. Their reasons were that the disappointment felt by the blacks at the smallness of their gains from emancipation was constantly deepening, and that their posture towards the whites was becoming very unsatisfactory. It is impossible, of course, to foresee what ignorant and excitable Africans may do. Still I think a war of races a most improbable event. The blacks have sense enough to know that there would be no chance of their coming victorious out of such a conflict; for they would be outnumbered by the whites, if all the Southern States are regarded as a single unit, which they most assuredly would be for the purposes of such a war; and they would be comparatively unarmed, without resources, and without organisation. They also know that, even if they were able to exterminate all the whites in the South, they would gain nothing by this; for that then they would only be putting themselves in the position of the Indian races, to be ousted from the land whenever it suited the convenience of the North. And they are well aware that in any rising they might contemplate they could expect no help from the Northern force that was sent at the end of the war into each State of the South to coerce the whites and protect the blacks. The feelings of these men, I believe, are well known; at all events, I heard one of them in a railway car in the South give expression to his own feelings on this point, and he did it so as to include his comrades. 'They have sent us down here,' his words were, ' to look after the whites and take care of the blacks. But that is not what we are going to do. We are not going to help niggers to cut white men's throats. If they move a finger against the whites, we are not going to mind colonels or generals, but will shoot every d—d nigger in the place.' Nor is it possible to conceive the existence of any other feeling; for in no class in the United States is the antipathy to the negro race so strong as in that from which the army is recruited. This the negro knows very well.

But though I think that no war of this kind is to be dreaded, which would make very short work of the blacks, yet one cannot but think that their eventual extermination by moral and economical causes is inevitable. They have from the dawn of history been the chief export of Africa, but have never anywhere been capable of existing in a state of freedom on the same ground as any superior race. The superior race gets possession of all the means of living, all the trades, all the professions, all the land, and the inferior race is thus pushed out of existence. If Congress were to enact, and future Congresses to maintain the enactment, that south of the Ohio and Potomac no white man was ever to do any kind of field labour, or to follow the trades of carpentering or bricklaying, of shoemaking or tailoring, then there would be means provided for the subsistence of the black race, and it might possibly be kept up even in a state of freedom ; but as none of these occupations will eventually be left them, their doom is as certain as anything can be in the affairs of men. Already, if a builder introduces into his yard, or places on any work in which he is engaged, a single coloured carpenter or mason, every person in his employ will strike work unless the man of colour, however unexceptionable he may be in his conduct, and however skilful in his trade, is instantly dismissed. All the stevedores at New Orleans were a few years ago of the coloured race. Some whites having taken to the employment, began to insist on the dismissal of all coloured people; and now there is not to be seen a single coloured stevedore on the quays of New Orleans. And just so eventually it must be with field labour. The

South must be completely, or at the least largely, cultivated on the Northern farm-system: and then it will be seen that the whites will no more tolerate the companionship of the blacks in field labour than in anything else. A people who have not the means of living must die out, and so emancipation comes to be extinction.

Those who believe in the obliteration of the black race will speculate on the time required for such a consummation. Suppose then each generation is only able to leave behind it half its own numbers, this would bring the blacks to the vanishing point at about the end of a century, by which time the white population of the United States will probably outnumber that of the whole of Europe. The rate of decrease, however, may be much more rapid. Persons now living can recollect the time when a considerable quarter of the city of Boston was occupied by these people; but now, without emigration, they have almost entirely disappeared. This is attributed by the people of Boston to several causes. In a state of freedom they bring up very few children. The mortality also among them is very great, especially from consumption; and then there is the fact that in the second, or at latest the third generation, the mixed race becomes quite incapable of continuing itself. These facts are distressing to contemplate; but nothing is gained by refusing to look facts in the face, of whatever character they may be. It is an analogous fact that the red man has been swept away from the face of the continent that was his own, all the way from Boston to the Rocky Mountains; and the work of annihilation will soon be complete from the Atlantic to the Pacific. But this ordinance of nature, that a civilised and a savage race cannot coexist on the same soil, is no reason why the inferior race should be treated with unfairness, unkindness, or contempt.

As to the fusion of the two races, history assures us that nothing of the kind has ever been accomplished, and that it is physically impossible. And it is fortunate for the progress of mankind that nature has put her veto upon it; otherwise that portion of the highest, and most advanced, and most richly endowed race of the human family, which has been placed on the grandest and most favourable stage for fresh development, would be sunk and degraded by admixture with the lowest race of all. The fact that in the long centuries during which the Greeks and the Romans occupied Western Asia and Northern Africa, they were unable to produce a mixed race capable of maintaining itself, may be suggested for the consideration of those who are advocating a scheme of 'miscegenation' between the Anglo-Saxon and the negro.

If we form our estimate of the condition of the South from considering the condition of its means of communication, we shall find it bad indeed. While I was there, some of its main lines of railway were running only one passenger train a-day. And, notwithstanding the infrequency of the trains, I observed in all the districts I passed through that there were very few passengers, and very little traffic. What ruin and desolation may be read in this single fact, when one remembers that a few years back the value of the raw produce exported from the Southern States amounted to between fifty and sixty million pounds a-year, and was greater than anything else of the

kind in the world. What a vast amount of travelling
must such a vast amount of business have given
rise to! for not only was fifty or sixty million pounds'
worth of cotton, rice, sugar, turpentine, and tobacco
to be sent out of the country, but there was also
an equal value in food and manufactured goods to
be brought in; for in the South they hardly grew or
manufactured anything, except what they exported.
Everything they consumed was imported. One cannot
but contrast the stirring life which all this
must have caused in every town, harbour, and
railway, with their present deadness. The rails
from Petersburg to Weldon are very much out of
order, but one despairs of being able to convey in
words an adequate idea of the state of disorder in
which they are between the latter town and Wilmington.
It was over this line, of 162 miles in length,
that, during the war, the blockade-run goods and
munitions of war were forwarded to Richmond and
the front. At that time there were but small means
for repairing or replacing worn-out rails. And as
the trade of Wilmington is now dwindled to nothing,
and this road is off the main line of communication
with the South, there have as yet been no inducements
or funds to set it right. The jolting on it is
so great that the passengers are incessantly being
thrown to a height of several inches from their seat;
and that at last produces in some the effect which a
gale at sea would have upon them. I believe that no
English railway carriage with only four, or at most
six wheels, could keep on such rails; but American
carriages, having never less than eight wheels, have a
much firmer hold.

CHAPTER VIII.

FIRST SIGHT OF A COTTON FIELD—SPANISH MOSS—A NIGHT ON THE RAILS—MANY KINDS OF SAMENESS IN AMERICA—MAIZE—ORDER OF SUCCESSION IN THE FOREST—ITS EXTENT—EVERGREENS IN THE SOUTHERN FOREST—POOR LAND IN THE SOUTH MAY BE MORE PROFITABLE THAN RICH LAND IN THE WEST—DEADNESS OF CHARLESTON —ITS HOTELS—A CHARLESTON SAM-WELLER—THE NAPLES OF THE UNITED STATES—FEW ENGLISH TRAVELLERS—SUFFERINGS OF SOUTHERN FAMILIES—WANT OF SCHOOLS—HOW THE DEFICIENCY IS BEING SUPPLIED—BLACKS SHOULD BE PUT ON SAME FOOTING AS WHITES—DIALOGUE WITH BLACK MEMBER OF CONVENTION— ANOTHER CONVENTION—ABLE BLACK MEMBER—SOUTH CAROLINA ORPHAN ASYLUM.

ONE cannot behold for the first time what one has heard and read about all one's life without some little emotion. I felt this when I saw for the first time a field of cotton. It was between Petersburg and Weldon. There is not much to attract attention in the sight itself as seen in winter, when there is nothing to look at but a large enclosure of dead bushes, each about the size of an ordinary gooseberry-bush, only with fewer branches, and every branch leafless, straight, and black, with every here and there a pod of cotton, that was missed at the time of harvesting, showing its white wool, with which the whole field is spotted. 'This insignificant plant, then,' I said to myself, 'is cotton; and this is the way in which it is cultivated. The plant which has created so much wealth, and caused so much bloodshed; which was the main support of slavery, and so the main cause of the late war; which clothes so large a portion of mankind; which has built so many ships and factories; upon which so much of the prosperity of England is founded; and which has affected so largely the commerce of the world; and the influence of which is now felt in every quarter of the globe.

The traveller has pleasure in recalling moments of this kind. I shall not easily forget the delight I felt at the first sight of the Spanish moss. It was in the first gray of the morning, and I was looking out from the railway car, shading off with my hands the light of the lamps that were still burning, that I might be the better able to see through the window, when I beheld for the first time this curious parasite, of which one had seen such frequent mention, hanging in slender streamers of three or four feet in length from the boughs of the trees. I immediately left my seat, and went to the outside of the car. I found we were passing through a cedar swamp on a tressle-bridge of many miles in length. We passed through several such swamps in the course of that day, and wherever this was the case, the trees, of which the swamps were just as full as the dry land, were always covered with this moss. Old trees were entirely enveloped in it to the extremities of their branches. As you approach the Gulf, the trees on the dry land as well as those in swamps are shrouded in it. Its streamers are occasionally two yards long near the coast. It is of a pale ashy colour, and gives you the idea of the accumulated cobwebs of a thousand years.

American ladies having been well broken in to the publicity of their system of railway travelling, make the best of it, and seem quite unconcerned about what would appear to those unused to it its disagreeable incidents. Never but with one exception did I pass a night on an American railway without finding a sleeping-car attached to the train. It was in the South, and there happened to be about forty people in the car, of whom eight or ten were married ladies travelling with their husbands: like everybody one sees in America, they were young, and of course, as all American young ladies are, were better-looking than the generality of the fair sex. English ladies would probably, under circumstances of so much publicity, have unnecessarily and unwisely endeavoured to keep awake. But their American sisters passed the night as comfortably as might be, each laying her head on her husband's shoulder for a pillow, and with their arms round each other, or with their hands locked together. In the morning, when the train stopped an hour for breakfast, they made their *toilette* in the carriage, there being generally abundance of water in a railway car, with a mug to drink from, and a basin to wash in. They appeared all to have with them brushes and combs, and towels and soap.

In travelling in the United States one is very much struck with the great amount of sameness that is met with in many things. In outward nature this is very observable. You go from New York to Charleston on what appears to be one level. Throughout these nine hundred miles you have no cuttings or embankments; at all events I do not recollect having had to go through or to go round a single hill. Again, you may go up the valley of the Mississippi on another longer level; and if you start from Chicago to cross the

Prairie and Plains, you cross another thousand miles of level ground. Again, throughout all these long levels, adding to them the space between Charleston and New Orleans, there is in the soil a great sameness of colour. Except in the black soil of the Prairies, and occasionally in the river bottoms—of which latter you see little in railway travelling—yellow, of slightly varying tints, is almost universal, whether the soil be sandy or clayey. And then the forest which clothes this soil of the same colour and of the same level, is also everywhere itself the same. The predominant trees are fortunately the unfailing pine, and almost equally unfailing oak. Sameness, too, but not quite to the same extent, characterises the Great Lake region. There are glorious exceptions to this general sameness in the Alleghanies, the Rocky Mountains, and California; but these are not the situations in which the great masses of the population have formed their homes. De Tocqueville and others have observed a similar sameness in the ideas and customs of the Americans themselves; and this they attribute to the completeness with which the principles of democracy have been carried out both in their polity and social arrangements. I have already noticed the extraordinary sameness of their language, which, throughout the whole continent, admits of no dialectical difference and, in passing, how great are the changes this single fact implies have taken place in the conditions of human life, when we recollect that in that little plat of ground of ancient Greece every little town had a dialect of its own. The universality with which any form of expression, any social practice, or even any state of feeling, is abandoned or adopted throughout the vast Union, is to those who observe these matters a very interesting fact in American civilisation. The extent to which they are readers of newspapers is not the cause of this, though of course it somewhat contributes to it. The real cause is the urgent and uncontrollable desire in every American to talk, and think, and live, and dress, and feel, and to do everything just in the same way as other people; as we say here, to be in the fashion, only that they apply the idea of fashion to everything. Changes of this kind are wrought in America almost as if by magic. There is in this a great balance of good, although it is so great a check upon individuality, because it keeps the whole people advancing together as one man.

In the agricultural reports of the United States maize is set down for so many million bushels as almost to transcend the power of belief on this side the water. How can so much be grown? how can so much be used? are questions which occur to us. But after one has seen something of America the feeling is changed into one of wonder at the inexhaustible merits of this grain, and of its incalculable utility to man; and one ceases to be surprised at finding it grown everywhere throughout the Union on so large a scale. It is quite impossible that America could have risen to her present greatness without it. While the hardy pioneer of civilisation was subduing the forest, which reached from the Atlantic to the valley of the Mississippi, there was nothing that could have met his wants as maize did. As soon as he had felled the trees for his log cabin, before the ground was cleared, or prepared sufficiently for any other crop, he would put in his seed for a crop of maize, which would be ready in a few months, perhaps before his log house was finished, and would supply with food his family, and pigs, and any other stock that he might have, till the next harvest. And when ripe, it did not, like wheat and other grain, require immediate harvesting; for nature had provided it with a thick strong stem to support it against the wind, and with a sheath which kept it effectually from the rain. And its yield, as it thus grew among the stumps of these forest clearings, was very great. And now that the land has been cleared, it still holds its ground as the chief crop almost everywhere, and apparently as almost the only grain crop in many districts. It is everywhere largely used as human food in a great variety of ways. It is the winter food of the cattle, horses, and mules, which latter do all the heavy work from Kentucky to New Orleans. The pork crop, too, of the United States, which is one of its largest items of produce, is only a certain portion of the maize crop in another form. The same may be said of the enormous quantity of poultry produced everywhere throughout the country. It is only transformed maize. Of all grains it is the easiest to grow, the easiest to harvest, the easiest to keep, the easiest to transport. It is good for man and for beast. It will grow on any soil, and will yield in the rich bottoms of Ohio and Illinois a hundred bushels an acre—and on some of these lands it has been grown for twenty years in succession—and on the poor sands of South Carolina will yield between twenty and thirty bushels, a quantity that is highly remunerative, where the land costs nothing, and an old negro and an old mule are all that are required for its culture.

In America a head of maize should be the national emblem.

It did not strike me that the succession of trees in clearing forest land was quite so regular as is commonly stated. I saw, for instance, a different succession on the two sides of the same fence. The original forest on both sides had been exclusively pine. Where the forest had been entirely cleared off, the succession was again pine. But where the large trees only had been removed the succession was oak. This went some way towards showing that the amount of light and air decided which was to come up.

In the Carolinas the forest is, along the railway, everywhere more or less continuous: still it is all owned, as appears from the fencing. The better trees are everywhere being cut for building, or fencing, or firing; and the larger pines have all been tapped for turpentine. One is surprised, at first, to see so little land cultivated along the line of railway. The reason however is that, as a general rule, the good land is along the banks of the streams which run from the Alleghanies to the sea, that is, from west to east, while the railway runs from north to south, so that in travelling along it you only get occasional glimpses of the way in which culture is in these parts beginning, for it is hardly more, to encroach on the forest.

In these latitudes the forest becomes a little diversified by the appearance of several evergreens. One of the commonest is the evergreen or live-oak. I frequently saw from the cars a small tree having very much the appearance of our bay. There is an occasional magnolia. There are several evergreen shrubs, and some creepers. In swampy places there are long reaches of cane-brake. This is the Bambusa gracilis, which we sometimes see in this country in gardens, in spots where moisture and shelter can be combined. These cane- or bamboo-brakes are evergreen impervious jungles about twenty feet high. But the most interesting form to Northern eyes is that of the little palmetto palm. Its fan-like leaf, however, is all that can be seen of it, for its trunk scarcely rises above the ground. In some of the swamps around New Orleans it and a kind of iris are the most conspicuous plants.

The question of the colonisation or resettlement of the South by the North is simply one of £. s. d. Will it be more profitable for a Northern man to grow cotton in the South, or wheat, pork, beef, &c. in the West? People say Northern emigrants will never go to the poor lands of the South till all the good land of the West is taken up. This is quite a wrong way of putting the case between the two. A man would not go to the South to grow wheat, beef, and pork. That can be done cheaper in the fertile West. But it is not impossible that an equal amount of capital and labour embarked in the cotton culture of the South might produce a greater return. In that case the poor soils of the South might be preferred to the rich soils of the West.

One infers how much more completely the fabric of society rested on slavery in South Carolina than it did in Virginia, by the fact that three fourths of the devastation caused by the great fire at Richmond have been already repaired, while nothing had been done to repair the damages done by the great fire at

Charleston, which destroyed the whole of the centre of the city. Literally not one single brick has yet been laid upon another for this purpose. There stand the blackened remains of churches, residences, and stores, just as if it were a city of the dead.

Still, even here I was surprised at the number and magnitude of the hotels. I had taken up my quarters at the Mills House, where I suppose there were three hundred guests. I saw another, the Pavilion, quite as large; and I was told of a third, the Charleston Hotel, which was described to me as being much larger than either of the two just mentioned.

Before I reached Charleston there had been some wet weather, and the streets were muddy. I therefore used two pair of boots the first day I was in the place. The next morning the Sam Weller of the hotel refused to clean, or as he called it, to shine, more than one pair. I remonstrated with him, but it was to no purpose, as he was quite persuaded of the force of his own argument, 'that if everyone in the house was to wear two pair of boots a-day his work would be doubled.' Boots was a Paddy, and, since his naturalisation in the land of freedom, had become sure that he had as much right to form opinions for himself, express them, and act upon them, as the President himself. I carried my grievance to the manager. He promised redress, but the boots were not cleaned, that is to say, not in the hotel. I mention this as it was the only instance of *insubordination* I met with in this class in my tour through the United States.

Nature has done much for Charleston. Its fine harbour is formed by the junction of two large navigable rivers, the Ashley and the Cooper. It is free from yellow fever, the scourge of Mobile and New Orleans. The orange and oleander grow in the spaces between its streets and its houses. Hitherto it has been the chief winter resort of those in the Northern States who were unable to bear the severity of their own climate, and of those from the West Indies who were unable to bear the heat of theirs. Thus the victims both of heat and of cold met in Charleston, and each found in its delightfully tempered atmosphere exactly what he sought. And the society of these visitors, combined with that of the rich proprietors of the State who had their residences here, made it a very gay and pleasant place. Of course America, hard-worked and consumption-scourged above all other nations, ought to have its Naples; and it will be equally a matter of course that the Naples of America should temper gaiety with trade, and combine work with idleness, and should not be entirely a population of do-nothings, of Lazaroni, and of pleasure-seekers. Still, the feeling that came over one at Charleston was, How far off this place is from the world! It was not the distance that caused this feeling, for it is only nine hundred miles from New York, while Chicago, where one has no feelings of this kind, is three hundred miles further off. Perhaps fifty years hence, when probably a busy white population will be cultivating the land around it, there will be nothing in the place to suggest the thought that, when there, one is out of the world.

I was surprised at finding how few Englishmen had, at all events of late, been travelling in the Southern States. At Charleston, in a dozen folio pages of names in the guest-book of the hotel, which I looked at for this purpose, I could only see one entry from England. At Richmond I only found two English names in forty folio pages, and the address appended to these two names was Manchester. In the North I heard that Lord Morley, and Lord Camperdown, and Mr. Cowper—I do not know whether the Right Hon. W. Cowper was meant—had lately been through that part of the country inspecting the common schools. But during my tour through the United States, I did not fall in with a single English traveller, nor did I fall in with one either on my outward or homeward voyage. All my fellow-passengers on both occasions were Americans. Of course in the summer—though it may be questioned whether that is, so decidedly as most people suppose, the best season for travelling in the United States—I might not have found my countrymen so conspicuous by their absence. And yet there is no part of the world which Englishmen ought to find so instructive and interesting. What is there in the world more worthy of investigation than the existing condition of things, and the events that are now taking place, upon this great continent, which contains within itself everything that is necessary for the well-being of man, which is indeed a world in itself, and which stands in the same relation towards the Atlantic and Pacific oceans that this little island does towards the Irish and North seas; and which, whatever else may befall, will at all events be thoroughly Anglo-Saxon?

Wherever one went in the South, one heard instances of the hardships, the deadliness, and the evils of the late war. Of the family of which I saw most at

Richmond, the three sons had been sent to the army. Of these three one was killed, and another maimed for life. These were men who were no longer young, and many a day in their long marches, and when before the enemy, their commissariat having been utterly exhausted, they had had nothing to eat but a few handfuls of horse corn. There were regiments that did not bring home one fourth of the number with which they originally went out; the rest having died of disease, or fallen in battle. In the family of which I saw most at Charleston there were two sons, the eldest only eighteen years of age. They both enlisted in Hampton's cavalry, for all above the age of sixteen had to go. And so again at New Orleans the gentleman to whom I was especially consigned, and who had held the commission of colonel in the Confederate army, and had been a rich merchant of the place, told me that he and his whole regiment were frequently without shoes, and that on one occasion he went bare-footed for six weeks continuously.

One of the most lamentable results of the great cataclysm that ensued on the close of the war, has been that almost a complete end has been put to the education of Southern children. Formerly many were sent to the North, but now parents have neither the inclination nor the means to continue this practice. In the South itself schools did not abound; and of those which existed before the war the greater number have followed the fate of so many other Southern things. Some effort is being made to remedy this. In one of the Southern cities I had been advised to call on a gentleman who would be able to give me information on these matters. I found him at last, after some trouble, teaching a private school of his own. He was engaged in giving a French lesson. I remember him as a remarkably handsome and well-mannered man. On my saying something which implied astonishment at finding him so employed, he replied that his profession was that of a lawyer; but that since the war he had not been allowed to practise, because he was unable to take the oaths which the North had imposed on all who had held any office in the South during the war. But he added, 'I am not in bad company, for many of the best men in the South, beginning with General Lee, are employed in teaching.'

While I was in the South the conventions were sitting. These were assemblies elected under the new system of universal suffrage, including the blacks, for the purpose of drawing up new constitutions for their several States. Of course where the negroes were numerically in the ascendant, the majority of the convention were either negroes or negro nominees. I felt a repugnance to witness this degradation of the whites; still it would have been foolish to have let pass the opportunity for seeing what indications the blacks gave of fitness for equal political power; and, as the governor of the State I was then in offered to take me to the convention and introduce me to some of the members, I accepted the offer. We had been talking on the irrepressible subject of the negro, and I had said I thought the blacks ought to be put on exactly the same footing as the whites. He had assented to this idea, as it sounded very much like what he was there to maintain. But I am not quite sure that he altogether approved of my explanation, when I went on to say that what I meant was, 'that the negro should be left to work or starve, just as the white man was in New York, in England, and everywhere else; that I did not at all see why the negro should be petted, and patted on the back, and have soup given to him, while he was doing nothing, and have expectations raised in his mind that something would soon be done for him, which treatment could not in the end be of any advantage at all to him, while it was very costly to the whites.' His reply to this was the offer I just mentioned to take me to the convention and introduce me to some of the members who were among the leading partisans of the negro race in the State.

I was present for two hours in this convention; during that time no speeches were made; I was therefore unable to judge in this manner of the intelligence and *animus* of the black members. I did not, however, leave the convention without a short conversation with one of them. He was a man of unmixed African blood, and, seeing me conversing with the white whom he regarded as the head of his party, he left his place in the house, and came up to me and held out his hand. I extended mine in return. On taking hold of it, he accosted me with the words,

'Sir, you then believe that the franchise is a God-given right.'

I said 'that was not my belief.'

'Why?' he asked, rather astonished.

'Because,' I said, 'it was given to you by Mr. Lincoln and the North.'

'No, sir,' he replied, 'it is a God-given right.'

'If it is a God-given right,' I rejoined, 'how does it come to pass that so few of mankind have ever possessed it?'

He then inquired what limitation I would put to the 'right.' I told him that I did not think it wise or just that those who had no property should possess the power of imposing taxes on those who had property, and deciding how the proceeds of the taxes were to be disposed of; and that the argument would be strengthened, if these persons without property were also without the knowledge requisite for enabling them to read the constitution of their State. Instead of replying to this, he returned to his seat.

I give the above dialogue as a specimen of what are a negro's ideas on the great subject of the day in that part of the world. I afterwards heard that the gentleman who had been speaking to me was the most prominent negro in the State.

In the convention I have just spoken of there was nothing remarkable in the appearance of the members of either race. In another convention, however, where I spent a morning, this was not the case; for I did not see a single white who had at all the air of a legislator, or even the appearance of a respectable member of society. Here I heard a man who was black, or as nearly black as one could be, make several speeches. He assumed a kind of leadership, or at all events of authority in the assembly, to which, as far as I could judge, he was most fully entitled. He certainly was the best speaker I heard in the United States, or, indeed, ever heard anywhere else, as far as his knowledge went. He spoke with perfect ease, and complete confidence in himself, and

at the same time quite in good taste. He said
nothing but what appeared to be most reasonable,
proper, and fair to both races. He was for putting
an end at once to all ideas and hopes of confiscation
on the part of the blacks, and to the fears of the whites
on the subject, by some authoritative declaration; for
he believed that these hopes and fears were giving false
expectations to his own race, and causing much uncer-
tainty in the minds of the whites, which prevented
their setting about the re-establishment of cultivation
on their estates. He had a good musical voice, and he
could vary its tones at his pleasure. His thoughts
were clearly conceived and clearly put. I must not,
however, omit to mention that, though the traces of
white blood were so slight in the colour of his skin,
he had most completely the head and features of the
European—a high forehead, a thin straight nose,
and a small chin and mouth. His hair was woolly
in the extreme. I afterwards understood that the
whites in this convention, who were so greatly his
inferiors in debate, were almost all Northern adven-
turers and 'mean whites'; the whole of the upper
class having declined to take any part in forming the
new constitution.

I was taken over the South Carolina Orphan
Asylum. It is a large fine building in the town of
Charleston, with well-kept and extensive grounds
around it for the children to play in. The number
of children who are within the walls is two hundred.
They are fed, clothed, educated, and placed out in
life by the institution. The expenses were formerly
divided between the State, a numerous body of sub-
scribers, and the interest that accrued from some

very considerable bequests. But during the war these investments went the way of all other investments in the South. They were placed in Confederate bonds, which are now worth nothing. Pretty nearly, therefore, the whole of the burden of maintaining the asylum has since been met by the State alone, in its present condition of extreme impoverishment. All the children from the different class rooms were summoned together for my inspection, into a large room somewhat resembling a theatre, in which they are taught music and some other subjects collectively. Small and great, they all appeared to be very well under control. They seemed also to be happy and healthy, but with more (which in those who lived all the year at Charleston could hardly have been otherwise) of the Southern lily than of the Northern rose in their complexions. As might have been expected, there was not the animation and zeal one sees in Northern schools, worked at the highest of high pressures. But it is a noble institution: in it Mr. Memminger, the first Secretary of the Confederate Treasury, was brought up.

CHAPTER IX.

COLD IN SOUTH CAROLINA AND GEORGIA—CURIOUS APPEARANCE OF ICE—TIME NOT VALUED IN THE SOUTH—WHY AMERICANS WILL NOT CULTIVATE THE OLIVE—TEA MIGHT GROW IN GEORGIA—ATLANTA BOUND TO BE GREAT—CATTLE BADLY OFF IN WINTER—A VIRGINIAN'S RECOLLECTION OF THE WAR—HIS POSITION AND PROSPECTS—APPROACH TO MOBILE BY THE ALABAMA RIVER—MOBILE—THE HARBOUR—WHY NO AMERICAN SHIPS THERE—A DAY ON THE GULF—PONCHATRAIN—NEW ORLEANS—FRENCH SUNDAY MARKET—FRENCH APPEARANCE OF TOWN—A NEW ORLEANS GENTLEMAN ON THE EPISCOPAL CHURCH—BISHOP ELECT OF GEORGIA—MISSISSIPPI—THE CEMETERIES—EXPENSIVENESS OF EVERYTHING—TRANSATLANTIC NEWS—FUSION OF NORTH AND SOUTH—FRENCH HALF-BREEDS—ROADS—THE BEST IN THE WORLD—APPROACH TO NEW ORLEANS BY LAND—SUGAR PLANTATIONS—A PRAYER FOR A BROTHER MINISTER.

I LEFT Charleston at midday. It was a cold day, but there was no ice in the town. A few miles out of the town, on the Augusta railway, it was freezing sharply, the railway-side ditches were coated with ice, and the ground was white with hoarfrost wherever the sun had not touched it. I supposed that the warmer air from the bay had kept the frost out of the town. All through that day in travelling as far as Augusta, and for the next two days, I found the frost in the country between Augusta and Atlanta very severe. We should have considered them unusually cold days in England; and yet there was not a cloud to intercept a ray of the Southern sun. To my sensations it was colder than I found it on any other occasion during my tour in the United States. I mention this because it is satisfactory to collect indications of large districts of the South being adapted to white labour. No doubt the summer throughout this region is very warm, but here it was cold enough to brace up relaxed constitutions.

I here saw an effect of frost, which, I suppose from differences in radiation and evaporation, is never seen in England. Everywhere along the railway embankments and cuttings, the ice appeared to have shot out in rays or spikes, three or four inches in length, and then to have bent over. When the rays were shorter they remained straight. I asked a gentleman how the people of the country explained the phenomenon. 'Our explanation of it is,' he replied, 'that in these parts the land spues up the ice.'

A Southern man does not set the same value on time a Northern one does. The day, he thinks, will be long enough for all he has to do. I often saw trains stopped, not at a station, for the purpose of taking up or putting down a single passenger. I even saw this done that a parcel or letter might be taken from a person standing by the railway side. On one occasion an acquaintance with whom I was travelling that day, and myself, both happened to have had no dinner. We mentioned this to the conductor, and asked him if he could manage in any way to let us have some supper. 'Oh, yes,' he readily replied, 'I will at eleven o'clock stop the train at a house in the forest, where I sometimes have had supper myself. I will give you twenty minutes.' I suppose the other passengers, none of whom left their seats, imagined that we had stopped to repair some small damage, or to take in wood or water, for on returning to the car we heard no observations made on the delay.

Whenever I suggested to Americans the probability that their long range of Southern coast was well suited for the culture of the olive, the suggestion was met with merriment. 'There is no one in this country,' they would say, 'who looks fifteen or twenty years ahead' (the time it takes for an olive tree to come into profitable bearing). 'Everybody here supposes that long before so many years have expired he shall have sold his land very advantageously, or that his business will have taken him to some other part of the country, or that he shall have made his fortune and retired from business.'

The same objection does not lie against the culture of tea, for which the uplands of Georgia appeared well adapted.

Atlanta I thought the most flourishing place in the South. I saw several manufactories there, and much building was going on. It has 34,000 inhabitants. 'Sir,' said an Atlantan gentleman to me, 'this place is bound to become great and prosperous, because it is the most central town of the Southern States.' I suppose he had not yet been able to divest his mind of the idea that the Southern States formed a political unit, and must have a central capital.

The cattle of the South must, during the winter, be among the most miserable of their kind. I saw nothing at all resembling what we call pastures; and if such institutions (in America everything is an institution, even the lift in an hotel) are known in the South, they can be of little use at that time of year, for every blade of grass in America is then withered and dry. The cattle appeared to be kept generally in the woods, and in the maize fields, where of course they could get nothing but the leaves that were hanging on the dead stems. In the North, where the dead grass is buried in snow, and the cattle therefore must be housed and kept on artificial food and grain, they are sufficiently well off; while their brethren in the South become the victims of a more beneficent climate.

I sometimes repeat the remarks of persons I casually met, without noticing whether I accept or disagree with the statements they contain, or the spirit which appears to animate them, because what I thought about the matter is of no consequence, while by reporting occasionally what I heard I enable others to form some idea of what passes in the minds of the people I came in contact with. For this purpose I will report what a fellow-passenger said to me one night on our way through the interminable forest in Alabama. I had several times during the day had some talk with this gentleman, and had been much struck with him and interested in what he said. He was a handsome man—a very noble-looking specimen of humanity; and his manners and ideas corresponded to his appearance. At night we were seated together talking about the war, and the prospects of the country, when he gave me the following account of himself. He was a Virginian, and before the war had possessed a good property. Though disliking the Yankees (I am giving his own words) and their interference with the internal affairs of the Southern

States, he had at first opposed the war. But when his State had decided for it, he took up his rifle, and joined it unreservedly. Everything he had possessed had been lost in the war; but he was determined neither to complain, nor to be beholden to any man. It was not a pleasant thing, for one who had lived as a gentleman, to work for others; but that was what he was now doing, for he had become travelling clerk for a large mercantile house. The period of his agreement had nearly expired, and if it was not renewed, and he could get nothing better, he would drive a dray. He spoke bitterly of the Yankees, for their greed of plunder, and for their want of a sense of honour. When the South surrendered, they did it in perfect good faith; acknowledging that fortune had entirely decided against them, and determining to submit honestly to the award. But the Yankees would not believe in their good faith, and had sent into every Southern State a military dictator with an army, to oppress and insult the whites, and to keep them in subjection to the blacks. He had loved his country, and been proud of it: but now he had no country, no home, no prospects. He said the blacks fought with more desperation than the Yankees. He had been through the whole war, and had had plenty of opportunities for comparing them. He would rather meet three Yankees than two blacks. The black was easily wrought up into a state of enthusiasm, and would fight like a fanatic. The Yankee was always calculating chances, and taking care of himself. The West it was that decided the war; and he thought it should have arbitrated at first, and prevented the fighting. I lost sight of this fallen but brave-hearted Virginian on the steps of the St. Charles Hotel at New Orleans, to which he was so obliging as to guide me on our arrival at that city. He was then on his way to Texas.

The railway does not run into Mobile, but ends at a wharf, about twenty miles from the city, on the Tensas (pronounced Tensaw), a kind of loop branch of the Alabama, which it rejoins at Mobile. It is a fine broad piece of water, and its banks are clothed with the undisturbed primæval forest, which is always to the European a sight of great interest. On unloading the train I saw that we had picked up during the night a dozen fine bucks, which we were to take on to Mobile. I had observed in the early morning two or three small herds of wild deer feeding in the forest. They seem to have become accustomed to the locomotive. Even here it was freezing very sharply, and the buckets of water on board the steamer were thickly coated with ice. This frost, I found at Mobile, had killed all the young wood of the orange trees. The crew of the steamer were negroes, and I was surprised to see them on so cold a morning washing their woolly heads in buckets of water drawn from the river, and then leaving their wet hair and faces to be dried by the cold morning air. At the junction of the Tensas and Alabama there was a great deal of swampy land, partly covered with reeds, and much shallow water, upon which were large flocks of wild fowl. The river was here full of snags and sawyers, and its navigation was still further impeded by a fortification of piles the Confederates had driven across it during the war, to keep the enemy from getting up to the city. This approach to Mobile had more of the air of novelty about it than anything I had yet seen in America. It made me feel that I was really in a new world.

As I intended to make no stay at Mobile, I did not use any of the letters of introduction I had with me, thinking I should in a short time see more of the men and manners of the place, if I accompanied a travelling acquaintance I had made, in his calls upon the firms with whom he had to transact business. I was four times during the morning invited, not to liquor, that expression I never once heard in America, but to take a drink. There is much heartiness of feeling here, and everybody carries out, to the full extent, the American practice of shaking hands with everybody, which is a rational way of expressing goodwill without saying anything. I walked about a mile out into the environs to see the houses of the merchants and well-to-do inhabitants. I passed three hospitals, one for yellow-fever cases that can pay, one for yellow-fever cases that cannot pay, and one for general cases. The streets of the town were full of pedestrians and of traffic. In this respect it bore a very favourable comparison with Charleston, where nothing was going on. The population amounts to about 34,000. The Spaniards who originally settled the place have been utterly obliterated. On inquiry I found that none had remained in the city, being quite unable in any department of business to support the competition of the Anglo-Saxon, but that among the mean whites, at some little distance from Mobile, a few Spanish names were to be found. These remnants of the original settlers the Alabamans call Dagos, a corruption of the common Spanish name of Diego.

The great cotton ships cannot come to up to Mobile. There is, however, a magnificent bay, in the form of a great lake with a narrow inlet from the sea, in which they ride at anchor, waiting for their cargoes, at a distance of between thirty and forty miles from the city. I counted thirty-seven of these ships. They were almost all English. Some said there was not a single American among them. A few years ago far the greater part of them would have been American; but since they have taxed heavily everything received into the country, or manufactured in it, they have ceased to be able to build or to sail ships as cheaply as we can.

I shall never forget the day I passed on the Gulf of Mexico in going from Mobile to New Orleans. The air was fresh and had just the slightest movement in it. The sky was unclouded, and the sun delightfully warm. We have pleasant enough days at home occasionally, but this belonged to quite another order of things. And as the darkness came on, the night was as fine and bright, after its kind, as the day had been. Many sat talking on the deck till long after the sun was down. Some, I suppose, felt that this would be their only day on the Gulf of Mexico.

The communication between Mobile and New Orleans is not carried on by the mouth of the Mississippi, but by the Lake of Ponchatrain. This is a large piece of very shallow water, seldom more than seven feet deep, which communicates with the sea. A railway is carried out into the lake on piles for a distance of five miles. At the terminus of this long pier the steamers deposit and receive their passengers.

On entering the city, at the other terminus of this

railway, at half-past six o'clock in the morning, the first sight that attracted attention was the French Sunday Market. This is what everyone who visits New Orleans is expected to see. It is a general market, and the largest of the week. I do not remember ever to have seen a larger or a busier one. What attracted my attention most, on passing through it, was the great quantity and variety of wild fowl exhibited for sale. The *Marché des Fleurs* was very good. In short there was an abundant supply of everything. The shops in the neighbourhood were all open; and in the American part of the city also, I saw several open on the morning of this day.

New Orleans still retains very much of the air of a French city. Many of the streets are narrow, and paved (which I saw nowhere else in America) with large blocks of granite. This is brought from New England. Something however of the kind was necessary here, on account of the wet alluvial soil on which the city stands; it would be truer to say on which it floats. The houses are generally lofty, and their external character is rather French than English. The French language is spoken by a large part of the population. In the street cars, one is almost sure to hear it, coming often from the mouths of coloured people.

While at New Orleans I heard Dr. Beckwith, the Bishop elect of Georgia. His church is about a mile and a half from the St. Charles's Hotel, in one of the best suburbs of the city. In going I asked a gentleman, who was seated next to me in the street car, the way. He replied that he was one of the doctor's congregation, and would be my guide. This led to some conversation; he said 'that of late years, in New Orleans and elsewhere in the States, the Episcopal Church had begun to exert itself, and was now doing wonders in bringing people into its communion.' I told him that only a few days before I had seen it stated in an editorial of a New York paper, ' that the Episcopal Church was now quite the church of the best society in the United States; and that if one wished to get into good society, it was wise to join this communion.' He replied 'that statements of this kind read well in newspapers, and that of course there were some people who could be influenced by such considerations; but that in his opinion the most effective reasons for attracting people to the Episcopal Church was the character of the Church itself, and of those who did belong and had belonged to it. It was an historical church, with a grand theological literature of its own, and that, indeed, almost the whole literature of England appeared to belong to the Episcopal Church; and it had, which he thought the most potent reason of all, a definite creed and a dignified ritual.'

Dr. Beckwith's congregation consisted of about a thousand very well-dressed people. As is usual everywhere in Episcopal churches in America, there was an offertory; and I saw, as its pecuniary result, four large velvet dishes piled full of greenbacks, placed in the hands of the three officiating clergymen. Nobody gives less than a quarter of a dollar note. The Bishop elect preached. He is a very good-looking, able, and eloquent man. He ridiculed the idea of a 'psalm-singing' eternity, and affirmed that the possession of knowledge would be an immeasurably nobler means of happiness. But if we concede this, there will still remain the question whether the exercise of the feelings of the heart would not confer on the majority of the human race far more happiness than the exercise of the powers of the intellect.

I looked into another large Episcopal church on my way to Dr. Beckwith's, and found in it several young men teaching Sunday classes.

One gets so accustomed in the lakes, rivers and harbours of America, to vast expanses of water, that the first sight of the Mississippi at New Orleans bcomes on that account more disappointing to most people than it otherwise would be. As you cross the Levee, you see before you a stream not three quarters of a mile wide. The houses on the opposite side do not appear to be at even that humble distance. The traveller remembers how many streams he has crossed, particularly on the eastern and southern coast, some of them even unnoticed on the map he is carrying with him, but which had wider channels. And so he becomes dissatisfied with his first view of the Father of Waters. Still, there he has before him, in that stream not three quarters of a mile wide, the outlet for the waters of a valley as large as half of Europe. What mighty rivers, commingled together, are passing before him—the Arkansas, the Red River, the Platte, the Missouri, the Ohio, the Wabash, the Cumberland, the Tennessee! How great then must be the depth of the channel through which this vast accumulation of water is being conveyed to the ocean! On this last point I questioned several persons in the city, getting from all the same answer, that several attempts had been made to fathom this part of the river, but that none had been attended with success.

On my calling the attention of the stout, mediæval, coloured female who had charge of the baths of the St. Charles's Hotel, to the water in the one she was preparing for me,—for it was of the colour, and not far from the consistency of pea-soup,—she convinced me in a moment of my ignorance, and of the irrational character of my remark. 'Child,' she said, 'it is Mississippi river, which we all have to drink here all our lives.'

I visited the celebrated burial grounds of New Orleans, one in the suburbs, and three others contiguous to one another, in an older part of the city. None of them are more than two or three acres in size. In each case the enclosure was surrounded with a high wall, which was chambered on the inner side for the reception of coffins. The whole peculiarity of these burial grounds arises from the fact that, the soil being too swampy to admit of interment, the coffin must be placed in some receptacle above ground. Many of the trades of the city, and several other associations, appear to have buildings of their own in the cemeteries, for the common reception of the bodies of those who had in life belonged to the brotherhood. Most of the families, too, of the place appear to have their own above-ground tombs. They are almost universally of brick, plastered outside, and kept scrupulously clean with whitewash. It was on a Sunday evening that I visited the cemetery in the suburbs. It was very cold on that evening to my sensations, and so I suppose it must have felt much colder to people who were accustomed to the climate of New Orleans; still I saw many persons, sometimes alone, and sometimes in parties, sitting or standing by the tombs that contained the remains of those who had been dear to them, and the recollection of whom they still cherished. In some cases I saw one man, two men, or more than two, seated at a grave smoking. In some cases there would be a whole family. This I noticed particularly at what was far the best monument in the place. It was one that had been raised to the memory of a young man who had fallen in the late war. There was a small granite tomb, over which rose a pillar of granite bearing the inscription. A little space all round was paved with the same material, and this was edged with a massive rim, also of granite, about two feet high. Upon this were seated many of his sorrowing relatives, old and young. In the same cemetery I saw two other monuments to young men who had died soldiers' deaths in the Confederate service. On each of the three, the inscription ran that the deceased had died in the discharge of his duty, or in defence of the rights of his country, or some expression was used to indicate the enthusiastic feeling of the South. One was stated to have been the last survivor of eight children, and the stone went on to say that his parents felt that they had given their last child to their country and to God. These were all English inscriptions; but I saw some that were in two languages, English being mixed in some cases with French, in others with German. I saw no inscriptions that had any direct reference in any way to what Christians believe.

At New Orleans, fifteen hundred miles from New York, you get, in your morning paper, whatever was known in London yesterday of English and European news. And this department of an American journal contains a great deal more than we, in this country, are in the habit of seeing in the *Times* and other English papers, as the messages brought to us by the Atlantic cable; because we want intelligence only from the United States, whereas they wish to get from us not only what is going on in England, but in every part of Europe, and in fact in every part of the Old World.

As one is thus day after day, whether you be in the centre, or thousands of miles away, at some almost unknown extremity, of this vast transatlantic region, kept well informed as to what is passing over almost all the earth, one feels that there are agencies at work amongst us which in some respects render 'the wisdom of the ancients' a little obsolete. Formerly it would have been thought impossible to harmonise such discordant elements as the North and the South. How could they ever dwell together as brethren, who were locally so remote from each other, that while one was basking in a sub-tropical sun, the other was shrinking from the nipping frosts of the severest winter; whose institutions, too, and interests, and antecedents had in many essential points been very dissimilar; and whose differences at last had broken out into a fierce and sanguinary war? Could they ever be fused into a single homogeneous people? Down to the times of our fathers, it would have been quite impossible. Each would then have kept only to his own region, and known no influences but those which were

native to it. But now we have changed all that. A
few threads of wire overhead, and a few bars of iron
on the levelled ground, will do all that is wanted. For
extreme remoteness they have substituted so close
a contiguity that the North and South can now
talk together. The dissimilar institutions, interests,
and antecedents of the past, however strong they
may be in themselves, become powerless when something stronger has arisen; and this new power is
now vigorously at work undermining and counteracting their effects. And it is a power that will
also exorcise envy, hatred, and malice. Men are
what their ideas are, for it is ideas that make the
man. And every morning these two people have the
same ideas, and the same facts out of which ideas
are made, put in the same words before them. The
wire threads overhead do this. And if a Southern
man, from what he reads this morning, thinks that
his interests call him to the North, or a Northern
man that his call him to the South, the railway,
like the piece of carpet in the Eastern story, will
transport them hither and thither in a moment. It
ensures that there shall be a constant stream of
human beings flowing in each direction. Everyone
can foresee the result—that there must, sooner or
later, be one homogeneous people. Formerly the
difference of their occupations produced difference of
feeling, and was a dissociating cause. Now it will
lead to rapid, constant, and extensive interchange of
productions, by the aid of the telegraph and railway.
Each will always be occupied with the thought of
supplying the wants of the other. And this will
lead to social intercourse, and the union of families.

So that what was impossible before is what must be now.

Everything in the United States, except railway fares and the *per diem* charges of hotels, is unreasonably dear; and the hotels themselves participate in the general irrationality on this subject as soon as you order anything that is not down in the list of what is allowed for the daily sum charged you. I never got a fire lighted in my bed-room for a few hours for less than a dollar, that is 3*s.* 6*d.*; or half a dozen pieces washed for less than a dollar and a half. But the one matter of all in which the charges are the most insane is that of hackney coaches and railway omnibuses. You get into an omnibus at the station to be carried two or three hundred yards to your hotel. As soon as the vehicle begins to move, the conductor begins to levy his black mail. He is only doing to you what his own government is doing to him. And in America it seems to be taken for granted that one will pay just what he is ordered to pay. 'Sir,' he addresses you, 'you must pay now; three quarters of a dollar for yourself, and a quarter of a dollar for each piece,' that is of luggage. You have perhaps four pieces, being an ignorant stranger; if you had been a well-informed native you would have had only one piece; and for these four pieces and yourself you pay about 7*s.* In an English railway omnibus you would have paid 6*d.* or 1*s.* The hackney coaches are very much worse. I found a driver in New York who would take me for a short distance for a dollar and a half, but I never found so reasonable a gentleman in the profession elsewhere. At New Orleans there appear to be a great many hackney coaches, all apparently quite new, with a great deal of silver-plated mounting about them, almost as if they had been intended for civic processions on the scale of our Lord Mayor's show. Each of them is drawn by a very fair pair of horses. I once counted two-and-thirty of these coaches standing for hire, on a rainy day, at the door of the St. Charles's Hotel; and I was told that it was their rule not to move off the stand for less than two dollars, or to take one out to dinner, and bring one back, for less than ten dollars.

Books of travel in the United States generally contain some remarks on the personal attractions of the mixed race in New Orleans. From the little I saw of them, I can add that they appeared to me as *spirituel* as the French themselves. I am more disposed to believe that this is hereditary, than that it is the result merely of imitation. But with respect to their personal appearance, after having of late seen so many of the coarse and ill-visaged half-breeds in which an Anglo-Saxon was the father, I was much struck with their superiority in face and figure. The features of many might almost have been called delicate and refined; and it was so, strange to say, even when very perceptible traces of the African nose and lips remained, and these still surmounted with the African wool. I understood that this was also to a great extent the case where a Spaniard was the father. The reason of this difference I believe to be a very obvious one, that Frenchmen and Spaniards, having much smaller bones than the Northern nations, are better able on that account to correct, in their mixed descendants, the grossness of the physiognomy and figure of the African. The German half-breeds are still more unattractive than the Anglo-Saxon; the Scandinavian are worse; but the worst of all are those whose long-headed and high cheek-boned fathers come from the north of the Tweed.

No one without having seen the thing himself—and the jolting will impress it on his memory—can form any proper conception of the holes, the mud, and the pools of water which not unfrequently constitute what is called in America a road. At Augusta I had seen axles disappear in the main streets. But the most advanced specimen of this kind of means of communication I ever passed over, was in going to the station of the Mississippi and Tennessee railway at New Orleans. I could not see or hear that any attempt had ever been made to form a road. The traffic was great, and was of course confined by the houses to a narrow street. It was a natural swamp, and there had been lately a great deal of rain. My reflections on coming at last to the station were, that American horses were wonderful animals, and that in nothing did the Americans themselves show their inventive powers so triumphantly as in constructing carriages which could carry heavy loads day after day through such difficulties;—I do not say through such roads, because there was nothing but a collection of the hindrances to travelling which a road is made to remedy.

This is a subject on which the Americans themselves are very tolerant and easily satisfied. 'Sir,' said a gentleman to me, on the top of Wells and Fargo's coach, as we were passing over the Plains to Denver, 'Sir, this is the finest piece of road in the world.' As nothing had been said previously about roads, and as what we were passing along was merely a freight-track on the dry prairie, four inches deep in dust and sand and earth in fine weather, and as many or more inches deep in mud in wet weather, I intimated that I believed I had not heard rightly his remark. He then repeated his assertion even more emphatically than at first, 'that it was the best piece of road in the world.' I was beginning to explain to him, as courteously as I could, why I should hardly have ventured to call it a road at all, when he stopped me short with, 'Sir, we have no faith in European practices. I am a judge of roads. I have seen all kinds of roads; and I have seen roads in all kinds of places; and this is just what I said it was, the finest piece of road in the world.' Over this model road, sometimes with six good horses, never with less than four, we were able to manage about six miles an hour.

The railroad from New Orleans, for the first mile or two, lies through a most dreary dismal swamp. The water stands everywhere. The palmetto and the swamp cedar grow out of the water. The trees are completely shrouded with the grey Spanish moss. The trees and the moss look as if they had long been dead. One who enters the city by this approach (had ever any other great city such an approach?) must carry with him some not very encouraging thoughts. Whenever in the summer or autumn the wind blows from this direction, I suppose it will remind him of the yellow fever, the horrible scourge of the place.

The swamp I just mentioned is succeeded by sugar plantations, the costly machinery of which had been destroyed during the war. They now appeared to be used as grazing farms for cattle brought up from Texas. On one of these ruined plantations I saw some hedges of the Cherokee rose. This is an evergreen, and makes too wide a hedge, though its height may be an advantage in that climate. It is a common opinion in New Orleans that all these sugar plantations will eventually be re-established; but that this will never be done by the present proprietors, who are all ruined, and who will have to sell the land at a merely nominal price, which is all that the land without the machinery is worth. Those who will buy the land will be companies, or Northern men who will have capital enough to purchase new machinery, and to pay the heavy costs of carrying on the cultivation of the cane and manufacture of the sugar.

Americans are very careful not to give offence in what they say to others. An American bishop remarked to me that the only exception to this rule was to be found among ministers of religion, and among them only in their prayers. He mentioned, as an instance, something that had occurred at a public meeting at which he had himself been present. A minister had opened the proceedings with prayer. He was followed by a rival preacher. The latter, after dwelling for some time on general topics, at last came up to his opponent in the following way: he prayed that the gifts of the Spirit might be poured out on all his brethren in the ministry abundantly, and then added, 'and on behalf of our brother whose words we have just heard, we offer this special supplication, that his heart may become as soft as his head."

CHAPTER X.

MY ONLY DELAY ON AN AMERICAN RAILWAY—NO CONCEALING ONE'S NATIONALITY—RAILWAY COW-PLOUGH—PISTOLS—MEMPHIS—EMIGRATION FROM THE SOUTH DEPRECATED—TRUE METHOD OF RESUSCITATION—THE MINISTER'S STUDY—CONVERSATION WITH TWO MINISTERS—INVITATION TO 'GO TO CHURCH' 150 MILES OFF—LUXURY DOES NOT SAP THE MILITARY SPIRIT—MRS. READ—ENTRY INTO EDEN—SHARE A BED-ROOM WITH A CALIFORNIAN—HOW CALIFORNIA WAS CIVILISED—HOW A SITE UPON THE SWAMP WAS CREATED FOR CAIRO—DECLINE THE FOURTH PART OF A BED-ROOM AT ODIN—'BE GOOD TO YOURSELF.'

ONE hears a great deal of accidents on American railways, and they certainly appear to be very frequent, and often to be most fearful. It is not an uncommon consequence of a railway accident in winter that a great part of the passengers are burnt to death. This arises from the fact that an American railway car is a long box containing between fifty and sixty people, generally with a red-hot stove in winter at each end, and without any possible means of egress except by the doors at each end. The natural issue of this is that when an accident takes place, the carriages are forced close together, the doors are thus shut, and the stoves being overturned, or the crushed-in ends of the carriages brought in contact with them, the train is in a few minutes in flames. But as the Americans have more than thirty-eight thousand miles of railway at work, which is more than three times as much as we have in the United Kingdom, they are entitled to a good many accidents. My own experience, but it is limited to eight thousand miles, is in favour of the safety of American railway travelling. No train I was in ever met with an accident. The only delay I ever had to submit to was caused by a luggage train ahead having crushed a rail. And this delay of four hours was not altogether wasted time, for besides giving one an opportunity for taking a little walk in an American forest, it was the cause of one's hearing the following piece of wisdom: 'There are two things a man ought to bear well: what he can help, and what he cannot help;' and the following specimen of infantile Transatlantic English: 'Mother! Fix me good. Fix me good.' The first came from a gentleman 'on board' the train, whom his friends called General, and was addressed to some impatient passengers. The latter came from a little sobbing child of two or three years of age, who wanted to be placed in an easier position.

In my tour throughout the greater part of the Union I was never mistaken for a native. On some occasions, before I had spoken a word I was addressed as an Englishman. I could not imagine what it was that revealed my nationality. Was it my dress? or the look of my luggage? or was it my manner? It once happened—it was between Gordonsville and Richmond—that a gentleman in the train even went still further, by divining at a glance not only my nationality, but also that I was a clergyman; for he began, 'I suppose, sir, I am addressing an English clergyman.' I was puzzled, and could only be certain that it was not my dress that had enabled him to make the discovery. The single point at which their sagacity was ever at fault, appeared to be the motive which had induced me to undertake so long a journey (of course I am only speaking of the persons one casually meets in a railway car). In the South, and up the Mississippi, I frequently heard the supposition that I had come across the water to establish some kind of business. I was supposed on the prairies to be speculating in land; in the Rocky Mountains to have an eye to gold mining. But to go back to the original point. I was once told what it was that had betrayed me on that particular occasion, and to that particular gentleman. He had taken his seat at the same breakfast table as myself, at the Gayoso Hotel, at Memphis. We had not been talking together long, when he announced to me that I was an Englishman, and how he had made the discovery. 'Sir,' he said, 'it is impossible for a foreigner to escape detection in this country. His speech always betrays him. There is a harshness and a coarseness in foreign tones which an American instantly observes, because Americans themselves all speak with soft and musical intonations; it is natural to them.'

The railway cow-catcher, of which we used to see frequent mention in books of American travel, appears now to have been superseded by another contrivance with a different form; for in the United States nothing remains long in one form. The new form resembles that of the snow-plough, and it must act by partially lifting what it comes in contact with, and then throwing it off to the right or left, as it may happen. This cow-plough, though evidently superior to any contrivance for picking up or catching the cow, does not always do its work. Not far from the town of Jackson, we came up with one of these poor animals that happened to be lying on the rails. On this occasion the plough went over it, and so did the first two or three carriages; till at last the unhappy brute got fast fixed among the springs and wheels of the car I was in. The train was stopped, and the cow taken out, which, though horribly mangled, proved to be still alive. The conductor called out for the loan of a pistol to enable him to put it out of its misery. In an instant almost from every window on that side the train a hand was extended offering the desired instrument. On my making some observation on the number of pistols that were forthcoming ready loaded, at a moment's notice, the gentleman seated next to me replied, 'that it was quite possible that I was the only man unarmed in the train. That formerly in that part of the country many people carried revolvers, but that now, from apprehension of the blacks, in consequence of the frequent robberies committed by them, no one ever thought of moving without his six-shooter.'

Memphis is on a bluff of the Mississippi. How strange does this juxtaposition of the names of hoar antiquity and of yesterday sound in the ears of a European! And it will also seem strange to many that this city, whose name they had never heard mentioned, except as being that of a great city of the Pharaohs, has already a population of 84,000 inhabitants, and is so well situated that it is destined to become, under the reign of freedom, one of the largest of the second-class cities of the Union. A bluff is a river-cliff. It may be either an old and abandoned one (many miles of such bluffs are to be seen in the valley of the Platte, at considerable distances from the existing channel of the river), or it may be one at the foot of which the stream still runs. To the latter class belongs the bluff on which Memphis is built. It is of a soft sand, and large spaces of it have been escarped and graded between the city and the water's edge, in such a manner as to enable the traffic to be carried on easily. A great many cotton bales were standing ready for shipment on the great river steamers. As these bales were spread out over the quays, occupying in this way much space, they suggested the idea of a great deal of traffic. One might perhaps have counted a thousand of them. But then I remembered that the whole of them would be but a very sorry cargo for one of the enormous steamers, the General Robert Lee, or the General Putman, on board of which I had lately been, and which were the largest vessels, excepting the Great Eastern, I had ever seen. They had stowage, I understood, for three thousand bales, and yet as you looked through their gilded and splendidly furnished saloons, 180 yards in length, and saw how great was the number of sleeping berths they contained, you would have supposed they were constructed for passengers only.

In this most modern city with most ancient name, there were many fine shops and good buildings, but little that was continuously good; unoccupied spaces, or spaces occupied only with poor wooden tenements, were everywhere interposed. The streets were generally totally uncared for. This unsightliness and neglect are to be set down to the past, and not to the present state of things. They are some of the legacies of slavery.

I found that from Memphis, as from many other places in the South, a considerable emigration was going on. While I was there names of intending emigrants were being collected for a settlement in British Honduras: this however, I believe, was abandoned on account of the unsuitableness of the climate for white labour. As in their own State of Tennessee there is so much good land, and so delightful a climate, it could have been political reasons only that prompted this thought of leaving their country. For such persons Brazil appears just now one of the most favourable fields for commencing life anew; as the government is there offering, at a merely nominal price, in the hills in the neighbourhood of the capital, land well suited for coffee plantations, and where the climate is such as to admit of European labour. This has been done with the especial view of attracting some part of the emigration from the Southern States. No friend, however, of the unhappy people of the South would advise them to accept any offers of the kind. How much more manly would it be, and how much better would it be financially for themselves, and morally for their children and descendants, if they are prepared to labour with their own hands, to do so in their own country, and remain a part of the great Anglo-Saxon race, with all its rich inheritance of laws, literature, and traditions, than to cast in their lot with mongrel Portuguese and Africans!

Among the letters of introduction I carried with me to Memphis was one to the President of the Memphis and Ohio railway. He had just returned from a short stay at the Hot Springs Mountain in Arkansas. He is one of those gentlemen who are doing everything in their power to resuscitate the South by persuading the people to turn their attention to the varied and inexhaustible resources they possess within their own territories. As instances of this he showed me two specimens; one of a creamy white stone he had lately brought from the Hot Springs Mountain in Arkansas, and which could cut steel as readily as a file does soft iron. Of this stone he was having hones and grindstones made, which would probably be the best things of their kind anywhere to be had. The other specimen he showed me was that of iron ore from the Iron Mountain in Alabama. It looked almost like the metal itself. He said it contained sixty per cent. of iron, and that the Confederates had made use of it in the late war. This mountain is sixty miles north of Montgomery, and there is in its neighbourhood plenty of limestone, and of coal. For this district he expected (as who would not?) a great future; for not only is the consumption of iron in agriculture every year increasing, in the form of new machinery as well as tools, of which the South now stands greatly in need, but the place itself, from its contiguity to several large navigable streams, is admirably situated for a great manufacturing centre.

It is the custom in the American Church for the clergyman of the parish to spend a great part of every morning in a room annexed to his church. I always found this room fitted up as his library and study, with a fire in winter blazing on the hearth, and the minister himself seated at the table at work.

This arrangement has great advantages both for the clergyman and for his parishioners. He can study, and prepare for his pulpit, without any interruptions from his children, or from the ever-recurring little incidents of domestic affairs, to which, had he been in his own house, he would have been expected to give some attention; and his parishioners are more likely to call upon him in this room, knowing that he is there for the very purpose of seeing them, and that they shall not be disturbing anyone by their visit.

Having been requested to call on a clergyman of the place, I found him in such a room as I have just been describing, in company with another clergyman of the neighbourhood. Of course the conversation turned on church affairs. They told me that there were five Episcopal churches in the city; that the Episcopal church was not so active in the States of Mississippi and Louisiana as elsewhere in the Union. That the church of Rome was, in that part of the country, looking very far ahead, and buying large tracts of land, and founding educational establishments; that the Germans and Irish did not leave its communion. That church partisanship was a strong feeling in America; to take for instance our own church, there were everywhere men who were not members, that is communicants, but yet considered themselves as belonging to the Episcopal church, who would fight for every stitch in the surplice, and every letter in the Prayer-book. And that it was so in all the other churches. Much interest, they said, was taken in the ritualistic question, because it was becoming generally felt that our service is deficient in appeals to the senses; and that it wants variety and animation. That in the American church, though there is no canon forbidding *ex tempore* preaching, there is one which imposes on the clergyman the necessity of writing every sermon he preaches. The object of this canon is to enable the bishop to judge of the orthodoxy of any statements in the sermon with which the congregation may have been dissatisfied. This was thought necessary in consequence of the sensitiveness of some congregations, and the tendency in all American churches to lapse into some 'ism' or 'ology.' They told me that in some of the nascent States, as for instance in Idaho, the church was stronger than any other religious body. In this territory (I believe it is still in that embryonic condition), there is not a town or village without an Episcopal church. This has been brought about by sending out missionary bishops to plant the church in these new territories. The missionary bishop of Idaho, Dr. Clarkson, is one of the most active and successful of this new order. As this plan has succeeded so well, it is much to be regretted that it was not attempted long ago.

Americans are great travellers. It almost appears as if there was something in the air of America which makes one think lightly of distances, however great. I heard a lady at Washington talking of starting in a few days for California—a journey of more than five thousand miles—as if it involved no more than a journey from London to Edinburgh. I met another lady at a dinner table at New Orleans who had only that day arrived from New York, a distance of nearly fifteen hundred miles; and I entered Denver with two ladies who had been travelling continuously for about two thousand miles each—one from some New England town, and the other from New York. But I was never made so sensible of an American's disregard of distance, and of the slightness of the provocation needed for inducing him to undertake a journey, as I was by an invitation I received from a gentleman to accompany him one hundred and fifty miles out, and of course as many back, merely to hear a preacher he thought well of, and who he understood would be only at that distance from Memphis on Sunday. Now this gentleman was a lawyer who had come all the distance from Detroit to Memphis, on the previous day, on some matter of business, and would have to start on his return on Monday evening; and this was the way in which he spent the Sunday that intervened between two such long journeys, adding three hundred miles to what anyone but an American would have thought was already a great deal too much travelling.

It is a commonly received opinion, though perhaps more largely entertained by authors than by their readers, that the ever-increasing luxury of the present day has done much to weaken the warlike virtues. This opinion, I believe, is exactly the opposite of the truth, and is merely the echo of the opinion of those writers of ancient Rome who made and bequeathed to us a thoroughly mistaken diagnosis of the diseases and symptoms of the body politic of their own decaying empire. Our own late wars, but above everything of the kind in modern or ancient times, the late great American war, show how entirely false is this opinion. Never was a war before carried on upon so great a scale, in proportion to the population of the communities engaged in it; never was a war more deadly; and never before was a war so thoroughly voluntary in the cases of so large a majority of the common rank and file of the combatants. The history of the 7th New York Volunteers, a regiment of gentlemen who went out, at the beginning of the war, of their own free will, and went through the whole of it with all its hardships, sufferings, and deadliness, would alone disprove this opinion. The hundreds of thousands of men who in the North left their countinghouses, their farms, and their drawing-rooms, to risk health, and limb, and life for an idea, are just so many hundreds of thousands of arguments against it. And in some respects the argument from the South is still stronger, for there a still larger proportion of the people went to greater hardships, more cruel wants and sufferings, and to a deadlier warfare, inasmuch as the same regiments had more frequently to meet the enemy. In every family I visited in the South I heard tales of suffering and of heroism. I will only repeat one, because it shows what a lady even can do and bear in these luxurious times. A Mrs. Read, while assisting her husband at the siege of Vicksburg, had her right arm so shattered by a shell that immediate amputation was necessary. It was during the night, but she would not have anyone called off from other work to do for her what she was still capable of doing for herself; she therefore held with her left hand the lamp which lighted the surgeon to amputate her shattered right arm.

I arrived at Cairo by steamer at three o'clock in the

morning. It was a dark and gusty winter night. The rain was falling heavily. At the landing place there was not a light, not a conveyance, not a porter, not a negro even to direct us the way to the hotel. Self-help was the only kind of help any of the passengers got that night. As I scrambled up the slippery Levee, and then waded through the mud to the hotel distant about a quarter of a mile, I congratulated myself on my having sent on all my heavy luggage in advance, so that I had nothing with me but a hat-box and a hand-bag. But these impediments were more than enough for the occasion. As I struggled on I thought that if the author of 'Martin Chuzzlewit,' who was then giving readings in America, should revisit his Eden under such circumstances, he would not feel dissatisfied with the kind of immortality he had conferred upon it.

The stream of passengers at last reached the hotel. There was no want of light here. This had been our beacon, and we felt that we had made the harbour. It was a large red-brick building, with a large hall, and a large stove, red-hot, in the midst of it. I went straight to the clerk's counter, and entered my name in the folio guests'-book. I was among the first to do this, that I might secure a good room. No sooner, however, had I gone through this preliminary than the manager turned to me, and announced that the house could not allow me a room to myself that night, but that I must take one jointly with the gentleman who had registered his name before me. I hardly took in the speaker's meaning, for this was the first occasion of my life when the idea of occupying a bed-room with another man had been suggested to me.

I suppose I was so taken by surprise that I remained silent when I ought to have spoken, for I was next addressed by the gentleman himself with whom it was proposed I should share the bed-room. 'Well, sir,' he said, 'what do you intend to do? It is now past three; and if you don't accept this gentleman's offer, you will have to go out again into the street.' Having said this he took the key from the clerk, and turning to an attendant, told him to show the way to the room. I rather followed than accompanied him, thinking over, as I went along, what I had read of Cairo when, fifteen or twenty years ago, it was a nest of rowdies, robbers, gamblers, and cut-throats, floating upon a fever-and-ague-haunted swamp. I began to be somewhat reassured by the appearance and bearing of my companion. He was a clean-limbed and remarkably handsome man, apparently turned of forty. His moustache and beard were trimmed in the French style, and his bearing was frank and soldierly. On the other side, however, I observed that he had no luggage whatever. At last the door was reached and opened. The attendant entered to light the gas. While he was doing this my companion crossed the room. In crossing it he took off his coat, and kicked off his boots, and walked 'slick' into bed. This was done quietly and deliberately, but in less time than it took to light the gas. I felt that I was becoming uncertain as to the reality of things. Was I at Drury Lane, looking on at the transformations of a pantomime? or was I dreaming that I was at Cairo?

As the balance of probability did not appear to be in favour of either of these suppositions, I took off my boots, and placed them on the outside of the door. As I closed the door a voice came to me from the bed at the further side of the room. Its tone was manly and friendly : ' Sir,' it said, ' if that is the only pair of boots you have with you ' (it was so ; for I had sent my luggage on to St. Louis), 'I would advise you to keep them inside the room, and have them cleaned on your feet in the morning. The last time I was here I put mine outside the door, and never saw them again; and so I had to go barefooted till I could get another pair.' I thanked the speaker for his advice, and acted upon it. My next care was to provide for the safety of my watch and pocket-book, which contained three hundred dollars in greenbacks. This I did by putting them into the pocket where I had my handkerchief, which I then took out of my pocket, as if there was nothing in it (but the watch and pocket-book were in it), and placed it under my pillow. I have no doubt but that my companion saw through what I was doing, for he now addressed me a second time. 'Before you go to sleep, I suppose you would like to know who is in the room with you ; and yet I hardly know how to describe myself. For the last four or five years I have been on this side the mountains. For the fifteen years before that I had been in California ; and I began life in the old States as a lawyer. In the early days of California, I went out as one of a company for digging and mining. There were seven of us, and five of the seven were lawyers. I came over the mountains to help the North in putting down the rebellion. I made a great heap of money in California, and I have lost a great heap in bad speculations since I have been over here.

But I have got a scheme on its legs by which I hope to make again as much as I have lost. That, sir, is what I am—and I wish you good night. My name is——' I could not catch the word, but I afterwards ascertained it, and found that my first bed-room companion added modesty to his other merits, and had not told me how great a man he was in his own State.

It happened the next day that no train started for the North till half-past four in the afternoon; and as the rain of the previous night had turned to heavy driving sleet, I congratulated myself on the accident, although it appeared so disagreeable at the time, to which I was indebted for the acquaintance of the Californian. He had known California, he said, from the first influx of gold hunters. The rogues and desperadoes of all that part of the world were collected there; but there was some good stuff that came in at the same time. Society would have been completely turned upside down, and no decent man could have remained in the place, if it had not been for Lynch law and the use of the pistol. These two things set everything quite right in five years, in a way in which no other kind of law, supported by all the churches and all the teachers in the world, could have done it in fifty years. And now the State is as orderly a community as there is on the face of the earth. After the roughness of many years of Californian life, in the early days of the State, he found the hardships of the late war mere *bagatelles*. The war seemed to him only like an exciting pastime.

The capacity of Eden, for offering a field for such talents as those of Mr. Mark Tapley, was very much

CH. X. *How the Site of Eden was Created.* 161

diminished during the late war; for being at the junction of the Ohio with the Mississippi (the Ohio itself, not far above this point, is joined by three large streams), it became a very important military station. But it was necessary to create a site for a town, for the locality itself supplied nothing of the kind. This was done by raising a levee, forty feet high, and then, behind this, making streets in the form of embankments at right angles to the levee, these streets again being intersected by other embankments parallel to the levee. The whole space that was reclaimed was thus divided by these embankments into hollow squares, each of which is intended for a block of buildings. At present very few of these blocks have been raised, but the streets—that is, the embankments, with in some instances planked *trottoirs* at their sides—are finished. If the water should ever rise up through the ground, or the storm-water flow into the cellars and underground parts of the houses, it will be necessary to pump it out, for there can be no drainage in such a place. So in America, where no difficulties are recognised, are towns built in swamps.

One cannot help speculating on what will be the amount of inducement required for getting people to try to live and carry on business at this city in the swamp, for the fact that the traffic of the valleys of the Ohio and Mississippi join and diverge here will ensure its becoming rich and populous. And what will be the manners and customs of the place? Will it be merely that people living here will call for more whisky toddy and sherry cobblers, smoke more cigars, and play more games of billiards than they would elsewhere? How far will the beneficent railway go

M

towards redressing the wretchedness of the place by carrying off, for the night, for Sundays, and for holidays, all who might wish to have their homes on *terra firma*? Democracies are stingy and do not build beautiful cities in these days; so, however rich it may become, it is not likely ever to become a Venice.

The train in which I had left Cairo reached a place called Odin at eleven o'clock at night. We had to wait here for a St. Louis train till the next morning. This is an instance of what is called, in American railway phraseology, 'making bad connexions.' The gentleman who registered after me at the chief hotel at Odin happened to be my Californian acquaintance. Having entered his name, he said to the manager, pointing to me, ' This gentleman and I will have the same bed-room.' This was meant as a compliment; and I did not now feel as disinclined to the proposal, particularly as it came from him, as I had been a few nights before. The clerk, however, told him that the house was full, and that I was the last person he could accommodate. I was, upon this, shown to my bed-room, which turned out to be only the fourth part of a very small apartment containing four beds, three of which were already tenanted. My English inexperience and prejudices were still too strong for this, so I sallied out in search of another hotel. While thus occupied I had time to reflect, that there is not much more harm in spending the night in a room with three others, than in spending the day in a railway car with thirty or forty others. At last, chance conducted me to the same house the Californian had already reached; and we sat by the stove in the drawing-room, talking together till the small hours of the morning. There is an unconventional kind of frankness and manliness that is very pleasing in these Western men, who have gone through a great deal of rough life and hardship, and have never, for years together, been out of danger from Indians, or desperate white men, as sanguinary as Indians, and as little troubled with scruples.

For the words' sake I 'made a note' of a parting expression I heard used by a rough-looking and ill-clad ostler, who it appeared was not very comfortably assured of his friend's motives for leaving him to go to one of the most rowdy places in the Union. His friend had taken his place on the roof of the coach, which was in the act of starting, when he waved his hand to him, saying at the same time with an enviable neatness, that conveyed both his kindly feelings and his misgivings, 'Tom, be good to yourself.'

CHAPTER XI.

MISSISSIPPI FROZEN OVER AT ST. LOUIS—WHY THE BRIDGE AT ST. LOUIS IS BUILT BY CHICAGO MEN—GENERAL SHERMAN—IDEAS ABOUT EDUCATION AT ST. LOUIS—LIBERAL BEQUESTS FOR EDUCATIONAL PURPOSES—HOW NEW ENGLANDISM LEAVENS THE WHOLE LUMP—THE GERMAN INVASION WILL NOT GERMANISE AMERICA—ST. LOUIS—ITS RAPID GROWTH—ITS CHURCH ARCHITECTURE—AN IDEA ON MENTAL CULTURE FROM THE WEST BANK OF THE MISSISSIPPI—A THOUGHT SUGGESTED BY HEARING THE SKATERS ON THE MISSISSIPPI TALKING ENGLISH.

ON leaving Odin I saw the prairie for the first time. It was a sea of rich level land, and was here everywhere under cultivation. Since I had left Washington, I had not till now seen cultivation and houses everywhere around me, as far as the eye could reach. After some hours we came to undulating land where coal-mining was being carried on. There were several pits alongside of the rail. The seam of coal, I was told, is seven feet thick. At ten o'clock we reached East St. Louis. Only a few days ago I had been among the oranges, bananas, and sugar-canes; and now I looked upon the mighty Mississippi, solidly frozen from shore to shore, and saw multitudes of persons crossing and recrossing on the ice. So great is the range of climate in this vast country, and yet, by the aid of steam, so near to each other are the two extremes!

At St. Louis, the Mississippi is crossed by very

powerful steam ferries, and a passage across the river has for this purpose to be kept open and free from ice. The Bluff has been escarped to enable vehicles to get down to the water-side. The crush and crowd were very great, and to increase the difficulty of getting down, the face of the descent was at that time coated thickly with ice. I saw two loaded waggons capsize, and the coach I was in at one time began to slip, and we were only saved by the skill of the driver. The ferry boat took over more than a dozen coaches and waggons each trip, many of them having four horses. The city of St. Louis is on the further or western bank, and all the traffic of the city and of the vast region beyond it crosses at this ferry. It will not, however, be needed much longer, for the foundations are now being laid for a bridge, which, like that at Niagara, will carry foot-passengers and all kinds of horse-drawn vehicles, as well as the railway trains. It is a strange thing that this bridge is being built, not by the people of St. Louis itself, but by capital advanced by Chicago men. The reason is not far to seek. St. Louis, regarded as a considerable place, is ten or fifteen years older than Chicago. The moneyed men therefore at St. Louis are getting into years, and so have become cautious, and indisposed to try new investments. The Chicago men are still young: the enterprise of youth in them is not yet exhausted; and so they are ready to entertain, and even to accept, new ideas; and a proposal, however grand, or novel, or costly it may be, is not on these accounts appalling to them. In America, where everything is ever moving and changing, an elderly man is unfit for business.

At St. Louis I became acquainted with General Sherman. I mention this because it may be interesting to hear what were one's impressions of the man who conceived and executed one of the boldest and most arduous military achievements of modern times—that of marching his army down through the heart of the Southern States to Charleston and Savannah. He is tall and thin, without an ounce of flesh to spare. He gives you the idea of a man who is ready at any moment to tax his mental and bodily powers to any amount possible for human nature, and that they would respond to the demands made upon them without flagging, only that his frame would become more and more fleshless and wiry. If you had not known that he was General Sherman, still you would have thought him one of the kindliest and friendliest men you had ever met. His first questions were, whether there was anything he could do for me? any letters he could write for me to persons in St. Louis or Missouri? any information on any subject that it was in his power to give me? The letters of introduction he supplied me with he wrote with his own hand. He interested himself about my intended excursion to the Plains and Rocky Mountains, going over the route with me, and advising me what to see and what to do, and bid me not to hesitate about applying to him for anything I wanted that he could do for me. His physiognomy agrees with his military life in indicating that he is a man of unflinching determination. His first thought on undertaking anything appears to be, as it was with our Iron Duke, to master thoroughly all the details of the subject, to ascertain what will be wanted down to the minutest particular, and to provide for everything.

As the superintendent of schools at St. Louis, to whom I had a letter from Washington, was confined to his house by illness, I took a letter from General Sherman to the president of an institution at St. Louis that goes by the name of the 'Washington University.' It is not a university in our sense of the word, but an institution for working connectedly the different educational resources of the place, beginning with the elementary schools, and passing up through grammar and high schools to a kind of polytechnic institution, in which arts rather than sciences are taught, the arts in truth being little more than the principles and practice of different trades and occupations. This seems to us a low view to take of education and of a university. But it is what is first wanted in a new country, where every man has to work for his bread, and everything has to be done. Higher culture is not for the existing, but for future generations. So think the people who manage this institution. And so think the people for whose benefit the institution has been established, except that they have little or no idea at all, as yet, of the ' higher culture.' They are beginning to be intolerant even of the time and money spent in teaching law and medicine, and of the position assigned to lawyers and physicians. It was in this spirit that a gentleman said to me, on the prairie between Chicago and Omaha, ' What we want, sir, in this great country, is fewer graduates of law and medicine, and more graduates of the machine shop and agricultural college.'

This Washington University has had 800,000 dollars presented and bequeathed to it by citizens of St. Louis in the last eleven years; and as the war, and the collapse that followed the war, cover more than half of this period, the sum appears very considerable. This is in the spirit, and it is a very common spirit in America, of the times when our own colleges and schools were founded.

The president told me that he came from New England to settle at St. Louis thirty years ago. He rode all the way. At that time the country was so little settled that he would ride by compass a whole day without seeing a log hut or a human being. He brought with him to St. Louis the ideas and the traditions of New England. His son had, following the example of his father, moved on westward. He had crossed the mountains and settled in Oregon, on the Pacific coast. His son had been brought up at St. Louis in the ideas and traditions of New England, and had taken them with him. In this way it is that the New England element, which is a distinct character, is kept up and propagated throughout the whole West. Other emigrants bring with them nothing of so tough and perdurable a nature; New Englandism therefore must spread till it has leavened the whole lump.

In the West one is frequently confronted by the question, What will be the effect on the Americans of the future of the vast hordes of Germans which yearly invade and settle in the country? Whole districts are occupied by them, beginning in Pennsylvania, to the exclusion of the English language. In the Western towns you will see street after street in which half, or more than half, the names are German. They have their own hotels, their own newspapers, their own theatres. It seems a greater invasion than that of the Roman Empire by their fathers. That overthrew the empire, and for a time disorganised society; it, however, did not extend the language of the Fatherland into Italy, Spain, or France. But here is a continuous stream of between 200,000 and 300,000, every year coming, not with sword and torch to slay and to burn, or to perish themselves, but with the axe and the plough to clear away the forest, and to cultivate the soil. Every one that comes is taken up into that entity which will be the America of the future. What then will be the effect? Many Americans fear that it will not be good. 'Because,' say they, 'the Germans are deficient in spirituality.' That is the word they use. 'They have no religious devotion: this element appears to have been left out of their composition.'

I am disposed to think that they will have very little power to modify the future character of the nation. First, because they are all learning, and must all learn, the English language, which cannot but become their mother tongue. This being the case, they must imbibe the ideas current in America in that language; and so German ideas will fade away and die out of their minds.

Another reason I have for my opinion is, that the conflict is between Germanism and New Englandism; and it is carried on upon what may be regarded as the soil of New England. But New Englandism is a far tougher plant, and one of far more vigorous growth than Germanism, especially when transplanted to another world, very unlike that of the Rhine and of the Danube. For these reasons I believe that the German invasion will be absorbed and lost in America. It will not Germanise the Americans, but will itself be Americanised.

This applies to ideas, not to temperament, which is a matter of blood and nerves; and it is possible that the highly excitable American temperament may be somewhat calmed by the phlegm of Germany. But if this effect be produced, we can hardly expect that it will be lasting, for in time America will change the temperament of the German, just as it has changed the temperament of the Anglo-Saxon.

St. Louis is a large and well-built city of about 280,000 inhabitants. In the year 1836 it was only a French village of about 3,000 souls, almost all of whom were Canadians and Canadian half-breeds. In those days the wild Indian was close upon it. Now the French and the Indians are both alike obliterated, and railways reach between five and six hundred miles beyond it. It contains many churches, some of which are built in very good taste and style. I never saw red brick anywhere else used so pleasingly and effectively in pointed architecture, as in the spire of one of the churches in this city. I was also much struck with a stone church, the tower of which was not yet completed. Each window in the side aisles had a second window over it, in the form of a kind of window head or marigold. The main aisle had clerestory windows. All the windows throughout were filled with stained glass. This fine church belonged to the Episcopal communion. There are six Episcopal congregations in St. Louis. I here became acquainted with a clergyman who had just returned from a long tour through Europe and the East. It was strange, on the west bank of the Mississippi, on a spot where red men had sold their furs, and smoked their pipes, in the memory of the speaker himself, to hear expressed the opinion, 'that a man of culture and thought had not completed his education till he had seen with his own eyes the scenes in which the great events of man's past history had been enacted.'

While crossing the Mississippi on the ice, I could not hear unmoved the shoals of skaters cheering, and shouting, and talking merrily in good English, just as if it were all on the Serpentine in the Park; and I thought to myself that that small piece of water in the midst of London does not belong more completely to the English race than the Father of Waters himself does now, and must for ever.

CHAPTER XII.

INSTANCE OF AMERICAN KINDLINESS—RED-SKINS AND HALF-BREEDS ON THE RAILS—CINCINNATI AND ITS INHABITANTS—WHAT MAY BE MADE OF PIGS—THE INFLUENCE OF ITS PORK CROP—MACHINERY FOR KILLING AND CURING—IMPROVING EFFECT AMERICAN EQUALITY HAS ON THE HIGHEST AND LOWEST CLASS—CHURCHES ONLY UNPROSAIC BUILDINGS IN AMERICAN TOWNS—SCHOOLS—MERITS OF PHILADELPHIAN STYLE OF CITY-BUILDING NOT OBVIOUS—IN WHAT IT CONSISTS—AMERICA HAS BUT ONE CITY—NO. 24, G STREET, CORNER OF 25TH STREET.

ON leaving St. Louis for Cincinnati, I took the evening train, because, as far as Odin, the ground was the same I had lately passed over. On entering the carriage I met with an instance of American kindliness I should be sorry to have to pass unnoticed. When I applied for a sleeping berth, I found that they were all engaged except some on the upper tier. As the heated air accumulates against the roof, these upper berths are generally too warm; besides that, there is some difficulty in getting in and out of them. This difficulty would have been very considerably increased in my case, as I happened just at that time to be obliged to carry my arm in a sling. An American gentleman, and, as I afterwards found, a very well-known man in Chicago, observing this, came up to me, and insisted on my taking his lower berth, and letting him have in exchange my upper one. While at Chicago, I was laid under further obligation to this gentleman, which I must advert to when I reach that place. He was one of those who, during the late war, gave up their business, and left their comfortable houses for the tented field, that they might help to save their country from disruption; and he had had the good fortune to accompany Sherman in his memorable march through the South.

There were two red-skins 'on board' this sleeping car, on their way to Washington to transact the business of their tribe. They were tall, bony men, but their complexion was not of so dark a copper colour as I had expected. Their features were coarse and stolid, their only expression being just that of the obstinate tenacity of purpose, and of the power of endurance with which history credits their race. They were accompanied by two half-breeds, who appeared a great improvement on the pure stock. These latter played at cards hour after hour, and, when not so employed, sang together Heber's 'Missionary Hymn' and 'Three Blind Mice' alternately, equally unconscious of the poetry and sentiments of the one, and of the inanity of the other.

Everyone has heard of the Metropolis of Pigs. And it is rightly so called, for the greatness of Cincinnati is founded on cured pigs, in a far greater degree than that of Holland was on pickled herrings. Here are more than 200,000 souls maintained in life by breeding, fattening, killing, salting, packing, and exporting incredible millions of pigs. The 200,000 human beings are only 200,000,000 pigs in another form. The old and the young, the schools and the churches, the politicians and the men of science of this great city, are all created out of pig. Take

away the pigs, and they all disappear; double the
pigs, and they all are doubled.

And the influence of the pigs of Cincinnati is felt
all over the world. When an East Anglian farmer
sells his improved Essex or Suffolk hog, the price of
its bacon is affected by the greater or less number
of its brethren who grunted their last at Cincinnati
during the previous year, or, as the Cincinnatians
themselves would say, on the amount of the previous
year's 'pork crop.'

Of course, where so many pigs have to be disposed
of, one would expect to find in America some time-
and-labour-saving machinery; and I was told that, if
I went into any of the great factories—which, however, I did not do—I might see machinery in operation, by the aid of which a stream of pigs, that
walked into the factory at the front door, alive and
grunting, was made to issue, a few minutes afterwards, at the opposite door, ready packed for expor-
tation in the three forms of ham, bacon, and lard;
each in his passage through the building having
been stabbed in the throat, scraped, eviscerated,
jointed, and injected with bacon or ham-curing liquor,
all by machinery, and with the regularity of clockwork.

One of the most marked peculiarities of American
society is the total absence of all classes higher than
those of the merchant and professional man. One
sees the working of this in many different ways. For
instance, it evidently elevates the tone and character
of the classes which thus find themselves at the head
of the scale. It gives them a dignity and a bearing
they would not otherwise possess. If there is no

one higher in society than a retail shop-keeper, then by the force of his position he becomes brave and liberal, and his ideas become enlarged. I observed this at Denver, where there is no higher class. And I think the same observation would be made by any one who would go so far to judge for himself. There are good effects which the American system has upon those also who are most humbly placed. As they feel that they are theoretically, and in some respects practically, equal to those who are even the best placed in society, they endeavour not to disgrace or altogether to fall short of their position. This is a strong stimulus among them to education and self-improvement. It is what has suggested the efforts of many who have risen in life, and sustained them through many long years of patient industry and laborious enterprise. I have no reason to believe a word of all that I ever heard of the offensive self-assertion and obtrusive incivility of this class, for I never myself suffered from, or witnessed, anything of the kind. Where an Englishman is the complainant, I should be disposed to think that, in most cases, he had provoked the treatment he complains of, for no people are more careful about giving offence than Americans. This carefulness is taught in their schools, and is a tradition of American society, coming down from the time when, among an excitable people, the use of the pistol had always been simultaneous with the offence.

Another effect of the want in America of what we in Europe regard as the Corinthian capital of society, is the almost entire absence of the literary element. Not that the Americans have no writers or readers;

they have plenty of the former, and are a nation of the latter. But this leaves very little trace on American society, because they have no class whose only real work in life is intellectual. The chief source of supply for the literary element is, with us, that vast number of persons, constituting quite an order in the state, who live upon the rent of the land, associated with whom is perhaps a still greater number of families who live more or less on interest and dividends, that is, on realised personalty. The members of this class can only distinguish themselves in life by the exercise of intellectual powers. They have abundant leisure, and every appliance at their command for intellectual culture. Multitudes of them, it is true, never rise to any useful conception of the advantages and requirements of their position; still this, and this only, is what they are called to; and we cannot complain that their work is on the whole done badly. As a class they are highly educated. From them come almost all our statesmen, and a large proportion of our literary and scientific men. Their culture it is that with us gives to society its tone and colour. This intellectualising element is completely wanting in America. The effects of its absence are by the European never unfelt for a moment. He is always conscious that there are no statesmen, though plenty of politicians, no literary men, though plenty of writers, and no intellectual class, though much has been done successfully to cultivate intellect.

As was my custom wherever I went, I asked permission to visit and inspect some of the schools of this place. The superintendent of schools for Cincinnati was so good as to take me over the largest graded school in the city. We spent in it three hours. There were present about 600 children. The school was divided into six grades. In New York and most other places two of the grades would have belonged to the Grammar School. We began at the bottom and worked up to the top. They teach reading, as is generally now done in America, phonetically. This they think an easier method. They are not at all ambitious in their reading books, because they do not aim at conveying knowledge of things through the medium of reading lessons, but content themselves with creating the habit of reading correctly, and with attention to the meaning of what is read; and this is more likely to be secured, if the book consists of little interesting stories, than would be the case if it contained solid information. What in the upper grades they write to-day, is what they remember of an object lesson given on the previous day. This trains them to remember, to think, and to compose. There is no writing from copies, which children generally get through as quickly as they can, without any attention or thought. Singing is carefully taught, and so is elementary drawing, particularly in connection with the construction of maps. They begin the study of Geography, with the geography of the school-room, which is the North, the East, the South, and the West side : and then they go on to what is beyond. The geography of the United States is taught carefully. It often struck me in America that the geography of the rest of the world was almost ignored. In these schools the reading was very good, and from the readiness and correctness of their answers, it was evident that they were in the

N

habit of attending to what they were reading, and that they completely mastered its meaning. It is not to be expected that children, when they leave school, will keep up their reading, if they have not been taught to read with facility, and so far to understand what they read as to take an interest in it.

The key to the success of these schools, and of so many other city schools in America, is that they are graded, and that each grade has a room and teacher exclusively to itself. The whole time of the teacher is devoted to one class. No member, therefore, of the class can ever during school hours be idle. This system, too, naturally employs more largely than any other the oral method of conveying instruction. The teacher stands up before the class, and teaches it. The eye and the ear are always busy. There is no drowsiness, no whispering, no poring over books, or pretending to be poring over them. All the teachers in this school, excepting one, were women. The superintendent of the whole school appeared to attend equally to all the classes, and to be responsible for the state of each. Boys and girls are taught together in all grades except the highest. The district in which this fine school is situated is inhabited chiefly by German Jews, and more than half the 600 pupils were children of such parents. The Roman Catholic children were only six or seven per cent. of the whole. In the State of Ohio they do not, as is done in the State of New York, allow the Roman Catholics a part of the school rate for the maintenance of separate schools. If they wish to bring up their children in schools of their own, of course they are at liberty to do so, but they must pay for such schools themselves.

I observed at Cincinnati, and in some other cities, that the American Jews affect in their synagogues a Moorish style of architecture. As American cities can have no historical buildings, there is nothing in them to counteract the prose of commerce, and of the American method of laying out cities, except the churches. And as many of them (the practice being general among all the denominations) are embellished with towers or spires, their redeeming effect on the appearance of the town is very considerable.

As I am on the subject of American towns, I trust that my friends in that part of the world will excuse me for never having been persuaded by them to fall into ecstacies at the contemplation of the plan of Philadelphia, which they point to with feelings of enthusiasm, as the very perfection of taste and judgment in the art of building cities. There is, however, as far as I could see, nothing in Philadelphia which is not also in St. Louis and Cincinnati, and a hundred other cities in embryo, or in adolescence. The three cities whose names I have just mentioned are, saving their reverence, as like one another as three peas. They have no main street, but a number of parallel streets at equal distances from each other. These are numbered, first, second, third, &c. Another set of streets, again, exactly parallel to each other, cut the first at right angles. This second set of streets, in the three cities I have named, are called after different trees: Birch, Elm, Hickory, &c. This is everything. It is the very democracy of houses; for all the streets and blocks are equal. No one is larger, or wider, or in anyway better than another.

Of course the result of this must be that there is

not a particle of difference between one town and another, all having been cast in the same mould. It would be laughable, were it not tiresome, to have not a thousand cities in America, but one city reproduced over and over again, wherever you go. St. Louis and Cincinnati are about the same size, and have much the same kind of site, and I believe that if a man who had spent a week in each of these cities, were a month afterwards carried blindfold into one of them, and set down in the middle of the town, he would be unable to say in which of the two he was. I know no two things that are so like each other, except it be two farms on the Prairie, where every farm is just the fac-simile of every other farm; so that it is really impossible to guess how one living on the Prairie, unless he developes a new sense to meet the circumstances he is placed in, can ever distinguish his own home.

I venture to think that the Americans are under another mistake about their towns; they suppose that their method of parallel streets, not named but enumerated and lettered, is a great help to the memory, and facilitates very much the finding of any house one is in search of. Never did fallible mortals entertain so erroneous an idea. Instead of a name, Rivoli, or Cheapside, which readily fixes itself in the mind you have to remember a figure and a letter; and as neither figures nor letters suggest ideas, the thing is impossible. In truth, you have to remember two figures and a letter. For instance No 24, G Street, corner of 25th Street. There is no faculty in the human mind which enables one to retain this direction. In five minutes all certainty is lost as to whether it was

G or E, 25th or 26th—perhaps it was C, perhaps it was 36th.

In fact, the Americans have but one town, and in the nomenclature of the streets of this one town they have done everything the perverse ingenuity of man could desire to render it confusing.

CHAPTER XIII.

THE VALLEY OF THE OHIO—MUCH OF THE UNITED STATES WILL PRODUCE WINE—ILLINOIS AT NIGHT—FIRST VIEW OF LAKE MICHIGAN—CHICAGO—A SIGN OF OUTWARD RELIGION—'SMALL-POX HERE' —FIRE ALARM—LIBERALITY OF CHICAGO MERCHANTS—THE DOLLAR NOT ALL IN ALL—A CHURCH LIGHTED FROM THE ROOF—A HANDSOME AMERICAN—AMERICA HAS DEVELOPED A NEW TYPE OF FEATURES—CHICAGO SCHOOLS—AN EXCEPTION TO THE AMERICAN WAY OF DENOUNCING THE OFFICIAL CLASS—CHICAGO SUNDAY SCHOOLS—PROGRAMME OF ONE I ATTENDED—EXCELLENCE OF WATER AT CHICAGO—HOW SUPPLIED—LIFTING UP THE CITY—POST OFFICE ARRANGEMENTS—A DISADVANTAGE OF FREQUENT CHANGE OF CLERKS—AMERICANS ON ARISTOCRACY—HOW THE GERMANS, THE MASSES OF THE PEOPLE, AND THE UPPER CLASS FEEL TOWARDS IT.

THE valley of the Ohio pleased me—all things considered—more than any other district I saw in the United States. The land was generally very fertile, and much diversified with riverside levels and contiguous hills; with cultivated land, and woodland; with apple and peach orchards, and with wheat and maize. Its most novel feature was the space devoted to the culture of the vine.

In many parts of the Union, as in this State, California, and several others, a great deal of wine is already made; and the planting of vineyards is yearly extending. I tasted two wines, sparkling Catawba, and a red Californian wine, which are really good now, and which no doubt in course of time will become still better. The former was a little too sweet; but that is a fault, if it be regarded as a fault in America, which can easily be remedied by carrying the process of fermentation a little further. There is every prospect of a larger proportion of America, than of Europe, producing wine; in that case the same proportion of its inhabitants will become a wine, and not a beer, or spirit-drinking population. In Europe we attribute certain differences of national character to this difference in the beverage of a people. It appears as if, in this highly-favoured region, upon which Nature has heaped all her gifts, that nothing in the way of climate, occupation, or even food, which can diversify life and character, will be wanting. America will contain within herself all that other people, less bountifully provided, have to seek all over the world.

On passing through almost any part of Illinois after sunset, there are so many lights seen in every direction, glancing from the innumerable farm houses, that I could hardly help thinking, at one time, that the train was entering a large town, while at another, I was reminded of the gleaming on all sides from the shutterless windows of a scattered English village, during the first hour or two of darkness. And this is the way in which all these fertile North-western States are filling up.

On arriving at Chicago, my first thought was to see the Lake, one of the great fresh-water seas I had been reading of, since I was a boy. I was now within a few paces of it, and was only prevented by the houses from looking upon it. I had driven to the Sherman House, a large hotel on one side of the square in the centre of which stands the City Hall; and I had been told that the only good view of the city, and of the Lake, was to be had from the gallery round the top of the dome of this building. It was not long before I ascended the stairs that led to it; and as I stepped out on the balcony, the boundless blue water, reflecting the undimmed hazeless sky, and washing up almost to the foot of the building, and stretching away beyond the horizon, suddenly burst on the view. It was Lake Michigan. Imagination does much on such occasions. I felt satisfied. It was not only worth seeing, but it was worth coming to see.

Here, in these vast reservoirs, is Nature carrying on some of her hydraulic operations upon the grandest scale in the world. Here, too, at this very spot, at its southern point, the countless buffalo used to drink the water of the Lake, and here it was that the red man was waiting to welcome him; and now the white man is ploughing, and harvesting, and building cities all around its shores, and its waters are wafting to this great central depôt the produce of his labours, and then bearing it away again, to feed the millions of New England and of the distant seaboard cities, and even to aid the deficient supplies of Old England and France.

Chicago well deserves its reputation. Its stores, and private houses and churches, are good, and would be so considered in any city. Its stores are in buildings, two floors higher than the shops of Oxford or Regent Street, as is generally the case in all the large American cities. They have an air of solidity, and are not entirely devoid of external decoration. There are suburbs containing many good private residences, the best of which are to be seen in Michigan Avenue, along the shores of the Lake.

These are built of a cream-coloured stone, and many of them give one a favourable idea of the architectural taste, as well as of the wealth, of their inhabitants. From the gallery of the City Hall I counted twenty-three towers and spires; but this is very far from giving the number of churches, as perhaps the majority of them still being incomplete, or only temporary structures, are without these embellishments. In the central parts of the city, where all the buildings are good and massive, and the smoke—for here they burn bituminous coal—has put a complexion upon them something like that of London, you could never guess that you were standing in a city so young, that many of its inhabitants, still young themselves, remember the erection of the first brick house in the place; you would be more likely to suppose that you were surrounded by the evidences and appliances of the commercial prosperity of many generations.

On my mentioning to a 'citizen' of Chicago the number of the churches I had counted from the top of the City Hall, 'Yes,' he replied, 'we are a religious people outwardly.'

In this, one of the youngest cities in the world, I observed some regulations that would be worthy of adoption elsewhere. For instance, wherever in the city a case of small-pox occurs, a large yellow sheet is pasted to the door of the house, announcing in conspicuous letters, 'Small-pox here.' I could not but compare this wise regulation with our carelessness on the same subject at home. This very disease of small-pox, or scarlet fever, or any other infectious disease, may have struck down many of the inmates of a house; yet, according to our custom, it is allowable for the occupiers of the house, if they keep a shop, to invite customers to enter, and to sell them articles of dress, or of food, which in some way or other may become vehicles of infection.

Another very useful arrangement I found in operation here, is that by which the whole city is instantly informed of the existence of a fire, and of the locality in which it has burst out. The city is, for this purpose, divided into districts, each district being known by its number. In some central and conspicuous place in each, is a box containing an apparatus by which a bell may be rung in a room at the City Hall. In this room there are men constantly watching the bells. As soon as the bell of any district is rung, the watchers reply with a hurried kind of chime on the large bell of the City Hall, which can be heard in every part of the city. This is to announce that there is a fire. There is then a pause of half a minute, after which the number of the district is struck on the bell. This informs everyone of the exact locality of the fire. The policeman on duty in each district is the person whose business it is to go to the box and ring the bell. In order, however, to save time, it is competent for any respectable citizen to do this; for the place where the key of the box is kept is always mentioned on the outside of the box, and the keeper of the key is ordered to give it up to any respectable applicant. I was surprised to find how often during the night announcements of fire were made from the City Hall.

A few days before my arrival at Chicago there had been, in the best part of the city, one of those monster fires which are of such frequent occurrence in American towns. A fine hall belonging to the Young Men's Christian Association, and many of the largest stores in the city, had been completely destroyed. This gave the merchants of the place an opportunity for exercising the liberality which is one of the characteristics of America, and in no part of America exists in a higher degree than in Chicago. In a few hours after the occurrence, before the embers had ceased to smoulder, enough had been subscribed to rebuild the hall of the Young Men's Christian Association on a larger scale than that of the one that had been destroyed; and the merchants of the place had met, and had put down their names for considerable sums, to form a fund upon which their brother merchants who had been burnt out by the great fire, and lost their stock in trade, might draw for as much as was needed for rebuilding, and re-establishing themselves in business. Repayment was not to be thought of till the recovery of their affairs conveniently admitted of it.

It is commonly supposed that the Americans are entirely devoted to the pursuit of the dollar. It is true that they pursue the dollar more energetically, intelligently, and successfully than any other people, but no mistake can be greater than that of supposing that they pursue it exclusively. First there is no other country in the world in which the political sentiment is so widely diffused, and so deeply felt; where so much time and thought are devoted to it; where it calls forth so much hard intellectual work in the forms of writing, reading, and speaking. And this is true not of one, but of all classes, from the top to the bottom of society.

Nor is there any other country in which the religious sentiment works so vigorously and so spontaneously, and is so fruitful in great, obvious, and ponderable results. And this as well among those who labour, as among those who elsewhere are supposed to have almost the monopoly of thinking and feeling.

Again, in no other country do a million persons taken not from a horizontal, but from a vertical section of society, read so much; and there can be no surer gauge of the amount of pure mental activity than the amount of reading. The Americans are a nation of readers, and read far more than any other nation in the world. And not only do they read more, but what they read has more effect on them than is the case with any other people.

In the three great departments then of intellectual activity and life—politics, religion, and in the use of literature—this people who are supposed to devote their whole soul to the pursuit of the dollar, are greatly in advance of ourselves and of all other nations.

But whatever the amount of toil Americans may impose on themselves in getting money, it is not done with a view to saving. The American who hoards is a rare exception. They will make a good fight for the purpose of enlarging their business, and increasing their income. But, when this increase comes, it is used and not accumulated. All the world knows that there are no other people who spend so much on their families and houses, on travelling and entertaining, in hospitality and in charity.

On Sunday evening I attended a service at Trinity Church, having been attracted by the exterior of the building, which is a conspicuous object from some points in Michigan Avenue. I mention this because I observed a peculiarity in the means used for lighting it, which might occasionally be adopted with advantage in London, and large cities where sites are costly. I suppose the space was so confined by dwelling houses on the north and south sides, that windows in the walls of the aisles were inadmissible. This difficulty had been met boldly by enlarging the clerestory windows, and adding in the roof rows of quatrefoil skylights, filled with very dark stained glass. I should have been glad to have seen the effect of this by daylight. Nine tenths of the congregation I saw in this church that evening were gentlemen, from which I inferred that the service was intended mainly for the rougher sex.

What is conventionally regarded by us as the American type of features is not uncommon on the Eastern seaboard, but is seldom seen in the West. The clergyman whom I saw officiating in Trinity Church might have sat for the bust of a Greek philosopher. He had a massive head, with much refinement about it; a lofty forehead, a straight nose, and a magnificent beard. He spoke in a manly and soldierly way of what he had witnessed on the battlefields of the late war.

A new and completely distinct type of features has been developed in America. Of all races of men, that from which the Americans are descended has the greatest mixture and variety of features. We have no facial type. We have round heads and long heads; low, high, prominent, and receding foreheads; large jaws and small; our noses are infinite in multiformity; we have long and short, thick and fine, pug,

Roman, and straight, each in all degrees. In America, however, the whole of this variety has been lost and obliterated. The descendants of the most various-featured race of mankind have become one of the most uniform-featured race in the world. Whatever part of the country you may be in, you will find the same thing. As a general rule, the native Americans all have straight noses off straight foreheads, and small jaws. Their faces have been brought to one type, and that a far more intellectual one than what we are familiar with in the old country: it is almost the antipodes of that to which the conventional John Bull belongs. To be convinced of this, it is only necessary to look at the features of the passengers in a railway car, or at the Americans one meets in private houses, or at places of public amusement. The straight nose and forehead are everywhere the rule. I saw at Richmond a frame containing the photographs of the fifty Southerners who had most distinguished themselves in the late war. There was not a single pug, or short or Roman nose among them. It has been just the same with the Greeks; whatever race of people has inhabited the soil of Greece, has assumed the Greek type of feature. The present inhabitants of Greece are chiefly Bulgarians, but their features are Greek.

In America this transformation is observable chiefly in those of Anglo-Saxon descent. The French, both of Canada and Louisiana, retain their French features. This may give us some clue to the cause which has acted on our descendants. The French have retained French habits of life. They have not given in to and adopted the American love of excitement, love of work, and devotion to business, which never pause to enjoy life, but are always struggling forward, and doing something and doing it at high pressure. It is also observable that the descendants of the easy-going Germans retain their old European type longer than those who are of Anglo-Saxon parentage.

I was taken over some of the schools of Chicago by the Superintendent of Schools for the city. Those I saw were chiefly used by the children of German and Irish parents. They did not appear so quick as the children of native Americans: the variety, also, of feature, and more general fulness of face observable among them, indicated their foreign extraction. Americanization in these particulars takes place in the second or third generation. They were cleanly and orderly, and looked well clothed and well fed. In the Illinois system there are ten grades; the tenth is the lowest in the Primary School, and the first the highest in the Grammar School. No copy slips are used in these schools. They write at first from something set before them on the black board as I noticed was done at Cincinnati. When sufficiently advanced, they write each day from memory something they were taught on the previous day. In Chicago the number of children attending school is very much below the number of those who are of an age to attend. This is what might have been expected in a town that has grown to such dimensions in a single generation. Great efforts, however, are being made to overtake the work. The difficulty just at present is to get school-buildings quickly enough. It is certain that neither the city itself, nor their zealous and able superintendent, will fall short of the occasion.

The Americans are in the habit of speaking very disparagingly of their official class. I never heard one speak in any other tone on this subject. If the canon, that whatever all men, at all times, and in all places, affirm must be true, is to be accepted, then this class in the United States occupies a position of very bad pre-eminence. No one is spared. 'The President is a Judas Iscariot who has sold his country. Senators, and representatives, are a set of log-rollers and wire-pullers, who make, on an average of the whole body, £6,000 a year out of their votes in Congress. Judges receive such small salaries, that they must also receive bribes. Every town councillor (if that is the right title), every exciseman, every customhouse officer, every tax assessor, or collector, is open to conviction, if the argument used be the dollar. They work quick, for they know they have only four years for making their fortunes.' These are the mildest terms in which they inveigh against what they call the universal rottenness, from top to bottom, of the official class throughout the Union. On this very dangerous and delicate ground a stranger can only act the part of a reporter. He cannot give any comment, or even have any opinion of his own. I feel, however, that I should be guilty of foul ingratitude, if I did not give the results of my own experience and observation with respect to one class, at all events, of American public servants. I saw much of the superintendents of schools, and was everywhere struck with their devotion to their work, and with their ability. As far as I could judge, the public are well and faithfully served by these officers. And as the superintendent in each city is practically, though not theoretically, the doer of all that is done in the general management, and is responsible for the condition of all the schools in the city, his office is, in fact, second in importance to none.

On a Sunday, while I was at Chicago, the gentleman who had given up to me his berth in the sleeping-car to Cincinnati, took me to see one of the large Sunday-schools, which have been organised on a very extensive scale in this great Western city, and from which great results are expected. The one I went to see is held in a Congregationalist church. It is customary at the end of the meeting to give out the number of those who are present, as everybody is supposed to be interested in the maintenance and spread of the movement. At the meeting I witnessed there were 998 persons present, of whom 84 were teachers. They now have in the city 75 of these schools; of these, however, only five are organised on the scale of the one I am speaking of. One of the five is held in an Episcopal church, I believe that of the Holy Trinity. The pupils in these Sunday-schools are not confined to one class in society, or to children, or to the members of any particular communion. All classes attend them; so do many grown-up persons, and all religious denominations, except the Roman Catholics, are to be found among the taught and the teachers.

The work of the day commenced by singing three hymns, which were evidently intended to excite religious emotions of a highly enthusiastic kind. The leading manager then recited the Commandments, all present repeating, after each commandment, the petition of our Ante-Communion service. To this was added what follows the commandments in the American Episcopal service. 'Hear also what the Lord Jesus Christ says: "Thou shalt love the Lord thy God with all thy heart, and with all thy soul, and with all thy mind. This is the first and great commandment. And the second is like unto it, Thou shalt love thy neighbour as thyself. On these two commandments hang all the law and the prophets."' The last chapter in St. Mark's Gospel was then read, the chief manager reading the first verse, and all present simultaneously reading the second, and so on throughout the chapter. The object of their reading it in this alternate method is to prevent monotony, and to keep up attention. The pupils had been requested to commit five verses of this chapter to memory. These verses were now repeated simultaneously. This was all that was learnt by heart; and even the learning of this was left entirely to the discretion of each pupil. A prayer was then offered; but, as a preliminary to it, the subjects it was proposed to make mention of in the prayer were announced, with a few brief and pointed comments. The whole assemblage was now divided into classes of fourteen in each, with a separate teacher for each. This was done without a single person leaving his seat, by the simple process of reversing the back of every alternate seat; so that, where before there were a hundred pews holding seven persons each, there were now fifty holding fourteen each. The change was effected in a few seconds. Each teacher now commented on, and expounded to his class, the five verses that had been committed to memory. Then followed another hymn, and another short prayer, being founded entirely on the five verses which had formed the subject for the day's instruction. The whole was concluded with the singing of the Doxology.

This Sunday-school was divided into three grades. First came the infants. They were placed in a large room behind the west-end gallery, and over the porch. None of them could read. Nothing was attempted in this department except awakening the moral sentiments, and teaching a few facts of Christian history, and if possible a little Christian doctrine. This was done by telling the children little stories. Three of these I heard. My friend, who was the chief doer of all that was done and taught on the occasion of my visit, told these infants, in a very effective manner, well adapted to their little understandings, how he had spent on himself, after a long and uncertain struggle (which he minutely described to them), the first ten cents he had ever possessed; and how ashamed he afterwards felt of himself.

As soon as they can read, they are promoted into the second grade, which has its place in the gallery. After a time they are passed on to the third or highest grade, which has its place in the body of the church.

It is believed that this Sunday-school organisation has already effected a great deal of good, by bringing all classes together, and by influencing, in a way nothing else could, the destitute, the ignorant, and the reckless. And still more abundant fruit is expected from it in the future.

Who is there but will entertain bright hopes for America, where among the rural population the moral tone is sound and healthy, and in the cities there is so much zeal for doing good?

From the time I left New York till I reached Chicago, I had nowhere seen in the towns clear drinking water. At New Orleans it was of the colour of a mulatto, at Cincinnati of a mestizo, and at the intermediate places of the intermediate shades. At Richmond it had a kind of ochreous tint. The reason is the same everywhere. The rivers, with the water of which the towns are supplied, all run through a yellowish or reddish loamy soil—sometimes sandy, sometimes clayey; this is easily worn away, and carried off in suspension by the stream, and is largely added to, after rains, by the surface-washing of the country. At Chicago, by a boldly-conceived and most successfully carried-out plan, the whole city is supplied with the purest water. A tunnel, large enough for two mules to work abreast in it, was carried out for a distance of two miles beneath the lake. At this point they had reached water which is perfectly free from all the impurities of the shore; and here it is admitted into the tunnel in sufficient volume to supply all the wants of a population of about 280,000 souls. It is calculated that this tunnel will be ample for all that 100,000 more inhabitants will require. When the population has grown to this extent, a second tunnel will have to be constructed. The water is pumped up from the level of the tunnel to reservoirs that are above the level of the city: which latter is not the original level of the prairie, but considerably above it; for it having been found, after a great part of the city was built, that it was subject to being occasionally flooded, they raised the ground several feet. In doing this they did not pull down or bury any part of the streets and blocks of houses that were already completed, but lifted them up to the desired height by hydraulic machinery. In this way the Sherman House, one of the large American hotels (I stayed in it while at Chicago) was elevated to the level of the raised street, without a guest leaving it, or any interruption of its business.

A foreigner is much struck with the amount of business going on at an American post-office. Society not being in so settled and stationary a condition as with us, a far greater proportion of letters are directed to the post-office, and must be called for. A list of the names of the persons whose letters have not been called for is printed twice a week, and hung up in the post-office hall, for the inspection of the public. This list is divided into three separate parts—English, French, and German; each part is hung up by itself in its own frame, and there is a window of enquiry for each of the three nationalities. In the hall of the post-office, or rather in the screen that separates the office from the hall, are innumerable pigeon-holes, each with a door to the hall-side as well as the office-side. The key of the office side door is kept by the officials, of the hall side door by the person to whom the box has been assigned. Into this box that person's letters are put as soon as a mail is sorted; and he can go, or send at any hour of the day (or night), unlock his door, and take them out. He is not therefore obliged to wait for the general delivery, but can get his letters as soon as the mail arrives. There is, too, less chance of his letters being lost, for they never get into the hands of the letter-carrier. And, as everyone whose correspondence is of any consequence adopts this plan, the number and labour of the letter-carriers are much diminished. On account of the large amount of business always going on at the post-office, they separate the ladies from the gentlemen, assigning them a place for making enquiries, getting their letters, and buying stamps, quite distinct from that assigned to the men.

These are good arrangements. My personal experience, however, of the working of the office is not quite favourable. Two-thirds of the letters posted for me miscarried, and the remaining third I only got after a great deal of trouble. It is the rule in America that all officials must be changed as often as the President is changed; and this for the double reason of enabling the President to reward those who worked for his election, and because it is a principle in democracy that all good things of this kind shall be made to go as far as possible, which can only be done by making the tenure of each occupant short. I found that this had the disadvantage that the clerks were not retained so long as to enable them to become familiar with the letter Z. In consequence of this, in the direction of all the letters written to me from Europe, it was mistaken for an L; and in the directions of the letters written to me from New York, where it appears the Z is decorated with a crossbar, it was mistaken for an F.

The feeling of the Americans on the subject of aristocracy is very far from being the same in all classes or sections of the community. I have already made some slight reference to the way in which the German part of the population regard this institution. We must consider not only what they think, but also how much they count for in America. They count for a great deal; because, though they do not take a very prominent part in politics, still from their numbers, their intelligence, and their wealth, they form everywhere in the North, and in a still greater degree in the great West, a very influential portion of society. And as to this matter, there is no mistaking their thoughts and feelings. They hate aristocracy, as if it were the foul fiend in human society; and of all aristocracies they hate that of England the most, because they regard it as the purest type the world exhibits of this mighty evil. We may be sure, then, that there is nothing they would not do to humble the aristocracy of England. Theirs is a philosophical, instinctive, active, implacable hatred. And the vogue and influence of it is just in proportion to the strength of the German element in American society.

But far beyond the Germans in solid telling influence are the great masses of the native population. They may be described as a stirring, striving, half-educated people, as very much led by newspapers, and generally ready believers in local politicians. All these, too, have an active dislike to the idea of aristocracy, or (as it presents itself to their matter-of-fact minds) of privileged classes. They condemn it on two grounds. It is, they say, a ridiculous institution, for it assumes a superiority which it is impossible can exist; and it is an unjust institution, because it degrades the great bulk of society, by putting them in an inferior position.

Their ideas on the subject appear to be more closely connected with contempt than with bitterness. Still they are distinctly felt, and clearly defined. And they too would be ready, were there ever an opening for anything of the kind, to join in a crusade against privileged classes. They would be glad to lend a hand in the overthrow of any institution which embodies the denial of what they regard as the natural equality of man.

There remains the class which corresponds with what we call the Upper Ten Thousand—that is, the class of the refined and highly educated. Now, these persons do themselves form the aristocracy of American society. It is true that, speaking generally, they are all in business of one kind or another, some even in what we would speak of as retail business; but, in the almost total absence of anything higher, they constitute, and feel that they do so, a kind of social aristocracy. And though most of them would, theoretically, condemn aristocracies, yet they would have neither a contemptuous nor a bitter feeling against what they were condemning. Some of this class, following an inextinguishable feeling of human nature, have begun to look about, and see whether they are not connected by descent with old families of the old country. And this instantly gives rise to exclusiveness of feeling, because they are seeking for an advantage in which the multitude cannot participate. Here, therefore, it would be contradictory and inconsistent were there any strong feeling against aristocracy. Of themselves, such persons would be far more disposed to leave the thing alone, than to join in any endeavours to overturn it. But, practically, it is of little consequence, except to themselves, what this class thinks or feels. The majority disposes of everything in America; and the first step towards gaining its support in the race for power and place, is to suppress in one's self everything that would be distasteful to it.

For himself an American claims the same social position which in Europe is accorded to the possessors of hereditary wealth and hereditary titles; and he grounds his claim on the simple fact that he is an American. It may be as well that we should recognise and that he should enforce this claim; because it is part of a system which has for its aim to elevate every individual in the population of a mighty continent, by awakening in each a sense of political responsibility, by opening every career to everyone, and by obliging all to think for, and to depend on, themselves. This is a grander effort than any other political system has ever before made for humanity; and it is being worked out under the most favourable circumstances, for in America there are employment, food, and position for everybody, and no old and firmly established antagonistic institutions to be fought against and overthrown in opening the course for the new order of things. Slavery alone was arrayed against it; but that having been swept away in a convulsion that was felt not in America only, but all over the civilised world, the stage is now everywhere perfectly clear, and the great experiment can be fairly tried.

CHAPTER XIV.

PRAIRIE FROM CHICAGO TO OMAHA—PLAINS FROM NORTH PLATTE TO THE MOUNTAINS—OMAHA, THE INTERSECTION OF THE PACIFIC RAILWAY AND THE MISSOURI—TEMPORARY BRIDGE OVER THE MISSOURI—INDIFFERENCE TO RISKS AFFECTING LIFE—A PRAIRIE FIRE—THE FOREST ON THE MOUNTAINS ON FIRE—FIRE THE CAUSE OF THE TREELESSNESS OF THE PRAIRIES—FIRST-FOUND ANIMAL LIFE ABOUNDING IN THE VALLEY OF THE PLATTE—'THE HARDEST PLACE, SIR, ON THIS CONTINENT'—ITS PREDECESSOR—HOW IT IS POSSIBLE TO ESTABLISH LYNCH LAW AT SHYENNE—MY FIRST NIGHT IN SHYENNE—A SECOND NIGHT AT SHYENNE—NECESSITY AND ADVANTAGES OF LYNCH LAW—'THE USE OF THE PISTOL'—A MAN SHOT BECAUSE 'HE MIGHT HAVE DONE SOME MISCHIEF'—NEWNESS OF ASPECTS BOTH OF SOCIETY AND OF NATURE.

I LEFT Chicago for the Rocky Mountains at 3 P.M. Twice the day wore out, and twice the night came down on the prairie, and twice the sun rose from the level horizon as it were out of the sea; and the third night was closing in upon us, before the iron horse, that never tires, could bring us to the farther side of the land-ocean, here 1,000 miles wide. And such is the scale of all alike, of plains and valleys, of rivers, forests, lakes and mountains, in the United States.

In this journey we crossed the Mississippi at Fulton, by a covered wooden bridge a mile in length, the Missouri at Omaha, and the north fork of the Platte, at a place called North Platte, by a bridge that appeared to be about half a mile long.

As far as Omaha—that is, for the first 500 miles—

The Prairie to Omaha.

and then again for some distance beyond Omaha, the prairie is generally of a deep black soil, capable of producing most abundant crops of anything. The first 300 miles is all settled. The remainder is taken up and partially settled, of course more closely in the neighbourhood of Omaha, and none of it can now be had in lots contiguous to the railway at less than thirty dollars an acre. This will give some conception of the inexhaustible agricultural wealth of the United States.

As the Platte is approached, you enter on the dry prairie, where there is not sufficient rain to admit of cultivation. There is, however, abundance of the finest grass for sheep and cattle, and this continues for 300 miles more to the foot of the mountains. This dry region is called 'The Plains.'

Of all the astonishing sights in this land of surprises, none takes one more by surprise than the town of Omaha. At home we have been taught to regard Chicago as the extremity of civilisation, and therefore as one of the wonders of the world. But when you have turned your back on Chicago, and been borne away into the western prairie by the locomotive for 500 miles, you find that you have reached a thriving town, of brick buildings and large hotels, containing now 16,000 inhabitants, and which is destined to become—probably in a very few years—a second Chicago. For, being on the Pacific Railway, the grandest of all railways, as well as on that grandest of all arterial lines of water-communication, the Missouri, which is navigable for a thousand miles beyond the town for the same steamer that might have ascended the stream from New

Orleans, it must soon become the depôt for the two greatest lines of American traffic—that between the East and the West, and that between the North and the South, which will cross here. It does not appear possible that anything can arise to prevent its expanding, with a rapidity unexampled even in America, into one of the great commercial centres of this vast and rich continent.

During the summer the Missouri had been crossed by a steam-ferry. But to save a little time in the transit, and the trouble of keeping a passage for the ferry free from ice during the winter, the railway had been carried across the river, as soon as the frost became severe, on two rows of piles, which rose only a few inches above the surface of the ice. This was merely intended for the three or four months during which it would be buttressed and strengthened by the ice. As soon as that should begin to break up, it would be swept away. In going westward, the train I was in was made to traverse it at a snail's pace, for fear of shaking it to pieces, but even with this caution it wavered and groaned alarmingly. On returning some weeks afterwards, when the ice was hourly expected to break up, the train I recrossed it in was the last that used it. Again we traversed it, at a snail's pace, feeling our way as we went; again we heard the creaking, and saw the bending and swaying of the rickety fabric, many fearing that this last journey would be the one too many, and that it would not be swept away by the ice, but shaken to pieces by use. In no other country would so reckless a disregard of risks, imperilling life, be tolerated. But here neither the public, nor the contrivers of these risks, nor the possible or actual sufferers by them, appear to give these matters a thought; or, if they do, they probably regard them from the commercial point of view—that it would be hard to interfere with anyone who was endeavouring to make money, and that the public ought to be left to decide for themselves whether it is, or is not, worth their while to run the risks to which they are invited. The day after I left Cincinnati, the 'Magnolia' steamer blew up, and more than eighty lives were lost. About the same time some terrific railway accidents occurred; but, as far as I could judge, no one seemed to think that on these occasions blame could attach to anyone.

At a distance of about sixty miles from Omaha, on the second night of my journeying through the prairie, I saw it on fire. It was on the right-hand side to one going westward, and did not reach up to the rails within a mile or two. The front of the fire, as we passed along it, was a line of five or six miles. The flames had not an uniform appearance. In slight depressions, where moisture hung longer, and therefore the grass and prairie plants were thick and high, the flames rose about fifteen feet; but where the blazing had subsided, the smouldering remains of plants that had more substance than the rest, appeared like rows of stars. There was smoke visible only where there was much flame, and the lazy masses of smoke were illuminated by the glare of the flames beneath. As in one place there was something burning above the general level, we supposed that it was the dwelling-house of some prairie settler that was being destroyed.

I also, during four days, saw the pine and poplar

forest, on the mountain above the town of Boulder, on fire. I was not so near to this as I had been to the prairie fire; but it did not strike me, judging however from a distance, that its effects were grander. There seemed a great deal more smoke than flame, which streamed off down the wind like large bodies of cloud. I heard, however, that sometimes the appearance of the forest burning on the mountains was very grand. I observed, wherever I penetrated into the Rocky Mountains, that a great part of the wood had been destroyed in this way. The fire generally occurs through the carelessness of persons who are camping out. The waste of valuable timber is thus enormous.

As one passes over the prairie, the conviction becomes irresistible that fire is the sole cause of the absence of trees. The prairie was once covered with trees, because when fire is kept off by cultivation, and the earth loosened by the plough, so as to admit light and air to a greater depth than before, young trees at once appear. Of course the parent trees must, at some time or other, have grown on the spot. All the seeds that were sufficiently near the undisturbed surface to germinate had germinated, and the young plants that issued from them had been destroyed by fire. Those seeds which chance had buried more deeply waited for the aid of man to give proof of their presence in the soil.

Again, both forest and fruit trees, when planted by the hand of man, thrive well in the prairie, if only fire be kept from them. And wherever in the prairie, as on the rocky faces of bluffs, or the banks of streams, fire cannot reach, on account of the absence of sufficient grass and undergrowth to convey it, trees—as pines, oaks, willows, and poplars—abound. The great accumulations of black vegetable mould are to be accounted for in the same way; they are formed out of the burnt and half-burnt vegetable matter left by the annual fires of no one can tell how long a period. In the valley of the Platte, this vegetable mould appears to have been carried away by the stream, which has ever been shifting its channel from side to side, between the bluffs which bound the valley— in so doing floating off the lighter portions of the soil, and leaving sand and gravel only in its deserted beds.

On the dry prairie between Omaha and the mountains I saw, for the first time, some of the *feræ naturæ* of America in abundance. Hitherto I had frequently observed that there was almost a total absence of animal life from the roadside. I could count up the rare occasions on which I had seen either bird or beast. I had twice seen colonies of a social crow resembling our rook. In Georgia I had seen two birds, one about the size of a thrush, and the other rather smaller than a sparrow. In Alabama I had seen some wild deer and wild ducks. In a journey of several thousand miles I had seen no other wild four-footed or feathered creature. I had attributed the deficiency of the latter partly to the severity of American winters, which had taught them migratory habits, and partly to the sparseness of the population in the Southern States; for though it is true that the presence of civilised man is incompatible with the existence of some species, yet there are other species to which man, by his cultivation of the ground, and as it were by the crumbs that fall from his table, becomes the chief purveyor, and whose numbers therefore increase almost in proportion to the degree in which a country becomes settled. But here, on this arid plain, and in midwinter, neither naturalist nor sportsman could have had anything to complain of. Animal life was in abundance. In the course of one day I saw from the windows of the car three herds of antelopes (in one of which I counted thirty-eight), two wolves, prairie-fowl in great numbers, plenty of a species of bird resembling our English lark, several hawks, and innumerable colonies of prairie-dogs. As their villages are frequently at a distance from water, these agile and amusing little animals are supposed to be capable of living without drinking. I saw nothing of the owls and rattlesnakes who have been admitted by the prairie-dogs to a joint tenancy of their subterranean homes. Doubtless, if one were to examine on foot the banks of the river, and the rocky bluffs that bound the valley, my small list might easily be made a large one. The valley was strewed for hundreds of miles with the bones of the buffalo, and marked with the still unobliterated basins which showed the spot in which he had rolled himself in the dry sandy soil on coming up out of the water of the Platte. Experience corrects the common error that animal life in any district will be found in proportion to the vigour of its vegetable life. Nowhere is vegetation more vigorous than in the mighty forests of South America and Western Africa, but they are very far from abounding in animal life. On the contrary, vegetable life is poor and scanty in Southern Africa, and nowhere in the world is there so great a number of species and of individuals of the larger quadrupeds. Something similar is observable in the dry valley of the Platte, the obvious requirement being not abundance of vegetation, but enough of that kind of vegetation the animals require, and either that kind of covert, or such an absence of covert, as shall most conduce to their security.

Frequently, when I had mentioned my intention of going to the Rocky Mountains by way of Omaha and Denver, I had been cautioned against Shyenne city—'Sir, it is the hardest place on this continent;' by which was meant that it contained a choicer collection of hardened villains, and a larger proportion of them to its population, than any other place, and that, in consequence, it was harder there than anywhere else to keep out of a scrape. It is called Shyenne, because nine months before I was there, at which time it had three thousand inhabitants, the Chien or Dog Indians had scalped a white man on what was then the open prairie, but is now the site of the city. Nine months had sufficed for building and peopling the city. City on the Plains may mean a single house. At a place called 'La Park,' where there was but one wooden shanty, I heard a gentleman ask its proprietor 'if anyone was then talking about building a second house in that city?' Shyenne city is built entirely of wood. There is no company that will insure any goods or houses in the place. What so suddenly called it into existence was the opening of the Pacific Railway to this point. Here, then, everyone coming from the Pacific and Ultramontane States takes the rail for the East, and everyone leaving the rail for one of those States takes his place in one of Wells and Fargo's coaches. There are therefore people always arriving from both directions, with plenty of money. It is also the natural rendezvous (as there is nothing behind it for five hundred miles back to Omaha) for all those who are employed beyond it in the construction of the railway through the mountains, to spend their money at, and for many too of the goldwashers and gold-miners from the mountains. All these are the birds of passage of the place; but they it is who attract the two classes of permanent inhabitants, if such a word is suitable to any residents in a town only nine months old. Of these two classes one is respectable, the other not. The respectable class is that of the tradesmen; the one that is not consists of the rowdies, gamblers, and desperadoes, who have always formed the scum and dirt on the top of the foremost wave of advancing civilisation in America, and which that wave has now borne on to this place, and thrown them into it all together.

The same causes, in the winter of 1866–67, made a place called Julesburg, about one hundred and fifty miles back from Shyenne, the point at which for the time extreme rowdyism, but of a lower class and on a smaller scale, was concentrated. Being then the extreme point of the Pacific Railway, the teamsters, freighters, and their hangers-on, and those from the neighbourhood who join such gatherings, were all here collected together. A town of waggon corals and wooden houses was soon formed in this way, containing about one thousand inhabitants—almost all men, and almost all reckless and violent characters. I asked a man who was himself connected with the freighting business, and had been part of last winter at Julesburg, how things had gone on at the place, and how order had been maintained? He said that at first no attempt at all was made to have things right, but that when it began to be known as a hell upon earth—almost every day two or three men being murdered or killed in rows—a few policemen were sent. They did not, however, prove of the slightest use, for they were quite unable to arrest anybody, or to hinder anything. If they had made the attempt, they would have been shot as readily as anyone else. When I was at the spot in February 1868, not a trace of the Julesburg of the previous year remained. Everything, both houses and men, had moved on to Shyenne. A prairie station on the railway alone marked the place where the town had been.

The difference between last year's and this year's headquarters of rowdyism arises out of the better chance Shyenne has, as it is situated at the foot of the mountains, of maintaining a permanent existence, and if so of rapidly becoming a flourishing place of business. This has attracted to it a large number of storekeepers, who of course set up, as soon as they were strong enough to do so, the reign of vigilance committees and lynch law. In such places these are the means universally adopted for enforcing honesty and order.

I reached Shyenne a little after dark. Having been fully warned of the character of the place, I had taken the precaution of enquiring what were the names of the two least rowdy hotels. The moment the train reached the station, I was off, bag in hand, for the first chance of a bedroom. On my asking, at the larger of the two, for a room I might occupy alone, I was told they had no such accommodation. I then went on to the other, where the same answer was given to the same enquiry. I was determined not to take the chances of a night with a Shyenne desperado, so I again sallied forth in search of a lodging—this time, however, not knowing where to turn. At last my from-house-to-house investigation brought me to a wooden structure, on which were painted the words 'The Wyoming House.' It was far from having an inviting look: in fact it had more the appearance of a drinking-booth than of a place where one could find a bedroom. But as it was the only house I had seen (hotels are here all called houses), I thought the best thing I could do would be to go to some tradesman, and take my chance of his telling me whether it was, or was not, a safe place. A chemist, it appeared to me, would be as little likely as any to be dependent on the rowdies; so I entered the first shop of that kind I could see, to make the enquiry. If I had looked in through the window, I should certainly not have opened the door; for the first object that met my eyes was a rough, lying on the ground in front of the stove. His hair and beard appeared not to have been combed for months, and by his side was lying a gigantic mastiff. But, as it was too late to recede, I turned to the chemist—a youth apparently of less than twenty years of age, who was seated on the counter—and put my enquiry to him. 'Wall, stranger,' he said, taking his cigar from his mouth, and speaking very deliberately, 'if it is a night when they have got no dance—for they give a dance twice a-week to the ladies and gentlemen of the city—I calculate you may get through; but if it is a dancing night, I calculate you will do better outside.' On looking in, and finding that it was not a dancing night, I applied for and was shown to a bedroom. On entering, however, I observed that the lock of the door had been lately forced, for it was hanging loose by a single nail. In a house that admitted of such proceedings, I declined to take a room the door of which could not be locked. After making some difficulties, the attendant showed me to another room. On entering it I turned the key, and as it appeared to act properly, I told him it would do, and took possession. But on attempting to get the bolt of the lock into the doorpost, I found that things were not so square as that it could be done in a moment, some violence having been used against this door also. While I was 'fixing' this matter, which I eventually succeeded in doing, I fancied I heard men and women gambling in the next room a great deal too distinctly; and on looking in that quarter I saw a considerable hole in the wall, which admitted of anyone observing from the next room what I was about. This I stopped up with a Chicago newspaper I happened to have with me. My last thought was to ascertain whether the window which opened at the head of my bed had any fastening, and whether one could escape through it in case of a fire—a matter that must always be attended to in these wooden towns. I found that it opened into a back courtyard; that it had no fastening of any kind; and that one might open it from the outside with a single finger. I did not like this, nor anything that I had seen in the house; but as Judge Lynch had hung up two men in the main street of the town only a few nights before, I thought that all the good effect had probably not yet evaporated, and so was soon asleep. The next morning, when I offered payment, the landlord demurred accepting it immediately, and beckoning to one of his men, sent him off to see if all was right. On the man's returning, and giving him a nod, he took my money. I asked what was the meaning of this. 'Oh,' he replied, 'it is not the custom to settle accounts here till you are sure that none of your blankets have been made away with in the night through the window.' Blankets here are hard to get, and of some value for camping out.

I passed part of another night at Shyenne, on my return from the mountains. The coach reached the chief hotel of the place at three o'clock in the morning. I had expected at that hour to find things tolerably quiet; but on entering, I had to pass, first some people in a state of riotous drunkenness at the bar; then about twenty men sitting or sleeping round the stove; and, lastly, a parcel of people playing and rowing at two billiard-tables. Beyond all these was the clerk's counter. On entering my name, and asking whether I could have a room to myself, I was assured that I could.

'Give me a receipt, then,' I said, 'for my bag and rug, and let me be shown to my room.'

'Is there any other passenger on board the coach?' the clerk enquired.

I told him there was one. He asked me to wait till he had come in, and then the boy—the new name for manservant—would only have to make one journey in showing us to our rooms. I assented. At last the other passenger came in, and the clerk gave his instructions to the boy. In doing this I observed that he only gave him one key, from which I instantly inferred that I was done, and was only to have, after all, a part of a room; but I decided to submit, for there were only three hours to be passed in bed, and my fellow-passenger was a highly respectable storekeeper of Denver; and if I had gone out of the hotel, at that hour of the morning, with my luggage in my hand, all the rowdies about the billiard-tables, the stove, and the bar, would have known that I was going in search of a lodging, and some might perhaps have followed me out. But on the boy's opening the door, and setting down the lamp, while he said, 'Gentlemen, here is your apartment,' I was no longer equal to the occasion; for now I saw— the possibility of which had never before crossed my mind—that I was expected to occupy the same bed with another man; and I gave vent to my indignation by observing, 'that it was really too bad to be billeted off to half a bed, when I had been promised a room to myself.' 'As to the room to yourself,' replied the boy, 'I know nothing about that, and the thing is passed; but it is very unreasonable in you to complain about having half a bed, when it is a bed that is intended to hold three people.'

I asked my fellow-passenger not to regard it as anything personal that I was unable to occupy the same bed as himself, telling him that I would lie down in my clothes. Our first care, however, was to arrange what we should do in case of fire, for part of the house we were in had been in flames only a few nights before. In such a place sleep was impossible. Our room was exactly over the kitchen, and the floor having been made originally of unseasoned wood, the heat had shrunk it, so that there were gaps everywhere. Through these came up all night from the kitchen the effluvium of beefsteaks and onions, which were being cooked incessantly for the gamblers, who would themselves have kept anyone awake with the noise they made, the chief part of it consisting of the most ingenious and horrible oaths one ever heard, or will ever hear, as swearing is everywhere else becoming obsolete. On coming down, a little after six, for the seven-o'clock train, I found a few persons still drunk about the bar; and all the rest of those I had seen three hours before were now asleep on the floor, on chairs, or on the billiard-tables. These are persons who do not care for beds, or who would rather spend the price of them in drinking and gambling.

I mentioned that in my first night at Shyenne, I calculated on the effect two recent lynch-law executions would have in keeping things quiet for a season. About that time I heard of five other executions of the same kind in that neighbourhood. There are people who denounce this method of maintaining order, but they do so without understanding the circumstances. At all events, a man has been known to exclaim loudly against it in New England, and before he had been in the West a month, to join a vigilance committee. The fact is that the ordinary method of administering law is quite impracticable in a place where you can get no policemen, no constables, no lawyers, no juries, no jails, no judges; and where, if it were possible to get the apparatus of justice, it would be next to impossible to work it. Some one or other would be bribed, or some flaw would be established in the evidence, and there would be time and opportunity enough, in one way or another, for the escape of the prisoner. Instead of this, here is a system which has no officers or jails, which costs nothing, and is very terrifying to evildoers by the rapidity and certainty with which it acts, and the mystery with which it is involved. It would be a very unnecessary and evil system in a settled community, but where none of the ordinary appliances of law are possible, and where at the same time all the scum of the great world behind is concentrated, it is a necessity, and a highly beneficial one. It does really what Napoleon III. claims to have done for France : it saves society, which without it would cease to exist, for it would be overwhelmed by these reckless and desperate characters. Everyone in America knows how completely in California it got rid of all the disorderly and dangerous elements which were collected there in such force, that it would have been quite hopeless to have attempted to deal with them in any other way. Just so, again, it was at Denver, a town on this side the mountains, of eight thousand inhabitants, now as orderly and well-disposed as any other eight thousand persons anywhere to be found. Four or five years ago Denver was what Shyenne is now. But lynch law has purified it, and in a way in which ordinary law has never purified any community in the world. All the rogues and violent fellows have been hanged, and all the suspected have been made to clear out. There are now no other such eight thousand souls in any part of the Old States. A man who knows both would rather leave his baggage out all night in the street at Denver than in any city of New England. This is the state into which a community has been brought when lynch law hands it over to ordinary law.

But lynch law is only half the system. It is always accompanied by something else, which I have heard described as 'the use of the pistol.' This has, from the first, been maintained in America long after Judge Lynch has retired from the scene. It is still not unknown in Washington and New York. But in the ever-advancing frontier of civilisation, it has all along been in active operation. Every man in the West goes always armed. And it is one of the most imperative of the laws of Western society, that, if a man insults you in any way, you are bound then and there to shoot him dead. Society requires you to do it, and if you do not, you will be shot yourself; for the man who has insulted you, supposing that you can only be waiting for an opportunity, will think it better to be beforehand with you. This is their substitute for the old European law of duelling, which required that if a man insulted you, you should give him a chance of shooting you also. The Western plan is that you should shoot him. It is enforced too by the same kind of social considerations, and attended by the same immunities, and its object is the same—to oblige men, at the peril of their lives, to behave themselves discreetly and politely.

The following incident was told me by a thoroughly credible eyewitness: it will show how cheaply society holds, in this part of the world, the lives of its troublesome members. A dozen or more men were seated, drinking and smoking and yarning, in front of the bar of a Shyenne hotel. One of the troublesome class, in whom whisky was just then overcoming discretion, took out his revolver, and, flourishing it about, announced that everyone present had to acknowledge that he was the finest fellow in the world. Just as he said this two gentlemen came in, and, not knowing what was passing, walked up to the bar, close to where the swaggerer was seated. This took off his attention from the rest of the company, for he now turned to the newcomers, and pointing his pistol at the one nearest to him, told him to make the acknowledgment. The gentleman, finding himself taken at a disadvantage, and thinking it most likely that, if he put his hand behind him for his pistol, he should, while doing so, be shot by the tipsy desperado, began to do as he was required. 'Well,' he said, 'you are a monstrous fine fellow; I had no idea there were such fine fellows out here.' While he was saying this, his companion took his own pistol from its sling behind him, put it to the swaggerer's head, and blew out his brains. As the man fell to the ground, and he deliberately replaced his pistol, he said, by way not so much of explanation as of comment, 'That chap might have done some mischief.' Not another remark was made or word spoken on the occasion. Those who were in favour of order said nothing, as they approved of what had been done; while those who belonged to the troublesome class were also silent, because they thought it wiser not to show their colours. When it suited the manager's convenience, he sent one of the boys of the hotel to dig a hole in the prairie for the corpse; and with that the matter ended.

Having breakfasted at six, I was out at the first dawn, and again, as I frequently did afterwards, saw the sun rise on the prairie. Till he was above the horizon, and it was full day, it was impossible to distinguish the prairie from the sea. The same effect is also at times during the day observable. In the morning I even saw something like rippling waves on the surface, resulting, I suppose, from the way in which the level rays struck upon the little inequalities of the foot or two of haze that rested on the ground. At a distance of forty or fifty miles the snowy range was already tinted with light, while the lower intervening ranges were still black masses. The aspects of human society, as well as of outward nature, are here so unlike anything with which the English traveller is familiar at home, that he is ever feeling conscious that new pictures are being added to the furniture of his mind.

CHAPTER XV.

THE ARMAMENT AND EXPERIENCE OF A GERMAN HERDMASTER—A STAGE-COACH ON THE PLAINS—THE PARTY IN THE COACH—THE ONLY COLONEL I MET IN THE UNITED STATES—THE COLONEL'S WIFE—A COLORADO HERDMASTER—A PHILADELPHIAN GRADUATE—TWO JOCOSE DENVER STORE-KEEPERS—ADVANTAGE OF HAVING ONE'S RIFLE IN THE COACH—A CALIFORNIAN'S ACCOUNT OF A SKIRMISH WITH INDIANS—MANNERS AND LIFE AT A HOUSE ON THE PLAINS—A LADY OF THE PLAINS—AMERICAN SOCIETY JUDGES MEN FAIRLY—BETWEEN SHYENNE AND DENVER.

WHILE I was waiting for the Denver coach, and watching the changing scene, a German, with whom I had had some conversation in the railway car for the two previous days, arrived at the coach-office. We were both to start at the same time by stage—he for 1,200 miles over the mountains; I to coast along the mountains to Denver, the point at which I proposed entering them. On meeting him he held out his hand, saying, 'Well, I see we have both got safe through the night. But,' he added, 'I was prepared for them if anyone had meddled with me, I had sixteen bullets ready.' As he said this, he drew aside his coat to show me his eight-shooting revolver hanging at his back; and then putting his hands into his breeches pockets, took from each a small four-shooter. This gentleman told me that he was doing very well as a stock-keeper in Oregon and Idaho; that he had had Durham cattle driven and carried by rail from

New York to these Pacific States, more than 3,000 miles, in which journey, of course, they had crossed the prairies and the Rocky Mountains. He knew all the Pacific coast well, having been in the States of California, Washington, or Oregon; in British Columbia, and in Sitka. Of British Columbia he thought nothing ever could be made, as there was no agricultural land in the colony. At Cariboo everything, even to flour, cost a dollar per pound. The Indians about Sitka were the largest men he had ever seen; few were less than six feet in height or 200 pounds in weight. I never met with one of this description of settlers who belonged to any branch of the Latin race; they are all Anglo-Saxons, Scandinavians, or Germans.

The coach started at seven o'clock, with six fine horses. There was no postilion for the leaders, as was customary in our coaching days. The driver divided the reins between both hands, and off we started at a gallop. Perhaps some of the Shyennese, who witnessed our dashing departure, would not have been sorry to have left the place with us. The coach was full. It was constructed (but without the befitting capacity) to carry nine persons inside and three outside. Experience only can enable one to comprehend how much packing and squeezing and contriving are requisite for arranging nine persons in a space barely sufficient for six. You must imagine a coach a size larger than our old stages; and when three persons have been jammed into the front, and as many into the back seat, a bench is let down from the side which reaches from door to door—and on this three more persons, to speak ironically, are accommodated.

Though it was mid-winter, I should have liked my neighbours all the better had they been a little further off. What then must be the effects of such proximity on an American summer-day, with the thermometer on the roof of the coach at 120°, and a cloud of prairie dust pouring in at the window? If one of these Western coaches—destined for its whole existence to work on the plains and mountains, and never to pass over a furlong of made road, could have been exhibited in London and Paris in '62 and '67, people on this side would have been astonished at the strength of their springs, and of the whole of their construction.

We were full inside, and two of the outside places were occupied. The party was composed of eight gentlemen and three ladies. First came a good-humoured jovial colonel, the only colonel I met in the United States, where I must have made the acquaintance of not far short of fifty generals. He had long been on the Indian frontier, and had conducted many an expedition against them. His professional warfare being now over, he had taken to gold-mining and trading in the mountains. As he lived somewhere up on the Laramie plains, he laid his account with having a few more brushes with his old dusky friends before the time came, not now far distant, when their name would only stand for what once had been. He was still in the prime of life, as everybody is in the West. He had one child—nobody has more in the United States. There was nothing characteristic in these particulars; nor, perhaps, was there in his practice of carrying with him in his journeys a wickered magnum, and two kegs of whisky. Their contents were of different degrees of proof, and of different qualities, adapted to the varying circumstances and different hours of the day. Strength was the special merit of the magnum, which was intended for after-dinner use. It was regarded as a liqueur, or stomachic. The qualities of one keg made it suitable for the early part of the day; the qualities of the other fitted it for the evening. But it did not appear that the Colonel carried about the magnum and two kegs for his own especial benefit; for whenever we stopped for a meal, and sometimes only when horses were changed, if the interval seemed a long one, the keg with the black hoops, or the keg with the green hoops, or the magnum was taken from the boot, and everybody near was invited to 'take a drink.' Even the man who was changing the horses was not omitted. Could it be that the Colonel was one of the proprietors of the coach, and therefore desirous of making things as pleasant as possible to the passengers? This could not be the case, for the names of Wells and Fargo, the great American coaching firm, were on the panels. The true explanation, I believe, was that on the surface—that the Colonel had a heart as large as his head was strong, and that heaven itself would be no heaven to him if he could not share it with his friends—his friends being all those with whom at the moment he happened to be in contact. There was another point, besides that of being content with the rank of Colonel, in which he was unlike his countrymen, and that was his English aversion to the inside of a coach.

The Colonel's wife acted as cicerone of the country to the inside passengers. She knew the names of all the conspicuous mountains, and how far off they were; what accidents had ever happened on the route, and where there had been Indian fights, down to the one of last summer.

Next in prominence came a Colorado herdmaster, and his sister, whom he was taking from her home in Pennsylvania to keep house for him on the plains, at a place called the Garden of the Gods. Everyone contributed what he could to make the day pass agreeably, and this gentleman's contributions consisted in scraps of poetry and little highflown speeches suggested by the sights and occurrences of the moment.

There was also a lady who had made seventeen voyages across the Atlantic and Pacific (I suppose with her husband), and was now returning from a visit to her relations in the State of New York. Her husband was the owner of a mine in the mountains. Whenever called upon she was ready with a song.

The seat next to her was occupied by a well-informed and gentlemanly man. He was a Philadelphian, and had graduated at some American university. I collected that he was going to the mountains to look after some mines in which he was interested.

Two Denver storekeepers (but as town is here construed into city, so is storekeeper into merchant) completed our party. Their forte was that style of humour which is known as American. For instance, apropos to a conversation on the long-sightedness some people are said to acquire on the plains, Mr. A. asks Mr. B., 'Whether he can see that fly on the top of that chimney?' Mr. B. replies, 'I am not quite sure I can see it, but I can hear it scratching its head.' Mr. A. having been silent for some time is supposed to have been asleep: Mr. B. therefore requests him 'to repeat the remark he had just been making.' To this sally he replies, 'If there is anything I have said which I shall hereafter have reason to regret, I am glad of it.'

One of these two storekeepers had a literary turn, and was in the habit of giving lectures in Denver and the mining towns in the mountains, where I saw several of his posters on the walls. He informed me that he had then in the press a humorous poem entitled 'Life in Colorado.'

The other had strong sporting proclivities, and never went a journey by coach or rail without his sixteen-shooter rifle in his hand, for the chance of an antelope, or wolf, or whatever might cross his path. The year before last he had found, on this very road and coach, his practice of never moving unaccompanied by his rifle of use. A party of about a hundred Indians came down from the hills yelling, and firing on the coach. The gentlemen who were in it —they were all armed—got out to meet them, as they could do little when huddled together inside, and the horses and driver would soon have been shot. After the second volley, the driver finding that the Indians were not scared, got scared himself, and insisted on their all getting into the coach again, and his being allowed to drive off. They got in, leaving two of their number dead. The Indians followed for some little distance, and killed one more. The gentleman who told us this incident of travelling in summer on the plains—in winter the Indians are never troublesome—received in the skirmish a wound from an Indian bullet, in the back of his left hand. The ball passed through, shattering the bone. The hole remains as a memento of the day.

Such are the kind of persons one meets in a coach on the plains; and such is the way in which they while away the time.

On my return from the Rocky Mountains we found a Californian waiting for the train at North Platte. He had just come over the Sierra Nevada and Rocky Mountain ranges in a sleigh, in mid-winter. For the greater part of the way he had been alone. One of his feet was frostbitten. He was a little man, but appeared capable of daring anything, and of going through a great deal. His eye was quick, and very unlike that of men bred in towns or quiet farms. At this very point, many years ago, he had tried to carry his waggons across the Platte when the waters were out, and the river ten miles wide; but, having failed in the attempt, he had gone up the stream till he headed the freshet. His rifle was never out of his hand. I asked him, seeing that the barrel was somewhat short, at what distance it would kill an antelope. 'It was not made,' he said, 'for antelope hunting, but it would kill one at eight hundred yards. It was the rifle used against the Indians. It was a sixteen-shooter.' I asked him if it had ever been used in that way. 'Yes,' he said, 'a few years ago the Indians were very troublesome, and thirty of us went out after them with these sixteen-shooters. They came on to meet us. There were four hundred of them, all mounted. At the first volley we fired, many of their saddles were emptied; still they persevered in attacking us, for a day and a night; but as they always had to retire to reload, and we had not, we had a great advantage over them. At last, when we had killed eighty of them, and they had killed nine of us, we got towards morning upon the top of a hill, where there was a kind of natural breastwork of rock, and they could not approach us without being exposed to our fire: they then gave up the game, and drew off. These sixteen-shooters cost in California forty dollars; but mine has so long been my companion day and night, and has so often saved my life, that I would not take any money for it.' As he said this he turned it round, to see if there was any speck of dirt or rust upon it, handling it gently as if he loved it.

Perfect ease and equality, without any obtrusiveness or vulgar assumption, appeared to me to be the true characteristics of the manners of the plains. I spent a day and night at a solitary house where the proprietor combined the two employments of cattle-breeding and inn-keeping. I happened to be at the time the only guest. The accommodation was not bad. It consisted of a large room, used for smoking and for the bar; of a better furnished room for meals; and of a drawing-room, properly belonging to the mistress of the house, but into which favoured guests were invited. I here found several files of local and American papers, and among them the 'London Illustrated News.' The herdsmen of the proprietor took their meals with the guests. Before sitting down they always washed their hands and faces, and combed their hair. There was nothing at all disagreeable in their conversation or manners. They spoke good English, as all Americans do, and were unconstrained, as all Americans are. I had noticed on the previous evening that they had remarkably good appetites, and at breakfast, the next morning, I 'made a note' of what it took to satisfy the broadest-shouldered and hungriest-looking of the party. First, he called for beefsteak: the lad in waiting brought him about a pound, with a little dish of fried potatoes. This he soon disposed of. He then called for sausages. His next plate was ham and eggs. This was followed by a dish of slap-jacks, a kind of pancake eaten with butter and syrup. He finished with a dish of dried apples stewed. This was at half-past six in the morning. At the same hour in the evening, he would have much the same kind of supper, and at noon much the same kind of dinner. But these men live out of doors, and chiefly in the saddle, gallopping over a plain four thousand feet above the level of the sea, with a very bracing and invigorating climate. The lady of the house had been well brought up in New England, and her manners were pleasing. She had no help, and did all the cooking herself. They had an only child, then just five years old, but whom—for children are very forward here—one might have taken for seven. His chief amusement, while I was here, was catching the pigs and dogs with an Indian lasso made of buckskin.

At La Porte, a city of three or four houses, a lady of prepossessing appearance got into the coach. The wife of the Colonel I have mentioned shook hands with her; and we had some pleasant conversation about the society of the plains and mountains. She was very decided in her preference for it over that of cities. She thought that life in old settled districts was mere existence and not life. She talked of the delights of camping out, and of long excursions of fifty or eighty miles on horseback. At La Park the Colonel handed her out of the coach. Supper was soon announced, and we took our places at the table, when the lady who had been conversing so pleasantly in the coach appeared behind my chair and asked me, in an easy and well-mannered way, what I would take. I saw now that she was the landlady of the little roadside inn at which we had stopped, and that she did the waiting herself. She supplied everybody with what they required, changed the plates, filled the glasses and cups, and brought whatever was wanted, all the time talking much as the mistress of a house would talk to her guests.

But though perfect equality is the first principle of Western life, yet the superiority of refinement and mental cultivation is fully recognised, and everybody readily defers to them. This, however, is only done on the condition that there is no assumption on the part of the person himself. To pretend to a superiority to others,—what we call, to give yourself airs, —is in American society, whether it be in the East or the West, an unpardonable offence; it is the sin against equality, which is never forgiven in this world, and which every true American trusts will not be forgotten in the next. Only leave it to them to discover your merits, and you will have no reason to complain of want of appreciation. They are a people who measure others much more fairly than we do.

The track from Shyenne to Denver lies along the foot of the mountains, and is about one hundred and ten miles in length. On your left is the boundless plain; on your right are the mountains, rising suddenly like a wall out of the plain. The first range is either scantily clothed with pine forests, or shows only the naked dark-coloured rock. Behind and above this is the snowy dividing ridge, which, however, in summer and autumn, has snow only on its highest peaks. In some places the lower range is of a bright red, as if the mountain were faced with red brick. From the picturesque point of view, the defect of the mountains is that they keep too much to the straight line. This is not observed when you get among them, but it is very perceptible from the plain, into which no outlying hills, or spurs, obtrude on this route. St. Vrain and Burlington are the most important places you pass. Each of them appears to have a population of three or four hundred souls: they are only separated from each other by a stream. But it is sufficient to render the land on its banks capable of cultivation; and this, in a region where there is so little land that can be made to produce anything except prairie grass, is sufficient to account for the existence of the two places. The other cities along the route are only wooden public-houses, where the coach changes horses, and at some of which it is arranged that the passengers shall have something to eat. It is to the credit of the landlords of these cities on the plains, that what they provide for their guests is good of its kind, which cannot be said of any one of the purveyors for the five hundred miles of railway between Shyenne and Omaha. At St. Vrain the outer range sinks so low that you are able to look into the valleys of the snowy dividing ridge. Fortunately, in the midst of this exposed part stands Long's Peak, the highest point of the chain. As seen from the plain, it appears to be a three-peaked mountain, and each of its three peaks has the appearance of being accessible. On enquiry at St. Vrain, I was told that there was a good path for pedestrians, and even for mules, to the foot of the mountain, and that it had been frequently scaled. The mountain to the south of Long's Peak appears to have a precipitous face of some thousands of feet on its side towards the Peak; and there is distinctly visible, lying between the two, a green park. A park in the language of the mountains is a large expanse of level grass-clad land up among the hills. There are many of them in this range. They are always well watered, and abundantly stocked with game. This park and this peak are, by the path I have just mentioned, forty-five miles distant from St. Vrain. The depression of the outer hills which admits them to view continues for about twelve miles.

CHAPTER XVI.

THE CITY OF DENVER—THE LADIES GIVE A BALL—MANNERS OF DENVER—' QUITE OUR FINEST GENTLEMAN '—THE PLAINS WILL BE TO AMERICA AN IMPROVED AUSTRALIA—THE ADVANTAGES THEY OFFER FOR FLOCKS AND HERDS—WILL SOON BE CLEAR OF INDIANS —MARKETS NOW OPENED TO THEM—SIZE OF THE RUNS—WEALTH OF THE REGION.

I EXPRESSED some of the surprise I felt at finding a place like Omaha, 500 miles beyond Chicago. But here, at Denver, is a busy, thriving town, 600 miles beyond Omaha. It has almost completed its transition from wood to brick. The stores and offices are now nearly all of the latter material. So is the new church of the Methodists, which besides has stained glass windows. In the church of the Episcopalians, the primitive wood still maintains its ground in the greater part of the building. The finest structure in the place is a seminary for young ladies, which has just been erected by Bishop Randall. The Methodists have a large seminary of the same kind, but externally it is very inferior to the Bishop's. The United States Government has also a Mint here, for the gold and silver extracted from the mountains. I inspected in the town three common schools; two for whites, one for boys, one for girls, and one for coloured people of any age; for I saw several adults in the room, seated on the same benches as the children. Denver, as far as I could judge, is well provided with everything. On enquiry, I found that a haunch of antelope venison sold for seventy-five cents —about half-a-crown of our money. The mountains are close upon the town, and present a view that is very grand. Golden City, which is in a gap of the first range, is distant from Denver only ten miles.

In so new and remote a place one would not expect to find everything, in the way of manners and customs, moving on precisely in the grooves of the Old World. For instance, I was just too late for a ball which the ladies of Denver, availing themselves of the fact that it was leap-year, had given to the gentlemen. It had been, I understood, a lively affair and a great success. The ladies selected their own partners (one, however, has heard of other instances of this), and took the gentlemen in to supper. As in all new settlements the fair sex must always be in a minority, some of the gentlemen must on this occasion have learnt, ' with pangs unfelt before, unpitied and alone,' what it is to be a ball-room wall-flower.

I arrived at Denver at 4 A.M. A few hours afterwards, as I was passing the door of the drawing-room of the hotel, a gentleman I had never seen before came out to meet me, and, conducting a lady up to me, requested me to take her down to breakfast. I afterwards became acquainted with this gentleman, and found that he was an ex-judge, who on the expiration of his term of office had resumed his practice at the bar.

When breakfast was over, the manager of the hotel invited me to accompany him up stairs to the ladies' drawing-room, that he might introduce me to the mistress of the house and some other ladies whom I should find sitting with her.

These ceremonies having been got through, I took a letter of introduction to the editor of the local news department of one of the Denver dailies. With the overflowing good-nature of his countrymen, he immediately placed himself at my service, showing me over the town, and introducing me to its notabilities. Hospitality here is plainly the order of the day; for wherever we went, invitations of one kind or another were immediately given. In a place like Denver, where even the tradition of social inequalities has been lost, and the idea and practice of equality that rule society have, in their passage across the continent, been distilled and redistilled a hundred times, you find the article in its purest possible form; men are valued only according to their personal qualities, such as their cleverness, their *bonhomie*, and their ability to make money. I give this as a preface to my Denver cicerone's description of one of the persons to whom he was about to introduce me. 'You must now,' he said, 'let me take you to Mr. A. He is quite our finest gentleman.' I had not had many minutes' conversation with 'quite the finest gentleman in Denver,' before I had reason for coinciding with the estimate of his fellow-townsmen; for among other offers of assistance and hospitality, he had given me an invitation to be his companion and guest in a long tour he was about to make in the mountains, but which, he explained, would on his part combine business with exploration and pleasure. Of course it is inconceivable that there could be any gentleman in Denver who was not in some kind of business, and 'quite the finest gentleman' of the place happened to be a grocer. But what of that? So is the senator for the State of New York; and Denver grocers can and do possess many of the personal qualities of gentlemen, though it may be supposed they are quite unconscious of the sense in which Charles II. used the word, when he replied to his foster-mother's request that he would make his foster-brother a gentleman, 'that he could make him a lord, but that God Almighty could not make him a gentleman.' Meaning that the being, or the not being a gentleman, was a matter of birth, and of birth only.

One who has seen anything of these enormous plains, cannot but speculate on their future. I came to the conclusion that in a few years they will be the Australia of North America. And as their soil and climate are very much better, they will support, at a far cheaper rate, a much greater number of millions of sheep and cattle. In the Valley of the Platte, for 500 miles, and down as far as Denver, though the climate is too dry for agricultural purposes, still the herbage is so abundant and nutritious that even in winter, when it is all dried up into the form of natural hay, herds of cattle are turned out to fatten upon it, which they do readily, without any shelter or any help from artificial food.

As you go further south, you get some regions still better adapted to grazing and sheep-farming, and some not so good, till you come to Texas, in which enormous numbers of horned cattle are raised already. That Nature does of herself supply everything that is needed, is proved by this having been the home of the buffalo, which has ever been covering these plains with numbers beyond belief. It becomes, then, a kind of rule of three sum: if Nature, unaided, supported without fail so many millions of large herbivorous animals, how many more will she support when aided by the care and forethought of man? Convert in your mind these countless herds of buffalo into sheep and oxen, and then multiply the result twenty fold, for that amount may easily be reached, when American flock-masters and herd-masters shall have taken possession of the plains, and parcelled them out into manageable ranches, turning the whole of the surface to account.

There are a great many streams, small and great, which carry the drainage of the mountains across these plains to the Mississippi; and in places where there are no streams, water may be obtained by sinking wells. Wherever I went I made enquiries on this subject, and looked myself into the wells; and I found that water was reached in the Valley of the Platte, and on the plains from Shyenne to Denver, at a depth of about thirty feet. Water for the stock might be pumped from such wells by horse-engines or wind-mills.

In the northern part of the plains, in most winters there is a short spell of very severe cold, and it is possible that the ground may for several days continuously be covered with snow. Both of these difficulties may be met. The first by enclosures that will keep the cold wind from the stock, the walls being of wood, or of wood and adobe, or of any material that is the cheapest on the spot; and the second, by laying up a store of prairie hay. This is already done by

Wells, Fargo, and Company, on these very plains, for the purpose of supplying provender for the horses of their numerous coaches. They have it cut by the hay-cutting machine that is getting into use in this country. The prairie hay looks hard and coarse, but in reality is of very good quality, and has the great advantage that it will keep for many years; so that what is cut this summer, if on account of the openness of the season it be not needed in the ensuing winter, will stand over for another year; in fact, it will remain good till it is wanted.

Heretofore there have been two hindrances to stock-keeping on the plains—the Indians, and the want of a market. Both of these are now in course of removal. In a year or two the Indians to the north of Shyenne and Denver will have ceased to give any more trouble. To the south of Denver they have already been cleared off to a considerable distance. With them, indeed, everywhere throughout the plains, as it has been with them all the way up from the Atlantic coast, their disappearance will only be a question of time. And the time is now at hand, for the white man has begun to settle on the plains, and the two races cannot exist together in the same region. And as to the want of a market, that deficiency is being removed by the peopling of the Valley of the Mississippi, and by the advance into the plains of the two branches of the Pacific railway. These lines will carry mutton and beef to the Eastern States, at a lower figure than that at which they can grow the meat themselves. They will also carry away the tallow, hides, bones, and wool. In the Eastern and Northern States stock has to be kept all the winter on corn and artificial food, while here on the plains its keep costs nothing, for it can be fattened very well for market on the natural grasses. What, therefore, the wheat-growing States of the North-west have done for those who were formerly the wheat-growers of the East, these States on the plains will do for those who are now the meat-growers of the East.

There will be this great difference between farming and stock-keeping—that is, between the proprietors of arable land in the old States, and the flock and herd masters of the plains—that it is impossible to farm on a large scale; it has, with exceptions hardly worth noticing, been so throughout the Union, a farmer seldom getting beyond what he can manage with his own hands and the assistance of his family; but here just the reverse will be the only thing possible. It will be here as it has been in Australia: a man cannot keep a few head of cattle, or a few hundred sheep. To make it pay, indeed, to keep his animals alive, he must have a large tract of land, and do the thing on a large scale. We hear of paddocks in Australia thirty miles square. I suppose on the plains a third of this size will be a sufficiently large run, and a much more profitable one.

As the tide of population has now reached the plains on their eastern side, and in some degree on the western and northern sides also, and as many have already got a footing upon them, I suppose, judging from the rapidity with which everything that pays is carried out in America, that in a few years this enormous district, twice as large as France, will be occupied, and by a class of men such as the Union does not now possess. They will be very numerous and very wealthy—quite the wealthiest class in the Union; and even if there is to be no resurrection for the South, which it is impossible to believe, they will compensate, speaking from the wealth-of-nations point of view, for its loss. I have seen some of the pioneers of the class, and, prophesying of those who are to follow, from the way in which the influences of the Plain have shaped those who have already come, I would say that they will be characterised by hardihood, generosity, and manliness. They will occupy with their flocks and herds a great part of Texas on the south, and of Nebraska on the north, with the whole of Arizona, Colorado, and New Mexico. This region will, like Australia and the districts of the La Plata, export enormous quantities of wool, tallow, and hides. But they will have a mighty advantage over those two great stock-keeping regions, that they will not be themselves the only consumers of their beef and mutton, but will have customers for as much as they can produce, in the inhabitants of a rich and populous continent, of which they will be the centre. In this way is some new source of wealth, and always on the grandest scale, ever being developed in the United States.

CHAPTER XVII.

THE ROCKY MOUNTAINS—GOLDEN CITY—GOLDEN GATES—MINING TOWNS—NEIGHBOURING MOUNTAINS STRIPPED OF EVERY TREE—WHAT GROWS ON THE MOUNTAINS—AMERICAN HORSES—ROADS AND BRIDGES THEY HAVE TO PASS—HOW, SIX-IN-HAND, WE WENT DOWN A HILL SIDE IN THE MOUNTAINS—A NICE DISTINCTION AS TO ACCIDENTS ON THIS HILL—CLIMATE—WIND-STORMS—BIRDS—DOGS.

I ENTERED the Rocky Mountains at a place called Golden City. It lies in a gap of the first range. Till lately it was the capital of Colorado, which honour has now been transferred to Denver. It is chiefly of brick—the proof, in this part of the world, of mature age in a town. I counted three churches in the place; the best of the three belongs, as I was told, to the Episcopalians. The population appeared to be about three thousand. A thick seam of good coal is exposed just at the foot of the hill close to the town. I had heard that I should find a place of this name, but I was not at all prepared for the brick, and the churches, and the population. There is a good hotel here, kept by an Englishman; but, judging from those I fell in with, the well-to-do people of the place were mostly New Englanders.

Just beyond Golden City the road passes through a grand defile, between precipitous mountains of dark rock; this, as it leads to the auriferous regions up in the mountains, is called the Golden Gates.

R

Up in the mountains I visited the three mining towns of Black Hawk, Central City, and Nevada. The district to which these towns belong had a population of fifteen thousand persons engaged in mining, but I found several of the mills not at work, and was told that the population had lately fallen off considerably. In the neighbourhood of these towns all the timber has been cut down for building and mining; and as everything that would burn has also been cleared off for fuel, every accessible mountain has been made as bare as a ploughed field. Their sides are covered with what appear to be gigantic mole-hills, but which in reality are the heaps of earth the miners have thrown up in prospecting— that is, examining the ground for auriferous veins, which is done by digging holes ten or twelve feet deep. It will be a long time before the forest appears again, for at this altitude it was composed entirely of pine, and I could nowhere, on exposed places, find any young trees: I could find plenty of little seedlings, but they all were dead or dying, I supposed from their inability to bear without protection the wind, or the cold, or the drought. I saw some magnificent trees of, I believe, a kind of spruce, and a kind of silver fir, on the hills, from which it would have been difficult to have removed them if cut down. They were of great height, and very straight, though of course nothing like what we hear of as growing on the western slopes, and down to the Pacific coast. On the lower hills I saw abundance of a white-barked poplar, of a kind of alder, of birch, and of willow. Gooseberry bushes in places covered the ground. I heard that currants, raspberries, blueberries, and some other small edible fruit were to be found in equal plenty. I saw large spaces on the hill sides, where the undergrowth was chiefly Berberis aquifolium. In the valleys of the outer ranges there was a great deal of the small cactus I had seen in the plains, clothing the surface for miles together. This species must be capable of bearing very severe cold, for 20° below zero is a point that is occasionally reached here.

American horses are, speaking generally, better than ours. Their average character is higher. Though we probably in most classes have some animals that are more showy, and even better adapted to their work, yet certainly they have fewer poor brutes. With us everything that is in the form of a horse fetches money, from the stylish pair which everybody notices in the Park, down to the costermonger's pony. Manifestly inferior animals do not appear to be bred at all in America. There is a point they do not fall below, and that point admits of bone and blood enough to be noticed.

Their horses have another merit also. As a general rule, they do just what is required of them, and nothing more. It is rare to see one that jibs, or shies, or stumbles, or misbehaves himself in any way. I cannot say whether it is that, being sounder in body, they are sounder also in mind; or whether it is to be attributed to some superiority in the American method of breaking in their horses; or whether the moral effects of maize are superior to those of oats; though indeed I see from the returns that in some parts of the country a large quantity of the latter kind of grain is raised.

As American drivers have more confidence in themselves and their fortune than any drivers in the world, and are ready at any moment to run any risks, this rationality and docility of their horses is a valuable quality. One frequently does not know which to admire most, the skill and nerve of the driver, or the intelligence and training of the horses. In passing over the plains you find that only some of the streams are bridged. The bridges, however, appear to one who is new to the country to be very inadequate to what is required of them. They generally consist of two long pine trees laid from bank to bank, or, if the stream is wide, from pier to pier, and then covered with a corduroy of cross pieces, sometimes a little dressed; the interstices are filled up with prairie hay, which is strewed over the whole structure. To save material and cartage, these bridges are made just wide enough for the wheels of the coach. I do not think there could have been a foot to spare on either side. There is no side railing of any kind. The driver, with four or six horses as it may happen, generally takes them at his best pace. Any hesitation, or a false step, or any kind of misconduct in any of the horses, would lead to a mishap. But then, mishaps never occur, or only so seldom as just to show that such things are not impossible. This, however, is a momentary affair, and by the time that one has noticed that the cross pieces are not fastened, but are starting and dancing under the feet of the horses and the wheels of the coach, the other side is reached.

In the mountains I saw a specimen of American driving that would have astonished our old stagers of the Exeter, or the north road. We were crossing one of the inner ranges, and had been slowly toiling up a long hill, at a rate I suppose of not more than four miles an hour. At last we reached the summit of almost naked rock. The descent on the opposite side was very rapid—seven hundred feet in little more than half a mile. This has been accomplished by a series of zigzags constructed on the face of the hill, in the rudest possible way. The trunks of pine trees were laid longitudinally on what was to be the outside of the road. On the inner side some of the rock was picked down and blasted, and laid on the pine trees; and thus a road was made, as in the case of the bridges I have mentioned, to a very little greater width than that of the coach. The zigzags were short, and consequently the angles were close together. In the middle of the roadway the rock everywhere obtruded to a height sometimes of five or six inches. Any other people would have made the road more carefully, and of more durable materials, in the worst places would have put some kind of parapet to it, and would probably have used mules for the coach, making those sure-footed animals walk down the hill. But an American would consider it insufferable that the safety of the public should be ensured at a loss of a few minutes' time daily, and that a dollar more than was absolutely necessary should be spent on a road which might in a year or two be superseded by something better, or not wanted at all. And so the way they manage it is to construct a road of the narrow scantling and in the rude fashion I have mentioned, and then to drive down it, with six fine horses, at a rate of not less than eleven miles an hour. As soon as we got to the top of the hill, the horses were put under the whip, and away we went. As we turned the corners at full speed the team appeared to be coming back on the coach; and as we rattled down the inclines the sides of the hill looked like precipices. If one horse had stumbled on the pieces of rock projecting through the road, or got frightened, or become unruly in any way, or if a piece of harness had broken, or the brake had given way, a capsize would have been inevitable, and we should have rolled over to the valley beneath.

There was an hotel at the bottom of the hill, and while we sat down to dinner (I think people must sometimes arrive at the hotel without much appetite), another team was put in for another stage, through ravines and along the edges of precipices, which would require American horses and American driving.

The hill we had just come down is called the Guy Hill. At Central City, where I was staying the next day, I asked the landlord of the hotel if anyone had been killed lately on the Guy Hill. 'No,' he replied, 'no one had been killed, he was glad to say, for two or three years, but every year several persons had died of accidents on the hill.' These accidents happen when snow is on the ground, and the horses cannot see their way, or when it is covered with ice, and they cannot get a foothold. I afterwards walked up this road, and a closer acquaintance with it only increased the respect the way in which I had been brought down it had made me feel for American horses, drivers, and coaches. I also went over the old road that had preceded it, and which was nothing but a gully of smooth rock down the side of the

CH. XVII.   *Climate in the Mountains.*   247

hill. I was unable to conceive how any vehicle could ever have been got up it or down it.

The fame of these American whips is not confined to their own country; for I am told by an Australian friend, that in that part of the world it is the custom to engage the services of one of them where the roads are unusually difficult.

Though it was February when I was in the mountains, the climate was so bright and warm, that it did not appear strange to see the gold-washers at work in slush and water. And yet there had been so severe a frost in the previous month, that the gulch was still thickly frozen over, and these hardy men had to break through the ice to get water for washing the dirt in which the gold is found. But though there is here a great deal of open fine weather in winter, yet at this season very severe frost, though generally of short duration, may be expected, and also extremely violent storms of wind, often accompanied with snow. A storm of this kind drove me out of the mountains, as I was afraid, which actually did happen, that it would bring enough snow to block the roads for some days. I made a run for the plains, and when I reached them, I found the storm still raging, and saw the dust it raised looking like a dark haze several yards high. As the wind blew from the mountains, I did not suffer much inconvenience in running before it for twelve miles, till I reached shelter. But the next day, when it was over, I saw teamsters who told me that they had found it impossible to move on across it, and that they had been obliged to anchor their waggons to moorings driven firmly into the ground, sheltering their cattle and themselves on the lee-side. These wind storms on the plains are not so bad for man as for beast, for the nostrils, mouths, and eyes of the horses and bullocks suffer much from the sharp sand.

Three species of the crow tribe are, I found, common by the road side in the mountains in winter: the blue jay, which is seen frequently in flocks; the magpie, which is marked very similarly to our own—it appears, however, to be a somewhat larger bird, and to have a larger tail; and the raven. In the summer, as there is then an inexhaustible supply of small fruit of different kinds in the valleys, and on the hill sides, I should expect to see a great variety of birds.

Almost in every house I entered in the mountains and in the contiguous plains I found an enormous dog. Some were pure mastiffs; others of mixed breed, in which the Newfoundland blood predominated. The mastiffs were larger and more powerful animals than I ever saw at dog-shows in London or elsewhere. Their size, however, imparted no air of nobility to their appearance and bearing, but much of savage brutality. The motive, I suppose, for keeping these Cerberuses is protection from wolves, and from the two-legged assailants of life and property.

CHAPTER XVIII.

ROCKY MOUNTAINS A FIELD FOR SPORTING—GREAT VARIETY AND ABUNDANCE OF GAME—WILD FRUIT—EXCELLENCE OF CLIMATE IN THE SHOOTING SEASON—HOW THE MOUNTAINS MAY BE REACHED, AND HOW MUCH SEEN BY THE WAY, IN 15 DAYS FROM LIVERPOOL—COST OF THE EXPEDITION—THE BEST CAMPING-GROUND IS THE SOUTH PARK, AT FOOT OF PIKE'S PEAK—THE ROUTE BY CHICAGO AND DENVER RECOMMENDED—OTHER ROUTE BY ST. LOUIS AND LEAVENWORTH—ROUTE INTO THE PARK—THE NORTH PARK EASIER WORK—THE MORE ENTERPRISING MAY GO TO LARAMIE PLAINS—WILL DETERIORATE EVERY YEAR.

THE Rocky Mountains are just at present the best sporting-ground in the world. They have both feathered and four-footed game, and fishing sufficient to satisfy the keenest sportsman. I saw the herds of antelope running about like flocks of sheep. The elk is very abundant. A few mountain buffalos are to be had : it is a smaller and darker-coloured variety than that of the plains, and plenty of what is here called the mountain rabbit, but which is larger than our hare, and in winter, when I saw it, is nearly white. A bear may occasionally be met with. The Rocky Mountain sheep is so rare that it must not be taken into the account. Among vermin there is the wolf, a brute that will sometimes attack a man. As he sneaks off he looks like a lean and smoke-begrimed sheep. There is also the cayotte, a smaller animal, about the size of a jackal, and which makes itself heard a great deal at night.

As to the feathered game; on lucky days you may get a wild turkey, and every day you will find plenty of prairie fowl, and quail in still greater abundance.

The fishing will be confined to the speckled trout; but this is to be had in any quantity you choose to take out of the water; and wherever you may be camping out on the mountains, you will always be on the banks of a stream, or have one near you.

Incredible quantities of small edible fruit are to be found everywhere. They consist of gooseberries, currants, raspberries, blueberries, and some other kinds, all of them being called collectively, in the language of the mountains, berries. I mention them here, because, when people are camping out, they supply materials for tarts and puddings, and, if it be required, for dessert.

The next question to that of game is the climate. It is just the most perfect in the world. In the months of July, August, and September, the three best for sporting in the Rocky Mountains, it is never known to rain. This is the experience of the people of Denver, of the mining districts in the mountains, and of many generations of trappers. And up on this high ground it is, at this season of the year, neither too hot nor too cold, but just what one would desire. It is indeed so pleasant, that it is the common practice of the people in the mountains and contiguous plains to camp out, as it is called, in the dry months; and the weather is so certain, that in these camping-out excursions the ladies accompany the gentlemen. The guns and fishing-rods of the latter supply the larder, while the former preside over the *cuisine*.

But how are people to get from the other side of the Atlantic to this sporting-ground, so grand in scenery, so rich in game, and so delightful in climate? Nothing can be easier. On the fifteenth day after leaving Liverpool you may dine in the Rocky Mountains on trout you have yourself caught, venison you have yourself stalked, and fruit you have yourself gathered. And could a fortnight be spent more delightfully? It would be a memorable fortnight in any man's life. It would include a voyage across the great ocean; a sight of New York and Chicago; a view of the lakes Erie and Michigan; the passage of the Mississippi and Missouri; five hundred miles of prairie, and as many more of the plains up the valley of the Platte; and the Rocky Mountains, a worthy finale of the whole. Instead, then, of the getting to the mountains being a difficulty, or any kind of obstacle to carrying out the plan, it is, if rightly considered, one of the greatest possible inducements for going. I suppose no other part of the world could in the same space and time present so many grand and moving sights; indeed, what greater sights are there in the world, except that there are some loftier mountain ranges?

The voyage across the Atlantic may be set down at that time of the year at eleven days. The trains take two days in going from New York to Chicago, and as many more in going from Chicago to the mountains.

As to the cost, the fare by the Cunard boats is about 25*l.* : it may be reduced to 20*l.* by the Inman line. From New York to Chicago there are two lines of railway; the ticket of one line costs twenty-two, and of the other twenty-five dollars; each charges eight dollars for a berth in a sleeping-car for the two nights, which gives one also a sofa to one's self in the day time. From Chicago to the mountains I cannot say what is precisely the fare, for I took a through ticket to Denver, which included one hundred and ten miles of coaching; I believe, however, that it is about forty dollars, which is a high fare for America. The fare by the steamer includes one's board. The cost, therefore, of actually reaching the mountains from Liverpool would be 31*l*., plus your keep during the four days you are passing from New York to Shyenne, which would not amount to more than four dollars a day, or sixteen in all, that is, about 2*l*. 10*s*. The whole cost, therefore, of getting to the mountains would not be more than 35*l*.

We may compare this with the alternative of taking a moor in Scotland. Out and home would cost 70*l*. If one did the thing well, and went to the best ground, it would be necessary to get, at Denver or Leavenworth, a span of good mules, with harness, and a double tilted waggon, fitted up with boxes that just pack close together, each in its own place. This, complete in everything, would cost about 600 dollars, or rather less than 100*l*. After three months' use it would sell for 80*l*.; because then the freighting season would be drawing to a close, and mules and waggon would not be much in request. The mules and waggon would thus cost 20*l*. Add to this the cost of a man to do the cooking and look after the mules. I suppose his services might be had for his board and a dollar a day. This, for ten weeks, would be seventy dollars for wages—say 100 dollars in all, or 16*l.* This gives, with the loss on the waggon and mules, 36*l.*, which, divided among three persons, the number the party would probably consist of, would add, in the case of each, 12*l.* more to the 70*l.*, bringing it up to 82*l.* For getting from Shyenne to Denver by coach, and by waggon from Denver to the camping-ground, for flour, whisky, sugar, and other sundries, reckon 18*l.* per head. The whole will thus be just 100*l.* But take 50*l.* more in your pocket for contingencies, and to enable you to see a little of the country on your way out, or on your return, and you will have had a season in the Rocky Mountains which will not have cost you so much as it would have done to have hired a moor and forest in Scotland, and paid a parcel of gillies, and kept house besides for two or three months; and you will have killed twenty times as much game, and had much more varied and interesting sport, and have had the choice of a district larger than the whole of Scotland, and seen some of the greatest sights the world has to show.

The best camping and sporting ground is a main point in the question. The South Park combines every advantage. The weather is sure to be good. There is plenty of grass, of water, and of game ; and there are no Indians or musquitoes : for though the latter are found on the ridges round the park, they are not found in the park itself. It is somewhere about twenty miles square. It contains also two small settlements, called Colorado City and Canon (pronounced Canyon) City. The topography is not given accurately in Appleton's maps ; for instance,

Pike's Peak, at the foot of which it lies, is represented as standing out on the plain quite detached, whereas it is only the highest peak in that part of the range. It is so much higher that from the neighbourhood of Denver it is the only point visible in that direction, and so becomes the steering mark for parties bound for the South Park. Colorado City is also put to the north of the peak, whereas it lies to the west of it.

There are two routes to the South Park, one by way of New York, south shore of lake Erie, Chicago, Omaha and Shyenne by railway: this is about 2200 miles; then to Denver by coach, which is 110 miles more; concluding with a waggon journey to the park, of about 75 miles. This is the route I would recommend for several reasons. There is far more to see upon it, and it can be done in less time. Instead of merely coming down to the mountains on a line at right angles to them, you would coast along them for nearly two hundred miles. You would pass close under Long's Peak, and through a very interesting part of the plain, in the neighbourhood of St. Vrain and Burlington. You might stop, if you pleased, for a day or two's fishing at La Porte and Big Thomson. You would see Denver, which is a place of much interest, and a good place for getting your waggon, mules, and stores, and the man to act as cook and waggoner, and where you would find everyone ready to be helpful in giving information and advice.

Or you might reach it in another way, by New York, Harrisburg, Pittsburg, Cincinnati, St. Louis, and the south branch of the Pacific Railway, which is now opened from St. Louis, by Kansas City, Leavenworth, and Lecompton, to a point called Pond Creek. By this route you would have to get your waggon and span of mules at Leavenworth, and would reach Pike's Peak and the South Park by the Smoky Hill track. In this way you would have to travel a great deal further by waggon; and though you would pass through a very interesting country, and see many stirring and busy places, yet in these respects it cannot compete with the more northerly route. Why, to have seen Chicago is in itself an education.

Whether you go by the Denver or the Leavenworth route, the best way of getting into the South Park is to strike the Arkansas River, and follow it up till you enter the park, in which you will find the head waters both of this river and of the Platte, separated by a divide of only five miles.

Or if you wish for something easier than the South Park, and which would enable you to dispense with waggon, mules, and a man of your own, you might take the North Park at the foot of Long's Peak. There is a good path to it from St. Vrain and Burlington, of forty-five miles; and I have no doubt but that, at the right season, you might find some gentleman, or some party, going up into the mountains for some little camping out, and who would be glad of your company. There is good shooting and fishing about Long's Peak, and you can see from the plains the grassy park at its south side.

Or if you are more adventurously disposed, you may still be suited. The Pacific Railway is at present opened for traffic as far as Shyenne. It is, however, completed for thirty miles further, to Forts Sanders and Halleck. This takes you into the very heart of the mountains. I had the offer of being carried on to this point, if I wished it, on a construction train, and I have no doubt but that the engineer or contractor would grant the same favour to any traveller who requested it. This would bring you almost upon one of the most celebrated sporting-grounds of the mountains, the Laramie Plains; or if you could not manage it in this way, or if you take waggon and mules, it would be better to leave the rail at Shyenne. You would then start at once from the present terminus of the railway, and after having kept a course of north by west for thirty or forty miles, you would find yourself on the Laramie Plains. This is not a park among the mountains, but a vast expanse of open table-land. One advantage you would have on this ground is, that a detachment of the United States army is quartered up here, and the officers are always ready to give any assistance in their power to gentlemen who are out on the plain for sporting. What calls for more enterprise in those who camp out on the Laramie Plains is that they are still open to Indian raids, and that they are exposed, as might be expected, to very violent wind-storms.

This year of 1868 the Rocky Mountains offer a greater combination of advantages than they have done hitherto, or ever, probably, will again. Till the opening of the Pacific Railway last year they were not to be got at; but their having now been rendered so easily accessible will lead to a great deal of the game being rapidly cleared off, both by shoals of vacation-ramblers from the old States, who will flock to them with tents and guns, for their yearly excursion, and by the immediate establishment of a trade in game between the mountains and the great cities of the north and east. I suppose that never again, after this year, will a haunch of antelope venison be retailed in Denver for seventy-five cents.

CHAPTER XIX.

HOTEL CARS, REAL FIRST-CLASS CARRIAGES—AN EDITOR ON HIS COUNTRYMEN'S KNOWLEDGE—AMERICAN GRANDILOQUENCE—OF WHOM THIS IS SAID—NECESSARY TO REPEAT SOME OF WHAT ONE HEARS—'HAVE YOU SEEN OUR FOREST?'—'THE PACIFIC RAILS WILL CARRY THE COMMERCE OF THE WORLD'—LARGE ACQUAINTANCE AMERICANS HAVE—AN AMERICAN ON LETTERS OF INTRODUCTION—NIAGARA—THE AMERICAN AND CANADIAN FALLS—WHAT IS IN THE MIND MAGNIFIES WHAT ONE SEES—THE STONE TROUGH IT HAS CHIPPED OUT—ICE-BRIDGE—HOW NIAGARA IS PRONOUNCED—A WEEK OF CANADIAN WEATHER—A SNOW-BOUND PARTY AT NIAGARA.

ON returning from the mountains, I left Chicago for the east in an hotel car. This kind of carriage combines a sleeping-berth with a travelling kitchen, and supplies you by day, just as the sleeping-cars do, with a comfortable sofa to yourself. In front of this a table may be placed when needed, on which you can have served in a few minutes whatever you please. In this way you may without leaving the carriage have all your meals for a journey of a thousand miles. No objection can be made either to the materials or to the cooking of what is supplied. These sleeping, hotel, and English cars are not merely devices for diminishing the inconvenience of a long journey, and enabling one to economise time, but they also act completely as first-class carriages. After you have paid for your ticket at one uniform price with all the rest of the passengers, you find in the train the steward of the sleeping-car (sometimes there is an office in the town), and pay him so many dollars more, and secure in this way a place to yourself, for night and day, in the special kind of car. It would give offence to call them first-class carriages; but from what has been said it will be understood that they do at all events incidentally supply this advantage. And as there is also a ladies' carriage, into which well-dressed gentlemen are admitted, and furthermore a caboose for negroes, emigrants, and very dirty people, in which the wound that is inflicted on their dignity is compensated for by a reduction of the fare, American railway trains, although they profess to put all their passengers on a footing of democratic equality, do in fact allow them to classify themselves.

Strange as it may sound, the traveller sometimes finds it difficult to carry on an argument with an American, on account of his complete ignorance of the subject upon which he will go on arguing; or, worse still, from his wonderful misconceptions, for some of which he may possibly be indebted to rural orators and rural newspapers. I was in this way myself often reminded of what a well-known American editor said to me—of course very much exaggerating the fact; still, however, his remark may have some grains of truth in it, 'that his countrymen were, and must long continue to be, in matters out of their own business, and beyond their own country, the most ignorant people in the civilised world.'

Another difficulty one occasionally meets with is that you do not know how much you are to discount from the speaker's grand phrases, in order to arrive at his own meaning; for it sometimes happens that the ideas that are in his own mind are very inadequate to the language he uses to express them. I was, for instance, for several days thrown into close contact with a very gentlemanly, well-spoken, well-mannered merchant, who had seen something of the world, for his business had frequently taken him to South America and to Europe. On one occasion he astonished me by affirming 'that the farmers, of all classes in the United States, possessed the finest intellects.' Anybody else would have meant by these words, that among them were to be found the most powerful and most cultivated intellects—minds great in imaginative power, or in the power of apprehending political, or speculative, or scientific truth. But of these uses of the intellect my companion had not so much as the germ of a conception. To nothing of this kind had his sight ever reached. What he meant by the finest intellect was just this: a mind capable of giving a pretty correct practical judgment on the ordinary occurrences of daily business. At another time the same gentleman startled me by the announcement 'that many of the blacks were very fine scholars.' After a time it became evident that he had no conception of scholarship beyond the elements of reading and writing, and the power of keeping accounts accurately. If a man had attained to the point of doing these things with ease, he had achieved everything; for my companion had caught no glimpse of anything beyond.

No one, I suppose, will so mistake my meaning as to imagine that I mention anecdotes of this kind with any wish to raise a laugh at the expense of the people I travelled among. It seems almost impertinent to remark that there are plenty of people in America who are very well informed, and plenty of people who express their ideas with perfect correctness. Their system, however, of equal education, and of equal chances to all, brings a great many to the front (and small blame to them for such a result), who—this I suppose to have been the history of the casual fellow-traveller whose expressions I have just repeated—never had any education but that of the common primary schools, and never afterwards had time for reading anything but newspapers, and never attempted to master anything except the details of their own business. This must be the case with many. Many others, however, there are, as is very well known, who have used what was acquired at the common primary school as a foundation for a solid and extensive structure of after acquisitions.

My object is to give a correct idea of America, and of the different kinds of Americans the traveller in the United States meets with, as they were seen by myself. If omissions are made, this object cannot be answered, and so what I might say would convey only erroneous conceptions. One is generally precluded from making any reference to what he saw or heard in private houses; but there are no reasons for silence as to what took place at tables-d'hôte, and in railway cars, on board steam-boats, and in coaches: all this was said and done in public. And besides, most of the people who in America make laughable observations would, considering the point from which they started, have had no observations at all to make, had their lot been cast on this side the water, or anywhere else excepting in the United States.

'Sir,' said a gentleman to me one morning at breakfast (we were seated together at a small table in one of the large hotels of a great city in the Valley of the Mississippi),—'Sir, have you seen our Forest?' 'Sir,' I replied, 'for the last thousand miles and more, since I left Richmond, I have scarcely seen anything else.'

'Sir,' my interrogator responded with an indignant tone, 'I am not speaking of the material, but of the intellectual Forest—of our Forest—the great Forest—the grandest delineator of the sublime and of the ridiculous in the united world.' I afterwards found that this grand delineator of the ridiculous was the actor Forest, who is not unknown professionally in this country, and who was playing in the town I was then staying at. I also found that his admirer was a dealer in ready-made clothes, who took his meals at the hotel.

'Sir,' observed to me a gentleman who was sitting next to me in a car of the Pacific Railway, 'these rails will carry the commerce of the world.' I requested him to repeat his remark. I then began to reply by saying, that I thought it not improbable that as much of what was used for tea in the United States as was grown in China would pass over them, when he cut me short with, 'Sir, it is not to be expected that strangers should understand the grandeur of our country, but these rails will carry the commerce of the world.' This dealer in prophecy was also a dealer in whisky.

Wherever you may be in the United States, you will not find it difficult to obtain letters of introduction to any town in the Union. If an American traveller were to ask an English friend at Ipswich for introductions to Exeter, Galway, Dundee, Carlisle, and Dover, his friend would not find it easy to comply with the request. But if the position of the two were reversed, and the Englishman were travelling in America, and were to ask his American friend for introductions to half-a-dozen places in the States, far more distant from each other than the places I have mentioned in the United Kingdom, the American would either be able to give them himself, or would easily find friends who could. This implies a vast difference in our social system. Ours is a system which isolates, theirs is a system which brings everybody in contact with everybody. One is astonished at the number of acquaintances an American has. For one acquaintance an English gentleman has, an American gentleman will probably have fifty or a hundred.

I will repeat here what an American gentleman at Washington said to me on the subject of letters of introduction. 'We Americans,' he remarked, 'are a busy people. We have not time to attend to general introductions. We gladly do what we can, but we cannot do what costs time. Still, however, if the letter is brought to us by one who has ideas, and who has the power of making us feel the magnetism of his ideas, we will give to him our time, and everything we have to give.'

Niagara is seen to advantage in a severe winter. It is impossible for ice to accumulate in front of the Canadian fall; but as vast masses are formed all about the American, the contrast between the two becomes far greater and more striking than in summer.

According to the figures usually given, the American is only one third the width of the Canadian; but this measurement gives no idea of the difference between the two, which lies chiefly in the fact that the sheet of water which comes over the former is so thin that it is everywhere broken, and white with foam; while in the Canadian fall it comes over in so deep and solid a mass, that it is green throughout the whole Horse-shoe. It is perfectly smooth, and there is not a bubble visible upon it. Every piece of wood that comes over seems to glide down its surface; the water itself being so unbroken as to appear almost as if it were stationary and had no movement in it.

I do not know any other grand object of nature where the interest felt at the moment in what is seen is so much heightened by what is not seen, as in these great falls. They are grand in themselves to the eye; but how much grander does the sight become, when it is accompanied by the thought that what you see is the collected outflow of all those vast lakes it has been taking you so many days to steam over and along, lakes on all of which you lost sight of the land, just as if you had been on the ocean itself, lakes larger than European kingdoms. Here you have before you, gliding over that precipice, all the water these great seas, fed by a thousand streams, are unable to retain in their own basins.

And behind you, in the seven miles from Queenston, you have in the deep perpendicular-sided trough, cut in the solid limestone rock, a measure of the excavating power of this descending flood, which has been for so many ages, just like a chisel in a carpenter's hand (the Horse-shoe fall is now a gouge), chipping out this deep and wide channel. When one reflects on the enormous weight of the falling water, surprise is felt at its not working at a greater rate than, as is supposed, that of twelve inches in twelve months.

When I was at Niagara there was what is called an 'ice bridge' a few yards below the falls, and which, as it requires a continuance of severe weather for its completion, does not occur, I was told, more frequently than oncé in every nine or ten years.

I stayed at an hotel on the American side of the Suspension Bridge, which is about a mile and a half from the falls. I was there three days, and during that time I met two Canadians who had all their lives been in the neighbourhood of the falls, and an American in business at the place where I was staying, who had not yet seen the great sight, and who felt no desire to see it.

I may here mention, that if we ought to pronounce Indian names in the Indian fashion, we shall cease to talk about the falls of Niăgăra. It was their practice to accent not the ante-penultimate, but the penultimate syllable. For instance, they talked of Niăgăra, and Ontărīo. In Ohīo, and Potōmac, if they are real Indian words, the true Indian pronunciation has been retained.

I have already mentioned that during the time I was in the United States I never found it uncomfortably cold. Nothing, however, of this kind could be said of my experience of the climate of Canada. The only ferry of those I had to cross, which had become impassable on account of the accumulations of ice, was that into Canada at Detroit. This was a bad beginning, and by it I lost a place I had paid for in an hotel car.

We had not gone far on Canadian soil before some of the iron-work of the engine broke, in consequence of the intense cold of the morning. At Niagara I was detained a day by a snow-storm. It was so violent a storm that it put an end to all traffic for twenty-four hours. The train I had intended using was to have left at 6.30 A.M. I struggled to the station, through the snow, that had drifted during the night to the depth of three feet, only to find that I had come to no purpose. During the whole of the day you could not see ten yards before you, the snow was driving and drifting so thickly. The next morning when I left for Toronto, the thermometer was standing at twelve degrees below zero; on the following morning, at Toronto it was nineteen degrees below zero. I left Toronto for the east by the first train that had been over the rails in that direction for some days. While I was at Kingston there came on a second gale of wind, but this time accompanied by blinding rain, every drop of which as it fell froze on the zero-cold ground and snow. I was staying with the Bishop of Ontario, and was to have been taken over the schools of the place, but the day was such that the scholars were not able to leave their homes. This rain continued all the next day, and, being a warm rain, it at last turned the snow, which was unusually deep, into such an amount of slush as one must see to believe. At last, after daily delays of many hours each, and several mishaps on the road, to be attributed to the mismanagement of the authorities of the bankrupt Canadian railway companies, I reached Montreal at the end of the week, when the weather suddenly, as in its other changes during the previous part of the week, became calm, bright, and warm. But when I mention the changes I experienced at the close of the winter in a single week, I must not omit an instance of unchanging persistence the weather had exhibited during the earlier part of the same winter. There had been forty-five days at Montreal (but I was told that there was no record of any other equal spell of cold), during which the markings of the thermometer had been continuously below zero. This winter, however, of 1867–68 will be memorable for its severity. In Minnesota thirty-six degrees, and in Wisconsin thirty-one degrees below zero had been reached.

During the day that I was detained at the Niagara Suspension Bridge Hotel, I had the company of about a dozen other travellers, snow-bound like myself. The storm was too violent to admit of anyone going outside; there was, therefore, nothing for us to do, except to sit round the stove in front of the bar and talk away the time. Everybody contributed what he could to the general stock of amusement, by making or repeating jokes, or telling stories and adventures, the latter, probably, sometimes participating in the nature of the former. I was called upon to give a detailed account of my run to the Plains and Rocky Mountains. When every other subject was exhausted, politics of course came up. This, as is usual, led to loud denunciations of what is called 'the corruption' of all the departments of the Government. 'But, Sir,' said one of the party to me, in a determined and fierce voice, 'the darndest corruption on this side creation is that of the British Government. You give your Cabinet ministers very little, but they all get rich.

There are plenty of people who want their help. It was this that enabled Lord Palmerston, during his long official life, to become so enormously wealthy. We Americans keep ourselves well posted in these matters. We have to transact too much business with your public men not to know what we have to do.' This was from the politician of the party.

'Sir,' said another to me, 'no man can be blamed for travelling in this weather, because no one would stir in it unless he had a big occasion.' The theory was plausible, but no one present acknowledged that he had himself been drawn away from home by 'a big occasion.'

In the evening I went into the ladies' drawing-room. I here found one English and two American ladies. They were all young, and all appeared to be on their wedding tour. One of the American ladies cried herself to sleep because her husband had left her that he might play at cards in the gentlemen's drawing-room. The other took her husband's absence for the same purpose very philosophically, consoling herself with a kind of dominoes she called 'muggins.'

CHAPTER XX.

EDUCATIONAL DEPARTMENT AT TORONTO—CANADIAN ARGUMENTS AGAINST COMMON SCHOOLS—A CANADIAN'S OPINION ON SECULAR SCHOOLS IN ENGLAND—HOW THE CANADIAN'S OBJECTIONS ARE MET IN THE UNITED STATES—UPPER CANADIANS NOT YET A PEOPLE—ADVANTAGES POSSESSED BY UPPER CANADA—SERVICE AT THE ROMANIST AND ANGLICAN CATHEDRALS—UNMANNERLY BEHAVIOUR PERMITTED ON CANADIAN RAILWAYS—BADNESS OF THEIR CARRIAGES—WHY CANADA IS NOT 'THE LAND OF FREEDOM'—YANKEE SMARTNESS IN TRAIN-DRIVING—PICTURESQUENESS OF VERMONT—TRAVELLING ON AMERICAN RAILWAYS NOT FATIGUING.

AT Toronto I was taken over the educational department for Upper Canada. It is very ambitiously housed, and combines so many objects, namely a general library, a collection and depôt of school-books and of school apparatus, galleries of art, chiefly for copies of celebrated pictures and pieces of sculpture, and normal schools, that I spent two hours in going through it. On my making some observation on the cost of the building, and of its contents, I was told that it might appear that too much had been spent on the department, but that it had designedly been carried out on this scale, and the building made imposing, and the galleries added, in order to give dignity and elevation to the idea of education in the minds of the people. A hope had been entertained that if the normal schools were brought under the same roof, a better class of young persons would offer themselves for the position of teachers: this hope had not been disappointed.

The arguments and facts which are in favour of the Canadian Common School system are to be heard at the department, the officers of which appeared to be able and zealous men. The system, however, has been very far from securing that unanimity which to the south of the great lakes exists on the subject of common schools. I will state this difference of opinion, and some of its causes, in the words of one of the leading men in the province, used in conversation with me on the subject. He said, 'that throughout Upper Canada their common schools had quite failed in winning anything at all like general approval. The Grand Jury of Toronto have for several years past made a presentment against the system, hanging the expression of their dissatisfaction on the peg of their visitation and inspection of the jail. Their dissatisfaction is shared very largely by the upper class, who pay a heavy tax for the schools, and yet find that those for whose benefit and elevation they were willing to be taxed do not send their children to the schools; but that, instead of this, the well-to-do tradesmen who could very well afford to pay for their children's education are now provided with it, almost gratuitously, at the expense of the community.

'Some towns in Upper Canada, as for instance Hamilton, have all along refused to establish common schools.

'Another difficulty about the system, besides its injustice, and its failure in its true object, is that it extinguishes private schools. When all the schools become of one kind, competition in excellence ceases, and everyone is content with a low standard of mediocrity. Every master knows that, so long as he is not more inefficient than his neighbours, his position is safe ; and that his salary, which is all that he at last cares about, will be paid him.

'The local superintendents, who are almost universally clergymen, have other things to attend to, and carry out their inspection in the most perfunctory manner.

'A cause that is doing much harm to the schools is, that everything connected with them is rapidly falling into the hands of the politicians. No party can now afford to forego an opportunity for strengthening itself by electing, or procuring the election, of party men as managers ; and these again, for the same reasons, are guided in the selection of teachers by party considerations. It is coming to this, that no one who has to do with the management, supervision, or teaching of schools, will be the fittest person for what he has to do, except by accident.'

This gentleman had studied the subject of education, as well in England as in his own country, and he gave me some of the opinions he had formed on the religious part of the question, or rather as to how he conceived the proposal for secular schools would affect the Established Church, in the following words. 'I think,' he said, 'the Church will lose nothing by the absence of a Church character in the schools. I never met with a clergyman in the old country, whether it was an archbishop or the incumbent of a small rural parish, to whom I put the question, who felt sure that the Church gained by the schools being in the hands of the clergy. No one will say that this attaches the children, when they are grown up, to the Church. For my own part, I feel sure that a system which would rigidly exclude both all Church and all denominational teaching would be a gain to the Church. This is necessarily true, if under the present system Church schools do less to indoctrinate those brought up in them with Churchism, than the denominational schools do to indoctrinate those brought up in them with dissent. My conclusion is, that if I were an English Churchman, I should not vote against the plan which would supplement your existing system with secular schools. It would do you no harm, and would give you many intelligent members.'

The way in which my Canadian friend's opinions about common schools differed from those held everywhere in the United States, supplies a means for measuring the social and moral differences of the two peoples. Not one of the above objections, whatever weight it may have in Canada, has any weight at all in the United States. There the first thing thought about is making the schools as suitable as possible for all classes, and this object is very largely attained, so that the upper class need not, and do not, hold themselves aloof from them. There, too, instead of noting with feelings and expressions of discontent that a great number of the lower class in the towns do not resort to the schools, great efforts are made to bring them in, by varying, and adapting to their wants and habits, the character of the schools, as is done at Boston and New York, and by getting as many people as possible to become volunteer workers in the effort to persuade such parents to send their children. I was, while at Washington, very much struck and interested by the account Mr. Barnard, the Commissioner of Education, gave me of the way in which this had been effected. And then, as to the deadness and inefficiency which show themselves in the public schools in Canada, as soon as competition with private schools ceases, an American public and American parents would not tolerate anything of the kind. And the American teachers themselves are so energetic and ambitious, that they would be the last in the community to succumb to such influences. The inefficient inspection the Canadian objectors complain of is a great evil, but is very far from being an irremediable one.

The fact is, that the inhabitants of Upper Canada are not yet a people. They are Englishmen, Scotchmen, or Irishmen, just as if they were still in the old country; and what would not have suited them there, they think will not suit them where they are. Unlike their neighbours, they are not possessed with the idea, that if they will only give themselves the trouble to attempt it, they can make anything bear its proper fruit. The American is the hardest worker in the world, never sparing himself, but always toiling on, in the faith that he will soon be able to bring all things right; and he generally succeeds in doing so. These are not yet the characteristics of the inhabitants of Upper Canada.

In Canada there is the stage, and there are the materials for a great nation. Its towns are more solidly built than those of the same size in the States, possibly on account of the greater severity of the

T

climate. The country is generally fertile. It is also very varied, full of lakes, and streams, and forests. It abounds in mineral wealth and in agricultural produce. Notwithstanding its seven months' winter, it is capable of ripening maize and maturing tobacco; and even, to speak of small things, through the medium of its peas, a crop which can rarely be grown profitably to the south of the lakes, it supplies no inconsiderable part of what is used for coffee among its neighbours. That product, however, of Canada, which most attracts the attention of the traveller, and is likely to make the strongest impression upon him, is the complexion of the Canadian ladies. It gives you more of the idea of transparency, otherwise you might have thought that it was of pearl.

On a Sunday, while at Montreal, in my way to the Episcopal cathedral of Christ's Church, I allowed time for witnessing the celebration of High Mass at the church or cathedral annexed to the Jesuits' College. As I left the building the thought in my mind was, 'I should like to ask the priests who have just been officiating, if they have, or can imagine, any reasons for believing that this service is either acceptable to God or edifying to man?' In the English cathedral the service was very well and impressively read by an elderly clergyman; but the young clergyman who afterwards occupied the pulpit was far too minutely acquainted with all that passes in the mind of the Almighty. No man could be so fully acquainted with what passes in the mind of his most familiar friend—hardly with what passes in his own mind.

One who has just come from the States may compare the manners and customs of the American travelling public with those of the Canadian. The former are very much in advance of the latter. The Canadian conductor, unlike his brother officer to the south, appears to make no attempt to keep things and persons in order for the general advantage. Anybody, however rough (and many Canadian travellers are in winter very rough indeed, perhaps because they are lumberers out for a holiday), is allowed to take his seat in the ladies' carriage. The shaggiest and most unmannerly fellows, sometimes with short pipes in their mouths, and in their shirt sleeves, are permitted to perambulate the train, staring everybody in the face; I suppose merely to show that they are lords of the situation. But what I found the most annoying of all was, that I hardly ever left my seat for a few moments without finding on my return that some one had pushed my luggage and rug on one side, and taken possession of my place. This I believe to be a practice quite unheard of in the United States; at all events, I never noticed an instance of it. The only case of drunkenness I ever saw in any railway car was on the Grand Trunk line of Canada: it was that of a dirty, uncombed rough, who was uproariously tipsy; but neither conductor nor anyone else took any notice of him.

Again; the worst carriages in the States are better than those on the great Canadian lines. All the former have good springs; but the Canadians are too strongly protectionist to tolerate American cars on their lines, and their own native cars have, as far as my experience goes, no springs at all. A Canadian assured me that there had once been a time when they had had springs, but that they had now stiffened or

worn out, or in some way or other gone to the bad.
The effect is that there is an incessant short, sharp,
rattling jar, which becomes very distressing. Their
home-made carriages must also be very deficient in
strength, or else their rails must be most alarmingly
out of order; for in one day I counted about a dozen
wrecks of trains lying by the side of the road. This
is not encouraging as one goes along and sees (the
ground being everywhere covered with snow) nothing
else but overturned and smashed-up cars.

Still, we must remember that in the great bridge
over the St. Lawrence, at Montreal, they have one of
the grandest railway works in the world. It seems
to be about a mile and a half long, and carries the
train over the rapids of the St. Lawrence through a
series of tubes supported by massive stone piers.

On crossing this bridge, on my return to the
States, I left behind me on the west bank more than
two feet of snow. In some places the fences were
entirely buried. On the eastern side, however, of the
river the snow was much thinner, and in less than
two hours we were passing over a country from which
it had almost disappeared. This was not lost on a
voluble little Irishwoman, the chief talker in a party of
Irish whom she had been endeavouring to persuade to
leave Canada and settle in the States. 'You see for
yourselves,' she said, pointing out to them how much
less snow there was than what they had left two
hours ago in Canada, ' you see for yourselves that
this is the land of freedom; for here, if a body
has no shoes, she can go without them: but in
Canada it is entirely too cold: faith, then, this is the
land of freedom.'

For the first sixty miles of this journey we remained in the execrable carriages of the Grand Trunk of Canada Company, and in the hands of their officials, whose way of doing things leaves on the mind the feeling that their object is to show how what ought to be done may be neglected. The instant the Yankees took charge of the train everything changed, as if by magic. You could feel at any moment that the train was being driven against time, and not allowed to go anyhow. The smartness with which the driver brought it into the stations, and took it out, never waiting one instant longer than was necessary for giving up the mail-bags, or whatever it might be the conductor had to do, showed the value he attached to the passengers' time, and to his own reputation for punctuality. I believe there were times when we were not stopped for more than thirty seconds. In a long day's journey, to feel that the train is handled in this way has quite an exhilirating effect.

All day long we were winding our way among the hills of Vermont, which rose above the valleys to a height of six or seven hundred feet. Every valley had its stream. The land appeared generally to be poor; but, as is usual in such cases, it was very picturesque.

I tried sometimes to make out why it is that five hundred miles by railway in America do not fatigue one so much as fifty in this country. More than once in America I travelled upwards of a thousand miles at a single stretch, but never on any occasion, in a tour of eight thousand miles by railway, did I feel, either during a journey or after it, anything like fatigue or discomfort, or have any sensation to remind me that I had travelled a single mile. The only explanation I could hit upon was that on English and European railways you are shut up in a little box, in which you cannot move about, and in which there are incessant draughts from a door and window on each side of you. The result is, that your feet instantly get cold, and cold feet affect the whole system disagreeably. In American cars, however, from the way in which the floors are fastened, and from there being no side doors at all, one's feet, with rare exceptions, even when the thermometer outside is below zero, are as far from being chilled as they would be in one's own house. Of course the American cars have also a stove at each end.

CHAPTER XXI.

BOSTON IS THE HUB OF AMERICA—MR. TICKNOR—PROFESSOR ROGERS AND THE TECHNOLOGICAL—MR. NORTON—PROFESSOR AGASSIZ—MR. APPLETON AND MR. LONGFELLOW—MR. PHILBRICK—A GRAMMAR SCHOOL COMMEMORATION—HUMILITY OF THE BETTER LITERARY MEN OF BOSTON—REGRET AT LEAVING BOSTON.

BOSTON is the hub of the world. So say those who, not being Massachusetts men themselves, are disposed to impute extravagant pretensions to the good old Puritan city. The hub, in the language of America, is the nave, or centre-piece of the wheel, from which the spokes radiate, and on which the wheel turns. As the Americans make with their hickory wood the best wheels in the world, they have some right to give to one of the pieces a name of their own. But, however, Boston need not quarrel with the saying. Nations, like individuals, are generally governed by ideas, and no people to such a degree as the Americans: and the ideas which have governed them hitherto, have been supplied from New England. But Massachusetts has been the wheel within New England, and Boston the wheel within Massachusetts. It has therefore been the first source and fountain of the ideas that have moved and made America, and is, in a high and honourable sense, the hub of the New World.

Among the celebrities of Boston with whom I was

so fortunate as to become acquainted, and to see in their own houses, I will name first Mr. Ticknor, the author of the well-known 'History of Spanish Literature,' himself now the father of American literature. His reminiscences of the history and society of his own country, and largely too of English literary society, for the last fifty years, contribute very much to enrich his conversation. I have a grateful sense of his hospitality, and of the other ways in which he assisted in making my visit to Boston most agreeable.

My next acquaintance was Professor Rogers, the head of the Technological Institute of Boston. A great deal has been spent by the city on the building in which this Institute is housed, and in providing it with an able staff of professors; and it has proved thoroughly well adapted to the teaching of all the different branches upon which it undertakes to give instruction. These are Physics, Chemistry, Mathematics, Mechanics, and Drawing, particularly as required by machinists, engineers, builders, and architects. Its objects are entirely practical; but it would be a gross mistake to depreciate them on that account. The knowledge imparted here is necessary for certain trades and professions; and it is better that this knowledge should be communicated well and correctly, than that it should be picked up imperfectly. It is better that those who carry on any business that is based on scientific principles should be familiar with its principles, than that they should go through life working merely by the rule of thumb. In the programme of the Institute Professor Rogers's department is Physics; but in fact the Technological Institute is Professor Rogers, and Professor Rogers (for he is so devoted to it that it has become a part of himself) is the Technological Institute, plus a great deal that is good, and refined, and generous.

I spent an evening with Mr. Norton, the editor of the 'North American Review.' I was much pleased with all that I saw of Boston society, but this evening at Mr. Norton's recurs to my recollection with especial distinctness. He, as the editor of the leading Review of the New World must for many years have had his finger on the literary pulse of America, and must know better than any other person what American writers can do, and what the American public appreciates. I was glad to hear that Mr. Norton contemplated spending twelve months in England with his family, though I regretted that he should find that a year of rest and of change of climate was necessary for him. It seemed to me, that both he and Professor Rogers were much overworked, and were also suffering from the withering aridity of the climate. A great part of the population of New England appears to be affected by the same cause—their vital organs are going through a process of desiccation. I trust that both these good and true workers in the literary society of Boston will before long be indebted for their restoration to health and strength to the moister and more merciful climate of the old country.

I was sorry that the shortness of my stay prevented my accepting an invitation from Mr. and Mrs. Agassiz. They are persons of whom it is impossible to know a little without wishing to know a great deal more. They had lately returned from their explorations in

Brazil, but more especially in the Valley of the Amazon. The popular narrative of the expedition (for it was composed of several persons) was written by Mrs. Agassiz, and has just been published. The more detailed and scientific account, by Mr. Agassiz, is eagerly expected. His character appears to be a most singularly transparent one. He has strong social instincts. In society he is evidently in his true element. But all the while, by the side of this keen enjoyment of society, you see that his soul has been constructed for making those discoveries in physical science, and acquiring those new ideas, he has so much happiness in presenting to the minds of others. His rich genial conversation and ready sympathies are worthy of the high position he holds in the scientific world.

To Mr. Thomas G. Appleton—the first American, I believe, who crossed the Atlantic in his own yacht—I am indebted for several kindnesses; among them for his taking me to his brother-in-law, Mr. Longfellow, who resides at Cambridge, about three miles from Boston. Mr. Longfellow's house is the oldest in the place, and has a good deal of curious antique carving and panelling. This is as it should be, for one can hardly imagine a poet living in a new, square-built, brick house, without a tradition or association.

In mentioning those whose names are public property, from whom I received kindnesses at Boston, I must not omit Mr. Philbrick, the Superintendent of Schools for the city. He allowed me to spend a morning in the Poplar Street Primary School, which was quite a model of its kind. It contained 300 children, divided into six grades. With few exceptions, they all come at the age of five, and leave at eight. He also took me with him to the yearly commemoration of the Adam Street Grammar School, in a distant suburb of the city. This is a mixed school for boys and girls, or rather for young ladies, for some of the latter were certainly not less than eighteen years of age. There were present on the occasion the superintendent, some assistant superintendents, or committee-men—I forget which was their title—and many of the parents of the children. The work consisted in recitations, singing, and reading extracts from a periodical written by the pupils and published in the school. The reciting was fairly done. No timidity was shown by any young lady who ascended the platform; but there was no boldness, or anything in any way unpleasing. There was only a degree of easy self-possession that would have been unusual in English ladies of any age. I mention this because the impression left on Mr. Fraser's mind by exhibitions of this kind appears not to have been favourable. As soon as the business of the day was over, Mr. Philbrick, being the chief official in the city connected with education, was called upon by the head-master to make a speech, or, as it is called in America, to deliver an address. After speaking for about ten minutes, he concluded by telling the company who I was, and with whom I was acquainted in the city, adding that he hoped I would give those present the pleasure of hearing me say something. I was a little taken by surprise at this summons, the heat of the room having almost put me to sleep. Otherwise one ought always to be prepared for such requests, because in America you may be quite sure that they will always be made. It is one of their institutions.

One hears a great deal about what is described as the arrogance and conceit of Americans. I never met with anything of the kind, except among classes which with us are generally too ignorant to know much, and too apathetic to care much about their own country. The upper classes are proud of their country, as they ought to be, and that is all. At Boston, however, I was struck, not with the arrogance and conceit, but with the humility of Americans. I am speaking now of the literary class; and I think the phenomenon is to be accounted for in the following way. These New Englanders are the most observant and the most receptive of the human family, and it is the first thought of all among them who have literary aspirations to travel in England and on the European continent. These are to them the Holy Land of thought. It is here that all the branches of literature, and all the departments of science, originated and were matured. All the creations of fancy, all the lessons and examples of history, all the familiar descriptions of outward nature, and of human emotions, come from this side. Here, then, are the shrines which the literary men of the New World must visit with the staff and in the spirit of a pilgrim. They feel an influence which their fellow-countrymen do not feel. But besides this, because they are New Englanders, they note and weigh every idea and practice they find in European society; and everything that approves itself to their understanding, they adopt readily and without prejudice. This is the reason

Humility of the Leading Literary Men.

why travelled New Englanders are generally so gentlemanly and agreeable. They understood what they saw abroad, and they have acknowledged to themselves that they have learnt much that they never would have known anything of if they had stayed at home. This, which is true of all, is doubly true of their literary men. One of the leading writers of New England described to me the craving that he felt for intercourse with minds cultivated as they are only in Europe. There only, in his opinion, men had time to think; there only had the critical faculties been trained; there only could you meet with broad and profound views on questions of literature, history, or policy. The whole of the literature of America was but a *rechauffé* of that of England, France, and Germany.

I regretted the necessity which obliged me to leave Boston before I had seen as much as I wished of its society. I did not feel in this way because it more nearly resembles European society than is the case in any other city of the Union—for one does not go to America to see what can be seen at home—but because I wished to know more of some with whom I felt that it would be a happiness afterwards to be acquainted, and because I was desirous of using every opportunity for arriving at some distinct conclusions as to the tendency of opinion and thought, more particularly religious thought, in the New World.

CHAPTER XXII.

AMERICAN HOTELS—WHY SOME PEOPLE IN AMERICA TRAVEL WITHOUT ANY LUGGAGE—CONVERSATION AT TABLES-D'HÔTE SHOULD BE ENCOURAGED—THE IRISH, THE AFRICAN, AND THE CHINESE—CAN A REPUBLIC DO WITHOUT A SERVILE CLASS?—WHAT WILL BE THE ULTIMATE FATE OF THESE THREE RACES IN AMERICA—NO CHILDREN—MOTIVES—MEANS—CONSEQUENCES—WHY MANY YOUNG MEN AND YOUNG WOMEN MAKE SHIPWRECK OF HAPPINESS IN AMERICA—THE COURSE MANY FAMILIES RUN—AMERICA THE HUB OF THE WORLD.

DURING the week I was at Boston, I dined for the last time in an American hotel; for the fortnight I afterwards spent in my second visit to New York, I passed in the hospitable house of Mr. Henry Eyre, a brother of the Rector of Marylebone, and a worthy representative of Englishmen in the commercial capital of America. With this exception, at the close of my tour, I made it a rule, from which I never departed, to decline all invitations to stay in private houses. My reason for doing this was, that I might come and go as I pleased, and have my time always at my own disposal. This gave me abundant opportunities, as my travels extended over 8,000 miles of American ground, for forming an estimate of their hotels and hotel life. With a few exceptions here and there, in some of the large eastern cities, the hotels are on the monster scale, and managed on the American system. The exceptions are called English, or European hotels, and their speciality is that you only pay in them for what you have. On the American system you pay so much a day for board and lodging; liquors and washing being extras. That the American system is the cheapest and most convenient, is demonstrated by its universality. The few exceptions that exist have to be inquired after and sought out. A traveller will also avoid them, because he is desirous of seeing the manners and customs of the people; and these can nowhere be seen so readily, and to such an extent, as in the monster hotels. They are a genuine production of the soil, are in perfect harmony with American wants and ideas, and are all alike.

Their distinguishing features are that the greater part of their guests are not travellers, but lodgers and boarders; and that they have one fixed charge for all, of so many dollars a day. The dearest I entered was the Fifth Avenue Hotel at New York, which charged five dollars a day; the board consisting of five such meals as no hotel in England or Europe could supply without bankruptcy. They are enabled to do this, because they have to supply these meals for several hundred persons. And they have this large number of guests, because multitudes of families, that they may escape the expense and annoyances of housekeeping, live in the hotels, and multitudes of men in business, keeping only a counting-house or a store in the city, do the same. The cheapest I was ever in charged three dollars and a half a-day. The service is so well organised in these hotels, that you may come or go at any hour of the night; and you can get your linen washed and returned to your room in a few hours. While dressing one morning at the Sherman House at Chicago, I sent out my linen to the laundry; on going back to my room at half-past eleven, I found that it had been washed and returned. This rapidity with which the washing of linen is performed in America enables one to travel with much less than would be requisite in Europe; and it explains why one often sees people travelling in America with no more than they can carry in a little handbag, called, in the language of the country, a satchel.

It does not, however, explain why some people in America travel with no luggage at all. Some of those whom I observed entering and leaving the cars in this light and unimpeded fashion, told me they had adopted the system because the work of the washerwoman had been advancing among them, not more in rapidity than it had done in costliness, so that it was now cheaper to get a new article, something at the same time being allowed for the old soiled one, than to send one of the same species to the laundry of the hotel. By acting on this idea they had escaped the necessity of taking with them relays of linen. I suppose this system must be an encouragement to the trade in paper shirt-collars. The difficulty as to razors, brushes, and combs, is easily met by the provision made in the barber's shop of every hotel. The Americans are full of original ideas, and they are very great travellers; it was therefore to be expected that they would be the first people to organise and perfect a system of travelling like the birds of the air.

The Americans having now revolutionised throughout the whole country the method of serving hotel dinners, passing at one step from what was the worst method of all to what is greatly in advance of the practice in this matter of all other nations, I would venture to suggest another change in a matter of still greater importance. It is evident that civilisation would have been quite an impossibility, if people had not met together at meals for the purpose of conversation. This alone rescues the act of taking one's food from its animal character, and associates it with the exercise of our moral and intellectual qualities. If we do not meet together, and converse, and exchange thought, and cultivate courtesies, our meals differ in no respects from the act of a horse or of a pig taking a feed. It is a strange mistake to suppose that there is anything intellectual or *spirituel* in hurrying through one's meals. The truth of the matter is exactly the reverse. To tarry at the table for the purpose of conversation makes every meal a school for the intellect, and for the promotion of the domestic and social graces. The savage hurries over his meals because he is a savage, morally and intellectually near of kin to the brute. If he could tarry over his meals he would have ceased to be a savage. All ancient and modern nations that have been highly civilised have acted instinctively on this idea. The Attic *symposia*, as well as the French *petits soupers*, rested upon it. Suppose meals are to be silently hurried through, they become mere brutish acts of eating and drinking, which any animal can perform as well as ourselves, and in much less time too. It is here that the Americans have a grand opportunity, in their widely diffused and generally practised hotel life, of which, it seemed to me, they were not availing themselves. You will see people day after day sit down to the same table,

U

take their food in silence, and leave the table without a word having been spoken. You may observe several tables occupied at the same time in your neighbourhood, and there shall be no conversation going on at any one of them. Those who sit at them appear to be entirely occupied either with their own thoughts or with attention to what they are eating. But it would make hotel life far more agreeable, and impart to it a far greater amount of civilising power, if it were the rule that people who meet at the same table might converse with one another, without any previous acquaintance, and without any necessity for subsequent acquaintance. Let it be understood that on such occasions conversation is the correct and the civilised thing.

No American will ever undertake any of the lower forms of labour—very few of the men before the mast in American ships are native-born. The class of agricultural labourers is unknown among them. What labour they have of this kind is supplied by immigration. No American would become a footman or hotel waiter. Their railways were not made by American navvies. In the North all the lower kinds of labour—but which, though they rank low as employments, are still necessary to the well-being, even to the existence of society—have hitherto fallen to the lot of the Irish, English, and German immigrants. Their place has been taken in the South by the blacks, and in the Pacific States by the Chinese.

This suggests two very interesting questions. The first is, Can a republic be carried on without a servile class? What would be the state of things in the American Union if it were deprived of the services of the Irish, the blacks, and the Chinese? Of course the loss would be much felt, and would very much retard the progress of the country; but I do not think that it would be a loss that would be irremediable and ruinous. As soon as the country begins to fill up, there will begin to appear in America the class that has existed in every country in the world, composed of those who have neither property nor a knowledge of any trade (which can seldom be obtained by those who have no property), and who therefore have nothing to live upon except their power of doing rude and unskilled work.

The other question is, What will be the future in the American Republic of these three races? The African, we may be sure, will either die out, which is most probable, or become a low caste, the pariahs of the New World: retail trade and a few of the lower kinds of labour and employment will be open to them. They will possess civil but not political rights. The Irish will be absorbed into the general population; and so one may speculate to what extent this will affect the American character. The Chinese can never be absorbed. What therefore will be the position that they will occupy in the Union fifty or a hundred years hence? Hitherto only one State has been open to them, that of California. Can anything be inferred from the position they have created for themselves in that State? I think we may be safe in supposing that, as they have already crossed the Pacific to the number of sixty thousand, when by the completion of the Pacific Railway the whole of the Union is thrown open to them, they will not remain cooped up in California. In a few years I believe they will be found in New York, and in all the large cities of the west and east. Voltaire said that the true wall of China was the American continent, the interposition of which saved it from European invasion; but it appears now that the American continent is the very point at which the European races will be invaded by the long pent up population of China. To what extent will this invasion be carried? and what consequences will result from it? One thing, I think, may be foreseen—the Americans will not admit these Asiatics, aliens in religion as well as in race, to political equality with themselves.

A recent writer on America has informed us that there is a disinclination among the wives of the luxurious cities of the Atlantic seaboard to become mothers. I found, after enquiry made everywhere on the spot, that this indisposition to bring up children is not confined to the wives or to the cities this writer's words indicate, but is participated in, to a large extent, by the husbands, and is coextensive with the American Union. It is just as strongly felt at Denver, two thousand miles away, as at New York, and results in almost as much evil at New Orleans as at Chicago.

The feeling—or, it might be said, this absence of natural feeling—may easily be explained. The expenses and annoyances of house-keeping are in America very great; and young couples, except when they are rich—and such cases must always form a small minority—generally escape them by living in hotels. Hotel living is always according to tariff, so much a week for each person. To a couple living in this way, and barely able to find the means for it, the cost of every additional child can be calculated to a dollar, and is seriously felt. As long as they are without children they may get on comfortably enough, and go into society, and frequent places of amusement. But if encumbered with the expense of a family, they will have to live a far quieter and less gay life. They cannot give up their autumn excursion, they cannot give up balls, and dresses, and concerts, and carriages. Therefore the husband and wife come to an understanding that they will have but one child, or that they will have no children at all.

Another reason for the practice, which would appear to affect the wife only, but which has frequently much weight with the husband also, is that the American lady's reign is not, under any circumstances, a long one. She has generally considerable personal attractions, but the climate and the habits of living are so trying that beauty is very short-lived. The young wife therefore argues, 'My good time will under any circumstances be short; why, therefore, should I prematurely dilapidate myself by having half-a-dozen children? And indeed what would that come to, but that I should have no good time at all, for the whole of it would be given up to the nursery? And by the time this would be over, I should be nothing but a wreck; my good looks will have disappeared, and I shall have fallen into premature old age.'

I met with husbands who themselves justified the practice on these grounds. They did not wish to have their wives, during the whole period of their good looks, in the nursery.

There is no secret as to the various means resorted to for carrying out these unnatural resolutions.

They are advertised in every newspaper, and there are professors of the art in abundance, judging from the advertisements, in every city. There is one large establishment in the most fashionable street in the city of New York, from whence the great high priestess of this evil system dispenses her drugs and advice, and where also she receives those who need her direct assistance. These things are so notorious and are so much talked of, that one is absolved from the necessity of being at all reticent about them.

No one, of course, would suppose that any practice of this kind, so abhorrent to our best natural instincts, could become universal: nor is it so in America: many denounce it. But still it spreads; and we cannot expect that it will die away, as long as the motives which prompt it continue to be felt as strongly as they are at present.

I will note one of the evil consequences of the practice. When those who have acted in this unnatural way are no longer young, and the motives which prompted their conduct have ceased to have any weight, the husband and wife find that there is no tie between them. They have no reason to respect each other. Each condemns the other, and is in the other's presence self-condemned. And this is one of the causes of the numerous divorces which so much astonish those who look into the social conditions of American life. Nature and our common moral sense will avenge themselves for such outrages.

A stranger travelling in America is not likely to receive letters to any except prosperous persons, and so, unless he is on his guard against it, his personal experience is likely to be confined to the bright and splendid side of society. But from the observations and enquiries I made, I came to the conclusion that there is no country in which the proportion of those whose destiny it is to suffer complete eclipse of happiness is so great as in the United States. Among men one chief cause of this appeared to me to be the irresistible attraction a life of heartless dissipation has for multitudes of young Americans. Why is this so? I believe their theory of social equality is responsible for some of it. They have a fatal craving to appear as fashionable, and to enjoy life as much as their wealthy neighbours. But I do not suppose that this will account for everything. After all, the careers that are open to city-bred young men are very limited. Practically for them there is not much beyond the counting-house and the store. Farming, the great employment of the country, is repulsive to them; and the ranks of the law are generally recruited from the hard-headed and enterprising sons of farmers. But be the cause what it may, there stands the fact that in the large American cities, and of course nowhere to such an extent as in New York, there is to be found a large class of young men of very limited means, who are living dissipated lives, and whose great aim is to appear fashionable—a detestable word, and a vulgar and unmanly idea, of which we in the old country have not heard much since the times of the Regency.

The case of the women who fail in life is more sad than that of the men, because, while they have less control over their own destinies, the failure in establishing a happy home is to them the failure of everything. The impracticable theory of social equality, I was again led to believe, was frequently the cause of such failures. These young women have been brought up in precisely the same way as their more fortunate sisters, at the same or at similar schools. This makes, in after life, the distinctions that meet the eye—of dress, equipage, and position—enter like iron into the soul; and so the determination to appear as others do becomes the rock upon which the happiness of many is wrecked.

These, however, are matters upon which a stranger will be very distrustful of his own observation, and will always hold himself open to correction from those upon the phenomena of whose social life he is commenting.

I will append to the foregoing remarks on the way in which many young persons in American cities make a wreck of their life's chances, an outline of the course I observed many families ran in America. The son of a farmer, we will say in Massachusetts, has some ambition. There is no field for ambition in New England farming. He therefore goes to Boston, or some commercial town, and becomes a lawyer, or a merchant, or a professional man of some kind or other. He rises to wealth and distinction, which are not so often secured by the city-born as by those who have the energy and vigour of new blood fresh from the country. He leaves his family well off. They never go back to the country. If any of the children have the energy and vigour of the father, they do not enter into business in Boston, but go out to the west, and help to build up such places as Chicago and Omaha. But if, as is generally the case, they have not energy and vigour enough for this, they go to New York, or some large city, where refined society and amusements are to be had. Some travel much, and take life easily. Some occasionally enter into political life. They marry city ladies, who are possessed of great refinement, but have very bad constitutions. They have two or three children with long thin fingers and weak spines. There is no fourth generation.

An Englishman cannot feel towards Americans as he does towards Italians or Frenchmen. Wherever in America he sees a piece of land being cleared and settled, or a church or a school being built, he looks on as if something were being done by and for his own countrymen. There is, however, one thing the evil effects of which he regrets to see everywhere, and that is the restrictions by which his American brethren are everywhere limiting trade and production. As he goes through their vast continent, and visits region after region, each capable of producing some different commodity the world needs, in sufficient quantities for the wants of all civilised nations, he rejoices at the greatness of their prospects, at the contemplation of all the wealth that God has given them. And he feels certain that the day cannot be very distant when they themselves will make the discovery that a dollar's worth of wheat, or maize, or cotton, or tobacco, or pork—and, when the plains shall be turned to account, of beef, or mutton, or wool—is exactly equal in value to a dollar's worth of manufactured goods, and two dollars' worth is exactly twice the value, and a hundred dollars' worth is of exactly a hundred times the value. And that when they shall have made this discovery they will strike off the fetters from trade and production, and by a single vote of their legislature increase the national wealth no one can foresee how many fold; and thus make themselves, what their vast and all-producing country, commanding both oceans and placed midway between Europe and Asia, is only waiting to become—the hub of the world.

CHAPTER XXIII.

ON AMERICAN COMMON SCHOOLS—CONCLUSION.

It was my practice, wherever I was staying, to visit some of the schools of the place. I have spoken of several of these visits in the foregoing pages. I will now give, collectively, the conclusions at which I arrived on the subject of education in America, after an actual inspection of schools, and much conversation with persons interested and engaged in educational work in every part of the Union, with the exception of the new States on the Pacific coast.

We have had the American Common School system held up before us for many years for our imitation. We have been told that, compared with it, our own efforts in the cause of education are discreditable and contemptible. We have been urged to look at what they are doing; to consider how highly they tax themselves for this purpose; to admire the effects of this system, as seen in a people, the whole of whom are now educated and intelligent. Of course the inference always is, that the best thing we can do is to go and do likewise. These are vague generalities, which an acquaintance with the subject will in some respects largely modify.

First, I demur to the statement that Americans

do tax themselves so highly for the purpose of education. It would be much nearer to the truth to say that there is no people on the face of the earth who educate their children so cheaply as the Americans; and therefore much more in conformity with the facts of their case, and of ours in this matter, to urge us to endeavour, by considering their example, to cheapen education amongst ourselves. I have now before me the most recent report of the Board of Education for the city of New York. It is for the year 1866. From this it appears that, taking together all the common schools of the city, the Primary, the Grammar, the Coloured, the Evening, the Normal, the Corporate, and the Free Academy, now the College of the City of New York, there are 227,691 children and young persons receiving education at a total cost for everything—including rents, purchases of sites, building, repairs, and salaries of officers of the board, as well as of the teachers—of 2,420,883 dollars, or about 30s. a head. Are the children of any city in England educated as cheaply ? These schools educate a considerable proportion of the children of the higher class, that is the professional men and merchants; speaking generally, all the children of the middle class, that is of the tradesmen; and as many of the children of the artisan and unskilled labouring class as their parents choose to send. This 30s. is a high average for American cities. I believe it is higher than any other in the United States. Tradesmen with us pay about 35l. a year for a child kept at a boarding-school, and about 15l. a year for the education given at day schools. In the great city of New York about

400,000*l.* a year is spent on the education of all classes, plus the cost of the few of the upper class who are sent to private schools. How much more, we may ask, is spent here on the education of 227,691 children of the different ranks in life of these New York children? There can be no doubt but that our unmethodical system, notwithstanding our numerous foundations, costs us much more than their system costs the Americans. Ours is the costliest educational system in the world; theirs the most economical.

This is still more apparent when we pass from the towns to the country. There the cost frequently falls below 10*s.* a head. The children educated in these schools are those of the proprietors of the land, but who cultivate it themselves as well as own it. Are the children of this class, in any part of the world, educated for so small a number of shillings a year? Why, in New York you have to pay as much for a pair of gloves, and more for a bottle of wine. In Illinois, one of the richest States in the Union, and whose population is probably better off than any equal number of people in any other country, the average cost for the children of the whole State is little more than this 10*s.* a head. And in Massachusetts, the State in which attention has been most carefully and for the longest time directed to the subject, and where everything is done that is thought necessary, the average for the town and country children actually at school is only 25*s.*

The fact is simply this. The rural population in America is the most homogeneous in the world. It is composed entirely of farmers, and of their sons and brothers who are the professional men and tradesmen of the district. Landlordism and tithes are unknown: so there is no one above the farmer-proprietor, and from New York to San Francisco there is no such class as our agricultural labourer, and so there is no one below the farmer. Now, how can a number of families of this kind, who are all completely on a footing of social equality, and also, if the word may be allowed to pass, pretty nearly of possessive equality, best educate their children? In a new country there are no foundation schools and few private ones—that is to say, to all practical purposes, no schools at all. There is, therefore, but one way of getting what they want—that is, by establishing schools of their own; and this can only be done by taxing themselves. There is no great sagacity shown in seeing this; and, as a matter of fact, everyone in America sees it. It is not seen more clearly in Massachusetts than it is in Ohio, or in Ohio than in California, or in California than in Colorado. I understood, indeed, that the schools of California (I had no opportunity of examining them myself) are the best in the Union; and the statement is not incredible, for the Californians are a people who will have nothing that is second-rate. One can hardly get now at any price a real Havana cigar in London or Paris, because the people of San Francisco will always pay the best price for the best thing. And in the territory, for it is not yet the State of Colorado, in the mountains, at Denver, and on the plains, two thousand miles away from Massachusetts, I saw the common-school system at work, in places where Judge Lynch is still the guardian of society in its infancy. No motive of patriotism or philanthropy can act in this universal and unfailing way. It can only be done by all, and in the same way by all, because it is obviously for the interest of all to do it, and because they could not get what they want in any other way. It is not forced on the rural townships by the general government of the State, but it permits them to tax themselves, if they please. And as they happen to raise the money they require by a tax, it becomes easy to ascertain exactly what the amount is; and the figures, as they include all that is paid for educating the children of a large State, appear to represent a very considerable sum, although, when it is looked into, it is seen to be the cheapest work of the kind that is anywhere done. The State of Illinois has now perhaps 10,000 schools, not far from 20,000 teachers, and about 600,000 scholars. The aggregate sum with which the people tax themselves for these schools and scholars appears very great, but in reality there are no other 600,000 scholars so cheaply educated. Our two schools of Eton and Harrow cost the parents of the children educated at them more than these 10,000 schools cost the people of Illinois.

And when we come to look into the working of the American school system in the cities, we see that nothing could be done without the motives I have spoken of, as never failing to bring about one uniform result in the country. The artisans, and tradesmen, and small professional men know that this is the best and cheapest way for them to get the kind of education they desire for their children. They are the great majority, and so of course the thing is done. There is a general tax, and common schools are established. And, as they have some advantages besides that of cheapness, they are used by many of the upper class—I mean merchants, bankers, and successful professional men, especially those who wish to stand well with the democracy. None can be excluded from the schools (indeed no one wishes it), and so they are open to the lowest class of the town population, with which there is nothing to correspond in the country. In truth, so far from wishing for any exclusion, great efforts are made to get hold of the children of ignorant and vicious parents, both from philanthropic and from self-interested motives, because in cities where every man has the suffrage, a vicious and ignorant population is doubly inconvenient and dangerous. Hitherto, however, the Americans have hardly succeeded in the towns better than we have, in their efforts to bring these children into their schools. At New York they have supplemented the common schools with a system of industrial schools, intended especially for those who would never enter the common schools. But all that can be said of them is, that they have met the evil they were intended to remedy to some small extent. At Chicago, I was told by the able superintendent of the city schools that there were 20,000 children in that city who frequented no school. And this is a growing evil in all the great cities of the Union.

The Americans, then, very wisely (in fact they could do nothing better, perhaps nothing else) have established, in the country and in the cities, common schools for their own children. What we are called upon to do is a totally different thing; and this I insist upon as another great distinction between what they have done, and what we are doing, in this matter. We have to establish schools for other people's children. With them those who pay for the school profit by it. With us those who will pay for the school will never derive any advantage from it. The point for us to settle is, How shall farmers and landlords be made to tax themselves for the education of labourers' children; and how shall the householders, and professional men, and tradesmen of a town be made to tax themselves for the schooling of the children of artisans and operatives? The Americans may be left to manage the business themselves, for it is their own affair. But we cannot: with us the law must be imperative, not permissive, and constant supervision will be needed; and to secure this right of supervision, it will probably be found necessary that the State should itself contribute largely towards the maintenance of the school.

The Americans possess an advantage in their schools to which there is at present no prospect of our attaining. The teachers of our elementary schools are taken from the humblest and most uneducated stratum of society, and have to be trained for their work. They have none of the traditions of mental culture, and their sentiments must in a great measure be those of their relations and friends. The humbleness of their origin does also considerably detract from the social position it would be desirable they should occupy. In America a like origin would not have the same effect; but here the daughter of a labourer or mechanic has not the influence with the parents of the children, or the respect shown to her, which would be readily conceded if she were the daughter of a farmer or tradesman; and it is from these two classes, whose social position is much higher in America than it is here, that the greater part of their teachers are drawn. They come from an educated class, and are entitled by their antecedents, as well as by their office, to some position, and they know how to assert it and maintain it. They have no more timidity or *mauvaise honte* than their friends. They are full of energy and ambition, and there is always animation in their teaching. It is quite impossible for any country to have better material for teachers than America has. And they appear to have an inexhaustible supply of it. 'Our half a million of teachers' is not an uncommon expression among them; but though this must pass for an American figure of speech, still what it implies is true, that whatever number of teachers may be required will always be forthcoming. I once heard an American bachelor in this country affirm that whenever he thought of marrying he should, other things being equal, give the preference to a lady who had for some years been a schoolteacher. I do not know to what extent this sentiment is shared by my friend's countrymen, or whether the lady-teachers of American schools are aware of the existence of this feeling in their favour; but at all events it shows that the social position of teachers is regarded as good.

Of course it is a mere truism to say that American teachers would be more efficient if they had had more special training. But whatever their deficiency may be in this respect, the advantages I have just spoken of as possessed by them are very manifest; and as soon as you enter an American school (this may be said generally of those in the North), you feel at once that you are surrounded by quite a different atmosphere from anything you are familiar with at home.

Another advantage their schools possess over ours is, that they are what, in American school-phraseology, is called 'graded.' This, unlike what I have just been mentioning, may be transplanted to our side of the water. I need not now explain what grading means, because I have spoken more than once of this method of arranging and teaching schools. It ensures much more careful teaching than our method, and that the whole of the school-time shall be devoted to study. I know that there are some who have recently said that it fails in individualising each case. I see, however, no force in this remark, because I was struck with the degree to which the very reverse of it resulted from the adoption of the method. It must be compared with the only other alternative for schools—that of the class system—and a little consideration will show that it is the class system perfected; for it is simply the assigning of one class to one person, and obliging that person to devote the whole of the school-time, from the first to the last minute, to teaching that one class. It prevents the scholars having any idle time while they are in school. It necessitates a great deal of oral teaching. It concentrates the teacher's whole attention on one point, as well as on one class.

It does also very much cheapen the cost of education. But this is not a benefit that will, among ourselves, be so understood and felt as that there should be any desire to secure it, until we have rate-supported schools. Our adoption of the rate to some extent, and in some form or other, can only be a question of time, for it is the only just method of supporting open schools; and the people will be averse to the schools in which their children are educated bearing an eleemosynary character. And when that day shall have come, then the majority of the rate-payers here, just as in America, will be in favour of the system, which, while it very much improves the teaching, will at the same time very much diminish its cost, by substituting where parishes are small one school for many.

Any remarks on American schools would be very incomplete if nothing were said on the exclusion from them of all direct or dogmatic religious teaching. The general rule is that a small portion, sometimes limited to ten verses, of the Holy Scriptures should be read daily, and that this should be followed by the Lord's Prayer. Some cities and districts allow more latitude for the prayer, a choice of certain forms that are provided being permitted, or even an extempore prayer founded on the Lord's Prayer. In some schools moral, as distinguished from religious or doctrinal teaching, may be founded on the portion of Scripture that has been read. Christianity, therefore, and the Bible are not ignored, as much being done as can be done in schools that are supported equally by many Churches differing from one another in their interpretation of the Bible. The masters, however, do not in all cases avail themselves of the opportunities allowed them for reading the Holy Scriptures and for prayer. Among the laity there is spreading a feeling of disapprobation at such omissions.

But what is the effect of this limitation of religious teaching? It must be remembered that these are all day schools. The children are present in school only during school hours. They are under the parental roof every night, at all their meals, and during the morning and evening of each day. The teacher, therefore, is not *in loco parentis*, as he is in the case of the child who boards and lodges with him, and is entirely entrusted to his care. The parents still have ample time and opportunities for all the religious instruction they desire to give their children, and then there is the Sunday, the Sunday-school, and the teaching of the ministers of religion. The question, therefore, as far as the primary schools are concerned, narrows itself to this—Is any irreligious effect produced by the absence of all direct dogmatic teaching from a school in which the children are only present a few hours a day, and where they go for the purpose of learning to read, write, and cipher, with a little geography and music? I do not think that much evil results from this, nor do I think that any very great amount of good would result from any attempt to alter the present system.

In the grammar school, where the instruction is not so mechanical, the conditions of the question are somewhat different. But even here I do not think that the tendency of the system is irreligious. I cannot believe that the cultivation of the intellect, even if there be nothing addressed directly and formally to their spiritual instincts, is, in the case of children so circumstanced as these, necessarily evil and hostile to religion. It would be so if they were confined for all the year, except the vacations, to the walls of a boarding-school, and the subject of religion never alluded to. But here again, as was observed with respect to the scholars of the primary school, the influences of home, of the church, and of the Sunday-school, ought to render the silence of the week-day school in a great measure innocuous. And this is the more likely to be the case with the scholars of the grammar school, as their parents do for the most part belong to a higher grade in society.

But if the system be tried in the most legitimate of all ways, that is by its fruits, I do not think that we shall have any reason to be dissatisfied with it. The sums raised voluntarily every year in the United States for the building and maintenance of churches, and for the support of the ministers of religion, is quite unequalled by what is collected in the same way among any population of equal amount in the world. It is impossible to ascertain a point of this kind, but I believe that it is far greater than what is contributed voluntarily by the whole of the Latin race. Almost the first buildings raised in the newest settlements are the churches. No one, unless he has experienced it, can tell what are the feelings and thoughts that spontaneously arise on finding yourself, as you enter such a place as Denver, beyond the prairies and the plains, as it were, welcomed by the Houses of God, which are the most conspicuous buildings of the place; and then, again, a few miles further on, as you pass through the first gorge of the mountains at Golden City, to find yourself surrounded by a cluster of three churches; and when you have got up among the little mining towns, perched like eagles' nests in the clefts of the mountains, still to find that the object which first of all attracts your attention is the little tower or spire, albeit of wood, that marks the building consecrated to God's service. I was astonished at the amount collected in the offertory at many of the churches in which I attended the service. I found the Sunday as well observed in America as I ever saw it anywhere else. I know that there are some facts to be set down on the other side, but they do not counterbalance what I have just been pointing out. And so the conclusion that I arrived at on this question was, that I should have liked some direct Christian teaching in the primary schools, and still more in the grammar schools, but this I knew was impossible. And on the whole I was not dissatisfied with the results of the American system of education on the religious character of the people.

Only one point remains—What, after all, do these schools teach? It has been lately objected to them that they aim at information, and not at the development of the faculties; and that they do not cultivate the taste. We are speaking of the common schools, and so of course are thinking of what school education in America does for the artisan and labouring class, and the lower stratum of the middle class; that is, children corresponding to those who are taught in our national schools, and those of a somewhat higher grade in society. Are the faculties (for that is the word insisted on by the most recent writer on the subject) of these two classes at all more developed here at home by our schools, than they are in America by their common schools? Or what fruit does our system bear among these classes in the refinement and the cultivation of the taste? Or, to put the question in the ordinary way, Are these classes better taught, rendered better able to use their wits, and rescued to a greater extent from the brutalising effects of ignorance among ourselves, or among them? Could the American system do more for these classes? If it could, I should be disposed to say it might do more for them on the very point where it is alleged that it does comparatively too much, that of giving information. But I do not say this because I thoroughly approved of so much time being devoted not in the least to imparting information, but to what is the main point in the schooling of those who must leave school very young—the teaching them to read, to write, and to cipher, with accuracy and facility. Among ourselves there is an enormous amount of failure in these primary matters; among the Americans there is very little failure in them. They teach their scholars to write with so much ease, that we may be sure they will never forget or lay aside the use of the pen; and they teach them to read with so much ease, and so much with the understanding, that we may be sure they will continue to read when they have left school. Do our schools accomplish this?

For 'the development of the faculties,' which are big words with rather indistinct meaning, I would substitute the concentration of the powers of the mind on special subjects, such as poetry, history, classical literature, philology, and the different branches of physical science, and I would say that the Americans as a nation have not yet arrived at the point where we may expect much either of this, or of 'refinement of taste.' At present all their mental strength and activity is required for the grand work of bringing a new world into subjection to man. They become settlers in the wilderness, or engineers and machinists, or merchants, or professional men, or newspaper-writers. All who enter on these employments are wanted in them, and can get a living by them. They invite and receive and remunerate all the energetic minds of the nation. But it will not always be so. As soon as the continent begins to fill up, and extension ceases, then multitudes of active minds will not find themselves called to the same employments as those of the present generation are. The battle with nature will then be over. By that time, too, wealth will have accumulated and become hereditary in many families. There will be many to appreciate, as well as many to devote themselves to art and literature. It is then that we may expect that the American mind and American culture will bear their fruit. They will then, I believe, have schools and styles of art of their own, and a literature of their own, as untrammelled as that of Greece, and richer and more varied than that of any other age or country. The day for these things has not yet come, but we see already the symptoms of the dawn; and when it has come, I think there will be no ground for complaining of 'want of development of the faculties,' or of 'want of refinement of taste' in America.

I trust that no word has been inadvertently set down in this book, should it be so fortunate as to find some readers among those who treated me with so much hospitality and kindness, which can in any way be displeasing to an American. If any from that side shall have accompanied me through its pages, now that the time for saying 'farewell' has arrived, my one wish is, that they may have come to look upon me somewhat in the light in which one of my Boston acquaintances told me a week's intercourse had brought him to regard me, that is, 'as one of themselves.'